THE UNIVERSITY OF MICHIGAN

SCHOOL OF EDUCATION

CENTER FOR THE STUDY OF HIGHER
AND POSTSECONDARY EDUCATION
610 E. UNIVERSITY, 2108 SEB
ANN ARBOR, MICHIGAN 48109-1259

Belongs To:
CSHPE Department
764-9472 (Priscilla)

The Uneasy
Public Policy Triangle
in Higher Education

The Uneasy Public Policy Triangle in Higher Education

Quality, Diversity, and Budgetary Efficiency

Edited by
David H. Finifter
Roger G. Baldwin
John R. Thelin

IXXI

AMERICAN COUNCIL ON EDUCATION
MACMILLAN PUBLISHING COMPANY
New York
MAXWELL MACMILLAN CANADA
Toronto
MAXWELL MACMILLAN INTERNATIONAL
New York Oxford Singapore Sydney

Macmillan Publishing Company
866 Third Avenue, New York, N.Y. 10022

Maxwell Macmillan Canada, Inc.
1200 Eglinton Avenue East, Suite 200
Don Mills, Ontario M3C 3N1

Macmillan, Inc., is part of the
Maxwell Communication Group of
Companies

Library of Congress Catalog Card Number: 90-20407

Printed in the United States of America

printing number
1   2   3   4   5   6   7   8   9   10

Library of Congress Cataloging-in-Publication Data

The Uneasy public policy triangle in higher education : quality, diversity,
    and budgetary efficiency / edited by David H. Finifter, Roger G.
    Baldwin, John R. Thelin.
        p.   cm. — (American Council on Education/Macmillan series on
    higher education)
    Includes index.
    ISBN 0-02-897145-0
    1. Higher education and state—United States.   2. Education,
    Higher—United States—Finance.   3. Education, Higher—United
States—Aims and objectives.   I. Finifter, David H.   II. Baldwin,
Roger G.   III. Thelin, John R., 1947-   .   IV. Series.
LC173.U53   1991
379.73—dc20   90-20407
                                                                    CIP

CONTENTS

FOREWORD

THOMAS H. KEAN

Speaking at the conference which spawned this book, I commented that some educators might consider quality, diversity and budgetary efficiency as compatible as Abbie Hoffman, Donald Trump, and Jerry Falwell. Although my speech attempted to dispel that comparison, I note that in the brief time since I made that remark, Trump defaulted, Falwell quit, and Hoffman died. If the recent flap over minority scholarships is any portent, America's colleges and universities are equally troubled.

Despite its faults, we still have the world's best system of higher education. It has given millions of men and women the opportunity to succeed. But we face new challenges. Taxpayers are demanding tangible results from their investment. Demographics show the need to boost recruiting of minority scholars on both sides of the lectern. And good teaching can no longer take a back seat to research in our faculty tenure system.

Having been on both sides of the handshake, I know that higher education and government need to reexamine their relationship if we are to remain a competitive, compassionate, and forward-looking nation. I am grateful to David Finifter, Roger Baldwin, John Thelin, and the College of William and Mary for opening the discussion. By heeding the essays they present, we can make this "uneasy triangle" less like Hoffman-Trump-Falwell and more like Tinkers-to-Evers-to Chance.

Thomas H. Kean
President, Drew University
Former Governor of New Jersey

PAUL SIMON

Last October I shared with my Senate colleagues a letter I received from a thirty-four year-old woman in Chicago, Gilda Amantea, who wants to be a teacher. She is raising three children and never graduated from high school, but not long ago she completed a GED program and is now attending classes two nights a week at Oakton Community College. She is active in her children's education, and is an elected member of her local school council. I think she would make an excellent teacher.

Completing her education one class at a time, however, will take many years—possibly too many. Tragically, financial assistance to students like Gilda Amantea is no longer a high priority of the federal government. The buying power of the Pell Grant has been eroded by half over the last decade. Guaranteed student loans, the alternative created for middle-class youth, are not a realistic choice for those in or near poverty, especially if they are not planning to enter a lucrative profession. And private aid has not filled the void left by the federal government.

The federal government must renew its commitment to education. We have a real chance to make that happen in the 102nd Congress with the five-year review of the Higher Education Act.

This book provides invaluable background on the opportunities and barriers we face in this review. From a variety of perspectives, it helps us think about how we can change the federal student aid system so that Gilda Amantea can realize her dream.

Paul Simon
U.S. Senator

ACKNOWLEDGMENTS

As the title of this book suggests, the role of public policy in higher education is complex and multidimensional. All three sides of the "uneasy triangle"—quality, diversity, and budgetary efficiency—interact with each other, generating both tradeoffs and opportunities for creative policymaking. This volume examines each of these dimensions and their interrelationships. The distinguished group of contributors identifies issues, dilemmas, and creative alternatives relating to federal and state policy and policy at the institutional level. While the topic is timeless, we now face important debates in Washington, D.C., in our state capitals, and in our educational institutions about the future of public policy and higher education. Our hope is that this volume contributes to the debate and the attainment of a sound policy prescription for the United States as we proceed through the final decade of the twentieth century.

A major undertaking such as this book and its preceding conference comes about as a result of the hard work and creativity of numerous individuals. We would like to thank several colleagues at the College of William and Mary—C. Lawrence Evans, Satoshi Ito, Anne M. Pratt, Julius J. Mastro, Ronald B. Rapoport, Kathleen F. Slevin—for their help with early planning of the conference. We also acknowledge the support and encouragement of several members of the administration at the College of William and Mary, including President Paul R. Verkuil, Provost Melvyn D. Schiavelli, Dean David J. Lutzer (of the Faculty of

Arts and Sciences), and Dean John M. Nagle (of the School of Education). Two individuals who were very helpful to this project were Gordon K. Davies, Director of the Virginia Council of Higher Education and Arthur M. Hauptman, Consultant for the American Council on Education. We are grateful to Jim Murrary, Director of Publications for the American Council on Education, who offered encouragement and guidance to this project. We are equally appreciative of the efforts by Lloyd Chilton, Executive Editor, Macmillan Reference, who offered ideas and suggestions and facilitated the project through various editorial activities. We also thank Bob Wilson of Macmillan Publishing Company for supervising the publication of the manuscript. We would like to thank several people who have helped in various clerical tasks including Karen Dolan, Nancy Lee Howard, Rita Scott, and Erika Finifter. We are indebted to Governor Thomas H. Kean and Senator Paul Simon for providing those attending the 1988 conference with thoughtful remarks and for writing forewords for this volume. Finally, we wish to thank the authors for the chapters of this book. The quality, diversity, and (relatively speaking) budgetary efficiency involved in the authors' contributions have not been the least bit uneasy.

CONTRIBUTORS

ROGER G. BALDWIN is associate professor of higher education in the School of Education of the College of William and Mary. His teaching and scholarly interests focus on curricular issues, faculty career development, and conditions in the academic workplace. Since completing his Ph.D. at the University of Michigan's Center for the Study of Higher Education in 1979, he has held administrative and research posts at Rollins College, the American Association for Higher Education, and Wittenberg University. Dr. Baldwin has served as a consultant on faculty issues to a variety of higher education and government organizations, such as the Great Lakes Colleges Association, the State Council of Higher Education for Virginia, the American Council on Education, and the Governor's Commission on the Future of Higher Education in Michigan. His publications include *Incentives for Faculty Vitality* (1985) and numerous articles on faculty careers. Dr. Baldwin is currently on leave from William and Mary to serve as special assistant to the Director of Education and Human Resources at the National Science Foundation.

DAVID W. BRENEMAN became the fourteenth President of Kalamazoo College, Kalamazoo, Michigan, on July 1, 1983, a position he held until 1989. Prior to that he was Senior Fellow in the Economic Studies Program of the Brookings Institution, where he specialized in the economics of education and public policy toward education. At Brookings since 1975, he coauthored two Brookings books, *Financing Community*

Colleges: An Economic Perspective (1981) and *Public Policy and Private Higher Education* (1978), and wrote on federal education policy for the annual Brookings series, *Setting National Priorities*. He also wrote *The Coming Enrollment Crisis: What Every Trustee Must Know*, a widely read 1982 publication of the Association of Governing Boards.

From 1972 to 1975, he was Staff Director of the National Board on Graduate Education at the National Academy of Sciences, writing extensively on economic and policy issues confronting graduate education. He also served as Executive Editor of *Change*, the magazine of higher learning. Dr. Breneman received his B.A. in philosophy from the University of Colorado and his Ph.D. in economics from the University of California at Berkeley, and he taught economics at Amherst College before moving to Washington, D.C. in 1972. Dr. Breneman is currently a Visiting Fellow at the Brookings Institution and will be a Visiting Professor at Harvard Graduate School of Education starting in Fall 1990.

WILLIAM J. BYRON, S.J. is president of The Catholic University of America, a post he has held since September 1, 1982. Earlier assignments included the presidency of the University of Scranton and a deanship at Loyola University of New Orleans. He has taught at Loyola of Baltimore and Woodstock College. Father Byron is the author of *Quandrangle Considerations* (1989) and *Toward Stewardship* (1975) and editor of *The Causes of World Hunger* (1982). He has published numerous articles dealing with economics, social ethics, and educational issues.

Father Byron is a trustee of Loyola University of Chicago, Chairman of Bread for the World, and a member of the Joint Commission on the Accreditation of Healthcare Organizations. He also serves on the boards of the Corporation Against Drug Abuse, the Medlantic Healthcare Group, the Overseas Development Council, the National Association of Independent Colleges and Universities, and the Education in Partnership with Technology Corporation of the District of Columbia. After service in military, Father Byron attended St. Joseph's College (now University) in Philadelphia for three years before joining the Jesuit Order in 1950. He holds degrees in philosophy and economics from St. Louis University, two theology degrees from Woodstock, and a doctorate in economics from the University of Maryland. He also holds a certificate from the Institute for Educational Management at Harvard.

GORDON K. DAVIES has been Director of the Council of Higher Education for Virginia since 1977. The Council is Virginia's planning and coordinating body for higher education. It has a combination of advisory and regulatory responsibilities.

Dr. Davies holds three degrees from Yale University: A Bachelor of Arts in English and a Master of Arts and Doctorate in the Philosophy of Religion. He joined the Council of Higher Education in 1973 as Associate Director. Prior to this, he has been a faculty member at Yale and a Dean at Stockton State College in New Jersey. From 1969 to 1971, he directed the Harvard-Yale-Columbia Intensive Summer Studies Program. In addition to academic experience, Dr. Davies spent several years selling computer systems for the IBM corporation and worked as a consultant designing personnel information systems.

DENIS P. DOYLE is currently a Senior Research Fellow at the Hudson Institute. For five years before that he was director of Educational Policy Studies and Human Capital Studies at the American Enterprise Institute; before that he was a Federal Executive Fellow at the Brookings Institution. Mr. Doyle's government service includes an appointment as Assistant Director for School Finance and Organization at the National Institute of Education where, among other duties, he oversaw major OECD/CERI studies and managed the Voucher and Experimental Schools programs. Before that he was an Assistant Director of the United States Office of Economic Opportunity. Mr. Doyle also worked for the California State Legislature and the State Office of Economic Opportunity.

Mr. Doyle is a recognized authority on education policy in both the United States and abroad and has written widely about education for both scholarly and popular audiences. He is a regular speaker at business and education seminars and conferences both in the United States and abroad. Mr. Doyle is the coauthor of three recent books on education: *Excellence in Education: The States Take Charge* (with Terry Hartle, 1980), *Investing in Our Children: Business and the Public Schools* (with Marsha Levine, 1985), and *Winning the Brain Race: A Bold Plan to Make Our Schools Competitive* (with David T. Kearns, 1988). In addition, he coedited, with Bruce S. Cooper, *Federal Aid to the Disadvantaged: What Future for Chapter 1?* (1988).

DAVID H. FINIFTER is associate professor of Economics at the College of William and Mary. He is serving as director of the Thomas Jefferson Program in Public Policy at William and Mary, a position he has held since 1987. His teaching and scholarly interests include the economics of education and public policy, human resource economics, evaluation and benefit/cost analysis, labor economics, microeconomics applied to public policy analysis, and econometrics applied to public policy analysis. Dr. Finifter has been on the faculty at the College of William and Mary since completing his Ph.D. in economics from the University of Pittsburgh. He also holds a B.S. degree at Loyola College of Maryland and an M.A. degree in economics from the University of Pittsburgh. He has published several articles and reports in the area of human resources and public policy on issues including federally subsidized employment and training programs, unemployment insurance policy, performance standards for employment and training programs of Indian and Native Americans and migrant and seasonal farmworkers, veterans' job training programs, and the Job Corps program. He has served as a consultant to several federal government agencies, including the United States Department of Labor, the Veterans Administration, and the Environmental Protection Agency. During 1978-79, he served as a Staff Associate in Employment Policy at the Brookings Institution and the United States Department of Labor.

ALAN L. GINSBURG is director of the Planning and Evaluation Service at the United States Department of Education. He received his Ph.D. in economics from the University of Michigan. He has published articles on a wide range of topics, including educational policy, educational evaluation, and school finance. Dr. Ginsburg has been involved in the development of major education legislation and is currently executive director of the Department's task force on Indian Nations At-Risk.

LAWRENCE E. GLADIEUX has been executive director of the Washington, D.C. office of the College Board since 1981. The College Board is a national nonprofit membership association that provides tests and other educational services for students, schools, and colleges. His office is the principal College Board liaison to the federal and state governments, and it conducts policy research on issues affecting educational finance and the goal of equal educational opportunity.

He has testified before congressional committees, served on various federal and state advisory committees, and authored or coauthored articles appearing in *Change*, the *New York Times*, *Journal of Student Financial Aid*, *Academe*, the *College Board Review*, and publications of the Academy of Political Science and the Brookings Institution. Mr. Gladieux is coauthor, with Thomas R. Wolanin, of *Congress and the Colleges: The National Politics of Higher Education* (1976). He is editor of *Radical Reform or Incremental Change? Student Loan Policy Alternatives for the Federal Government* (1989). Prior to joining the College Board, he served on the staff of the Council on Federal Relations of the Association of American Universities. He also served on congressional staff, as legislative assistant to former Congressman John Brademas of Indiana and executive secretary to an advisory task force for the late Senator Jacob Javits on educational and cultural exchange programs. Mr. Gladieux is a 1965 cum laude graduate of Oberlin College, and he received an M.P.A. degree from Woodrow Wilson School of Public and International Affairs at Princeton University in 1967.

MAXINE GREENE is Professor of Philosophy and Education and the William F. Russell Professor in the Foundations of Education at Teachers College, Columbia University. Her B.A. is from Barnard College; her M.A. and Ph.D. from New York University. She holds honorary degrees (D.H.L.) from Lehigh University, Hofstra University, University of Colorado at Denver, and Bank Street College of Education. Dr. Greene is a past President of the Philosophy of Education Society, the American Educational Studies Association, and the American Educational Research Association.

Author of about one hundred articles and chapters in the field of philosophy, curriculum, literature, social theory, and aesthetics, she has written five books, including *Teacher as Stranger* (1973), *Landscapes of Learning* (1978), and *The Dialectic of Freedom* (1988).

AMY GUTMANN is Andrew W. Mellon Professor of Politics at Princeton University, where she directs the Program in Political Philosophy. Gutmann's most recent book, *Democratic Education* (1987), is now being translated into Spanish and Arabic. She is also the author of *Liberal Equality* (1980) and editor of *Democracy and the Welfare State* (1988) and *Ethics and Politics* (1989). Gutmann is Vice-President of the American Society for Political and Legal Philosophy. Dr. Gutmann serves on the Board of Directors of the Salzburg Seminar and the Executive Board of the Center for Policy Research in Education. She has been a Rockefeller Fellow, a visitor at the Institute for Advanced Study, Vice-President of the Hastings Center, and visiting professor at the Kennedy School of Government, Harvard University. Gutmann received her B.A. from Harvard College, master of science from the London School of Economics, and Ph.D. from Harvard University.

TERRY A. HARTLE is the chief education advisor to the United State Senate Committee on Labor and Human Resources, chaired by Senator Edward Kennedy (D-MA). In this position, he advises the Committee about the design and impact of federal education policies and programs. Dr. Hartle received his Bachelor's degree from Hiram College (summa cum laude), Master's degree from the Maxwell School of Syracuse University, and Doctorate from George Washington University. He is a member of Phi Beta Kappa.

Prior to joining the Senate staff, he was Resident Fellow and Director of Social Policy Studies at the American Enterprise Institute for Public Policy Research. His research at AEI focused on policy-oriented studies of education and human capital development. Before joining AEI, Dr. Hartle worked for Educational Testing Service. As a research scientist, he studied educational finance, governance, and quality. As a Washington liaison for ETS, he worked in government relations with Congress, the Executive Branch, and special interest groups. Dr. Hartle has been a consultant to many public and private sector organizations. He has taught in the School of Government and Business Administration at George Washington University. Dr Hartle is the coauthor of *Excellence in Education: The States Take Charge* (1985). His articles have been published in the *Atlantic, Change, Public Administration Review,* the *Journal of Contemporary Studies, Public Opinion,* the *Washington Post,* and the *Los Angeles Times.*

ARTHUR M. HAUPTMAN has been an independent consultant since 1981 on issues relating to higher education finance and federal budget policies. Recently, his principal focus has been on ways to reform federal student aid programs, alternative financing mechanisms for paying for college, and an examination of why college tuitions and costs have grown so rapidly in the past decade. Mr. Hauptman recently authored *The Tuition Dilemma* (1990) for the Brookings Institution and *The College Tuition Spiral* (1990), a report to the College Board and the American Council on Education. He previously served on the staffs of the United States House Budget Committee and the United States Senate Labor and Human Resources Committee. He received a B.A. in Economics from Swarthmore College and a M.B.A. from Stanford University.

FRANCIS KEPPEL was Senior Lecturer in Education at the Harvard Graduate School of Education from 1975 until his death in 1990. He also served as Chairman of the Board of Lincoln Center Institute, the Lincoln Center's program for the arts in education. Mr. Keppel received the A.B. degree from Harvard University in 1938, studied sculpture for a year at the American Academy in Rome, and resumed academic studies while serving as an Assistant Dean at Harvard College from 1939 to 1941.

In 1948, following service in World War II, James B. Conant appointed the thirty-two-year-old Mr. Keppel Dean of the Graduate School of Education, Harvard University. From 1948 until 1962, he also served with a variety of national and international groups. From 1962 to 1966, he served as United States Commissioner of Education and later as Assistant Secretary of Health, Education, and Welfare (for Education). During his term of office, the Elementary and Secondary Education Act of 1965, the Higher Education Acts of 1963 and 1965, and other federal laws were enacted. Other positions held by Mr. Keppel were: Chairman of the Board of the General Learning Corporation; Vice-Chairman of the Board of Higher Education of the City University of New York; and Overseer of Harvard University from 1968 to 1973. At the time of his death he also served as Chairman of the Board of the American Trust for the British Library and on the Board of Governors of the International Development Research Centre in Ottawa.

MAUREEN A. MCLAUGHLIN is Director of the Postsecondary Education Division of the Planning and Evaluation Service at the United States Department of Education. This office is responsible for policy analysis and evaluation studies related to postsecondary education and federal programs. Before working at the Department, Ms. McLaughlin was a policy analyst at the Congressional Budget Office where she was responsible for policy studies in several areas, including postsecondary education. Ms. McLaughlin has a Master's degree in Public Policy from the University of Pennsylvania and a Bachelor's degree in Economics from Boston College.

WALTER W. MCMAHON is Professor of Economics and of Education at the University of Illinois at Urbana-Champaign. His Ph.D. in Economics is from the University of Iowa with both predoctoral and postdoctoral fellowships at the University of Chicago and at the London School of Economics. Dr. McMahon has published two books involving research on the efficiency, equity, and economics of expansion of education, and book-length education sector reviews for Indonesia and Nepal. He has also published approximately fifty-five refereed journal articles on the relation of education to productivity growth and to economic development, both in the United States and in the developing nations, as well as on why families invest in education and on achieving quality, efficiency, and equity in primary, secondary, and higher educational programs and financing. Dr. McMahon is a Senior Scientist Consultant to the National Science Foundation on the impact of federal budgetary changes on colleges and universities. He was at the Brookings Institution for a year and has also been a guest scholar at the London School of Economics, in the Research Department of the National Central Statistical Office in Paris, and at the IUI Econometrics Institute in Stockholm. He has recently been a guest scholar at Erasmus University in the Netherlands and has been the economist designing major USAID efforts in higher education and primary education in Pakistan, Malawi, and Nepal. He also has recently been a consultant to the *World Development Report* and to The World Bank on Latin American and African education projects. He is currently working on the human resources section of the next twenty-five year plan for the Government of Indonesia.

JOHN R. THELIN, Chancellor Professor and Director of the Higher Education Doctoral Program at The College of William and Mary, also is a member of the program faculties for Public Policy Studies and American Studies. In 1986 he received the College's Phi Beta Kappa Award for Faculty Contribution to the Advancement of Scholarship. An alumnus of Brown University, he concentrated in European history and was elected to Phi Beta Kappa. At the University of California, Berkeley, he was a Regents Fellow and received an M.A. in American history and a Ph.D. in Educational Studies.

From 1978 to 1981 he was Research Director for the Association of Independent California Colleges and Universities and a member of the National Institute of Independent College's state-national research group. He is author of three books, including *Higher Education and Its Useful Past* (1982) and (with Lawrence Wiseman) *The Old College Try: Balancing Academics and Athletics in Higher Education* (1989). He serves as Essay Review Editor of the *Review of Higher Education,* Associate Editor of *Higher Education: Handbook of Theory and Research,* and on the editorial boards for *History of Education Quarterly, Educational Studies,* and *Higher Education Abstracts.* Dr. Thelin is author of more than seventy articles and reviews, published in such journals as the *Review of Higher Education, Policy Studies, Academe,* the *Chronicle of Higher Education,* the *Wall Street Journal, History of Education Quarterly, California Historical Quarterly,* and the *Journal of Higher Education.* In 1989 the Spencer Foundation awarded him a three-year major grant for historical study of intercollegiate athletics as part of academic policy.

REGINALD WILSON was named Senior Scholar of the American Council on Education in October 1988. He joined the Council as Director of the Office of Minority Concerns on October 1, 1981. Prior to that appointment he was, for nearly ten years, President of Wayne County Community College in Detroit. Other higher education career positions he has held have been Dean, Director of Test Development and Research, Director of Black Studies, and Director of Upward Bound. He was a Psychologist in the Detroit Public Schools prior to that. Dr. Wilson has taught graduate courses in psychology and black studies at Wayne State University, the University of Detroit, Oakland University, and the University of Michigan. He is the coauthor of *Human Development in the Urban Community* (1967), the editor of *Race and Equity in Higher Education* (1982), and the author of *Civil Liberties and the U.S.* (1988). He is on the editorial board of the *American Journal of Education* and the *Urban Review.* Dr. Wilson received his Ph.D. in clinical and educational psychology from Wayne State University. He is licensed as a Psychologist in Michigan and in Washington, D.C. and does volunteer work with the homeless. He was honored as a Distinguished Alumnus of Wayne State University in 1980 and is a recipient of the Anthony Wayne Award and the Distinguished Service Medal of the City of Detroit.

ROBERT ZEMSKY serves as both the University of Pennsylvania's chief planning officer and as the director of its Institute for Research on Higher Education (IRHE). He received his B.A. from Whittier College and his Ph.D. from Yale University. He is widely published.

As director of the College Board's Comprehensive Undergraduate Enrollment Planning Project, Dr. Zemsky led the team that developed a market segment model based on the Board's extensive database. He (with Penney Oedel) wrote *The Structure of College Choice* (1983). Dr. Zemsky is also the principal designer of the Penn Plan, a nationally acclaimed integrated program that helps Penn students and their parents, in partnership with the University, finance their college educations. He has served as a principal planning consultant to a wide variety of institutions, including Indiana University, and as faculty assistant to the president of the University of Pennsylvania from 1971 through 1973, continuing as director of Planning Analysis until 1981 when he assumed his present responsibilities. Under a grant from the Pew Charitable Trusts, Dr. Zemsky serves as Project Director and principal investigator for the Trusts' Higher Education Research Program.

Since 1986 Dr. Zemsky has directed the development of a proto-type undergraduate coursework database, drawing on transcripts submitted by a nationally representative sample of thirty-five institutions. Dr. Zemsky serves as a Trustee of Franklin and Marshall College. He is a Woodrow Wilson fellow (1962-63, 1965-66), a recipient of a postdoctoral fellowship from the Social Science Research Council (1973-74), and has held visiting appointments at the Johns Hopkins University and the University of Michigan.

The Uneasy
Public Policy Triangle
in Higher Education

INTRODUCTION

The public policy arena is fraught with dilemmas among societal goals, and public policy toward higher education is no exception. The goals of quality, diversity, and budgetary efficiency are all clear priorities of federal and state policy. And yet there is an uneasiness or tension among these goals. This book is the result of a conference sponsored by the College of William and Mary's Thomas Jefferson Program in Public Policy and the School of Education's Higher Education Program and co-sponsored by the Virginia Council of Higher Education. The conference was held in Williamsburg, Virginia in October 1988 and featured nineteen speakers and panelists, most of whom are the authors of the chapters in this book. The papers have been revised for this volume.

The theme of this book is derived from the dramatic changes that have occurred over the past thirty years in the United States in the relationship between higher education and public policy. The demographic, economic, social, and political climates in which higher education functions have changed. These changes in higher education have, in turn, affected productivity and the ability of the United States economy to adapt to technological change.

This book is divided into five sections following the structure of the conference. Section I is entitled "Looking Backward: The Historical Context of Public Policy and Higher Education." The role of government in the higher education sector has changed dramatically over this nation's history. Higher education has a long history of direct and indirect subsidization at the federal, state, and local government levels. The subsidies come in the form of direct budgetary support by states to public institutions, federal guaranteed student loans, scholarship programs, work-study programs, funding of research projects for faculty and students at universities, and exemptions of property taxes by local governments. Along with this strong and varied way in which government has provided financial support for institutions of higher education has come varying amounts of accountability by the institutions and individuals who benefit directly from these programs. This section serves as a retrospective and prospective examination of the relation-

1

ship between public policy and the higher education sector. Authors include Francis Keppel, David Breneman and Maxine Greene.

Section II is entitled "The Tenuous Connection: Public Policy and Higher Education Quality." Traditionally, the higher education sector has been self-monitoring. Professional associations, accrediting organizations, and institutional self-study represented the common forms of evaluation and assessment. In recent years, along with the growth of federal and state funding of higher education, funding agencies have become more involved in quality and accountability issues. This has brought to the public policy arena questions relating to the autonomy of the educational institution, the difficulties of assessment measurement, especially when involving value added, and the importance of liberal arts and core curriculum versus a professional/vocational curriculum orientation. Authors include Gordon Davies, Amy Gutmann, and Denis Doyle.

Section III is entitled "The Goal of Diversity in Higher Education." The link between education and opportunity to succeed has long been thought to be a strong one in the United States. Public support for higher education in its many forms has often been justified by appealing to the principle of equality of opportunity. Success in this area would be measured, in part, by the diversity of income, ethnic and family backgrounds, and gender mix of students in higher education. Demographic projections point to a decline in the size of the student applicant pool in the years to come. Other demographic indicators point to a relative increase in Hispanics, blacks, and Asian Americans in this pool. Therefore, both to produce a sufficient number of trained people for our labor force needs in the future and to accomplish the narrower goal of filling up classrooms in the academy, it will be important to permit greater access to higher education for more people with diverse backgrounds. Mirroring these trends will be the increased desire and opportunity for diversity of college and university faculty, a wide range of curricular offerings, and the internationalization of campuses and curricula. The tradition of seeking equal educational opportunity and the compelling demographic trends make the issues of access and choice of growing importance in the United States. However, the relationship of diversity to educational quality and budgetary cost must also be considered as decision makers in the higher education sector and public policymakers set the parameters for the future. Authors include Robert Zemsky, Reginald Wilson, Alan Ginsburg, and Maureen McLaughlin.

Section IV is entitled "Budgetary Efficiency, the Federal and State Commitment in the Face of Severe Federal Budget Deficits." The most obvious role of government in higher education takes the form of student aid programs through the Higher Education Act. Pell Grants, student loan programs, and work-study are the main components of the federal aid package. In recent years, there have been cutbacks in the growth of these programs, a shift toward loans, an increase in targeting efforts toward the lowest income groups and therefore away from the middle-income groups, a greater awareness and enforcement of loan defaults, and an increase in the rhetoric of accountability for educational institutions. The coincidence of rising tuition levels in excess of other cost of living components and record-breaking federal deficits has put federal and state governments at loggerheads with educational institutions. Combine this with the cutback in the 1980s of support for research—especially basic research in the sciences, research and development in academia, and research in social sciences and humanities—and the growing importance of academic pork barreling, and the stage is set for a redefinition of the role of public policy in higher education. In the face of these budgetary problems, the goals of quality and diversity have often taken a backseat. Public higher education has responded to this by seeking more private support from foundations, corporations, and individual donors, with obvious negative impacts on the private higher educational sector. In addition, exploration of new forms of assistance is under way. Authors include Arthur Hauptman, Terry Hartle, and Walter McMahon.

Section V is entitled "Conclusion: Coping With the Uneasy Triangle—The Tradeoff Continues." This section includes a conclusion and two additional papers, one by Lawrence Gladieux and one by William Byron, S.J.

Higher education, and education in general, were important campaign issues in the 1988 presidential election, with each candidate laying claim to the title of "education president." As many feared, problems with federal and state budgets have dominated the story since that time. What this will mean for the quality and diversity sides of the triangle can hardly be positive. Nevertheless, pressures relating to United States competitiveness and demographic changes toward an aging and increasingly ethnic minority student body imply that these non-budget issues will become paramount in the 1990s.

We were fortunate to have Frank Keppel as one of our speakers and authors. Professor Keppel, who died February 19, 1990, was such an important part of higher education and public policy during his lifetime that we deem it appropriate to close this section with two quotes from an interview in a recent issue of *Change*.[1] Professor Keppel's remarks suggest significant changes in the social and political arena in which federal policy is made.

I got to Washington in December 1962. There was a lot of activity, including the Civil Rights Act of '64, the Elementary and Secondary

[1] Nancy Hoffman and Robert Schwartz, "Remembrance of Things Past: An Interview With Francis Keppel and Harold Howe II." *Change* 22, No. 2 (March/April 1990): 52–57.

Act of '65, plus the Higher Education Acts of '63 and '65. The Civil Rights Act started a rather muddled process I presided over, that of trying to get the Southern school districts to sign a piece of paper saying they'd be virtuous. By the summer of '65 the bite was being put on them, and we were trying desperately to push a lot of school districts, over 5,000 of them as I remember, to announce their virtue, if not their virtuous practice. (p. 54)

What comment on the federal role might be interesting from a fellow who's been looking back? I was reviewing a couple of national commission reports—*A Nation at Risk*, and so forth—for a piece I was writing, and one thought occurred to me. I read all the recommendations, and—let me put it this way—the recommendations are "to whom it may concern." Whereas, back in the '60s, they'd all have been addressed to the federal government. It's an interesting difference because it symbolizes a withdrawal in the '80s from federal responsibility...a great success, I guess, of Reagan. Today, the federal government is no longer *automatically* part of the solution. (p. 57)

SECTION I

Looking Backward: The Historical Context of Public Policy and Higher Education

Implicit in American democracy is an aversion to monarchy that obviously renders inappropriate the role of "Advisor to Kings." Setting aside royalty in favor of elected offices, Americans do have a sustained fascination with the notion of advisors who wear "multiple hats." Action and reflection are fused in an ideal of public service in which expertise and intelligence shift comfortably from academe to government to institutional leadership and back. Nowhere is this distinctive tradition more evident than in the authors in Section I, whose selections provide historical context for understanding public policy in higher education as a product of *both* experience and scholarship.

A common thread among the three contributors—Francis Keppel, David Breneman, and Maxine Greene—is that each is heir to the claim of *making* as well as *writing* history. They have been participants in and witnesses to, as well as analysts of, the formation of what we now call our national policies toward colleges and universities.

Francis Keppel's essay, "The Role of Public Policy in Higher Education in the United States," bridges two centuries of policy initiatives, from "Land Grants to Pell Grants and Beyond." Its recurrent message is that often higher education has been influenced *indirectly*, albeit *significantly*, by public policy, whether one looks at the Western Reserve of the late eighteenth century or the Serviceman's Readjustment Act following World War II. Such an interpretive survey is healthy for the higher education community in that it does keep us humble (more or less), with the historical reminder that although colleges and universities may be the hub of our professional universe, they are not necessarily the center from which federal public policy radiates. Keppel also provides another antidote to higher education *hubris*: his account recognizes the unexpected consequences of policy formulation. In retrospect, the evolution of federal policy toward higher education may appear to be smooth, even inevitable. In fact, it has been an uncertain process whose outcomes were seldom evident to lobbyists and policy proponents. Plans and schemes have more often than not taken unexpected twists. Perhaps the best historical case that illustrates this theme comes from John Whitehead's *Separation of College and State* (1973): in the early 1800s the New York State Legislature favored upstate Hamilton College by awarding that institution the proceeds from a state lottery; Columbia, having fallen from favor by dint of its New York City location, received the consolation prize of seemingly worthless land known as "Hockensack's Botanical Gardens." Today that "worthless" land by the calculations of 1810 is more familiar to us as prime Manhattan real estate—the source of a comfortable endowment long after Hamilton College had spent its lottery money!

The theme of "unexpected consequences" is at the heart of David Breneman's selection in his account of higher education and public policy's recent past. Looking backward from 1990 to 1960, the biggest surprise for higher education lobbyists was the relative failure of federal policy to embrace direct institutional support. Instead—and very much outside the formal strategies of higher education associations—a dominant story since 1970 has been the political success story of *need-based student financial aid*. Here was a strand of massive, expanded federal support for higher education that pleased elected officials on two counts: first, it meant that Congress was spared the task of choosing which institutions received (and did not receive) direct federal funds; second, by making student financial aid both portable and an entitlement, voters back home were made happy—as parents applauded the senator or congressman who helped make going to college affordable for the sons and daughters of voters. Ironically, the literature from the 1950s and 1960s showed little sign of anticipating this policy development that would come to characterize—along with federal research grants—higher education's public policy in the past two decades. And, David Breneman describes and analyzes a distinct yet related consequence: the emergence of state-level student financial aid as both a supplement and partner to the proliferation of federal programs. Since 1970, then, a major strand of higher education public policy has been a virtual revolution in public expectations about student financial aid.

Is there a danger that policy analysis now competes for the dubious claim of being the "dismal science?" If so, Maxine Greene counters that trend by reviving the Jeffersonian notion of philosophical inquiry and public debate on significant issues as central to the policymaking process. And, drawing from John Dewey, she uses historical and philosophical analysis to present an example of and case for an "articulate public." By her own writing and example, Greene shows how there can—and ought to be—a place for *active* civic discussion of the agenda that higher education sets forth to both federal and state governments. The significant education issues of our time—equality, equity, access—argues Greene, are too important not to include widespread, informed discussion. Indeed, the three selections in Section I serve the dual purpose of both identifying that void and providing informed discussion that stands as at least a good start in solving the problem of unexamined policies.

The authors of the selections in Section II make no claim to provide all the answers to issues of historical context and evolution of public policy associated with higher education. It is, therefore, fitting to introduce Section I with a query: Have we unwittingly defined "public policy" in such strict terms so as to overlook a rich historical legacy? Specifically, if *government* involvement in the nineteenth and early twentieth centuries was rather limited or haphazard, might we consider that an important strand in the American tradition is the role of *private* organizations in *public* policy? With this consideration, one then can contemplate the influence and consequence of, for example, the great foundations (Carnegie Foundation for the Advancement of Teaching, the Rockefeller Foundation, et al.) for shaping the nationwide options and directions that institutions, left to themselves and their individual resources, might not have made? Second, might we consider whether the Truman Commission Report of 1947 provided a manifesto of sorts for many of the themes—if not the particulars—of public policy for higher education in the decades after World War II? Such questions gain energy and interpretation from the lucid essays provided by authors Francis Keppel, David Breneman, and Maxine Greene.

1

THE ROLE OF PUBLIC POLICY IN HIGHER EDUCATION IN THE UNITED STATES: LAND GRANTS TO PELL GRANTS AND BEYOND

FRANCIS KEPPEL

INTRODUCTION: HAS THERE BEEN A CHANGE IN THE ROLE OF GOVERNMENT IN HIGHER EDUCATION?

Lawrence Cremin, in his account of the land ordinances of 1784, 1785, and 1787, pointed out in *American Education: The National Experience* (1980, p. 10) that, "far more important than the particular provisions regarding schools were the more general procedures for extending the American Government forms." When he later considered the Morrill Act of 1862 (p. 401), he wrote that the act "to establish Colleges of Agriculture and the Mechanic Arts provided further stimulus to the founding of new institutions and the expansion of older ones." The land ordinances carried out the Jeffersonian plan of how best to organize the newly available land by forming "distinct Republican states," in which education played its suitable, local part. The Morrill Act thought it to be in the national interest to stimulate educational institutions to strengthen the national economy through encouragement of state-managed institutions. These early actions of the federal government suggest that its underlying policies were to consider higher education as a means to achieve a larger governmental purpose of decentralization, in the land ordinances to build toward local and state self-government, in the Morrill Act to encourage state government to support institutions for agriculture and the mechanic arts.

Professor Keppel's death preceded final editing of this manuscript. The editors of this volume have made minor editorial changes from the original draft.

In neither case did the actions appear to have been based on a general public policy of building or expanding institutions of higher education primarily for their own sake. While educators, on patriotic or other occasions devoted to self-congratulation, have often suggested that federal or state governments have committed society to supporting colleges and universities on the basis of their inherent virtue, my own reading of history and personal participation in the formulation of particular public policies forces me to another conclusion: that public policy has used higher education as a means to an end, not as an end in itself. It has been assumed that colleges were trustworthy institutions that would benefit the students, and would adjust their affairs to accomplish public interests.

This conclusion makes me question the first sentence of the original charge given to me in writing this chapter:

> The role of government in the higher education sector has changed dramatically over this nation's history.

Certainly state governments have provided far greater financial support than in earlier days to a more diverse group of institutions. Certainly the federal government, since World War II, has decided to use a limited number of universities to carry out basic and applied research in the national interest. Certainly the federal government has also decided in the last quarter century to use higher education as a means of providing greater equality of opportunity for disadvantaged and minorities. But do these actions lead to the conclusion that "the role of government . . . has changed dramatically?" Does it mean that the United States' policies are directly comparable to the public policies of European nations in the support of universities, or that it is heading down the same road as that undertaken recently by Mrs. Thatcher's government in Britain?

As you will gather from my remarks so far, I have my doubts about the extent to which the role of government in this nation has "changed dramatically," particularly the extent to which federal policy has changed. Historical interpretation of events in my lifetime suggests differently. For example, as a junior staff member of the group that drafted the first version of the GI Bill of World War II, I was well aware that the basic motivations of the act included the fear of massive unemployment facing returning veterans and concern over a war-caused shortage of a college education generation—but by now many seem to believe that the government of the time acted to show its confidence in higher education institutions as such. The Higher Education Act of 1963 was designed to expand college facilities, lest children of the postwar baby boom would be unable to find a college to attend, which would not be politically or socially acceptable. The Higher Education Act of 1965 was part of the Great Society effort to provide something nearer equality of opportunity to the poor and the minorities. I even harbor the suspicion that the student financial aid legislation of the late 1970s was more designed to appeal to disgruntled middle-class parents than it was to support the needs of higher education, though the lobbies for higher education may understandably have been glad of the result.

Let me submit, therefore, that the federal role has not changed fundamentally—so far. But what of the future? What of the future policies of state governments, for whom the support of higher education is an increasingly heavy financial and management burden, increasingly seen as related to economic development? The charge to me for this chapter was:

> Along with this strong and varied way in which government has provided financial support for institutions of higher education has come varying amounts of accountability by the institutions and individuals who benefit directly from these programs.

Will these "varying amounts of accountability" so develop over time that they will combine in effect to change the role of government in higher education in the years to come? While the intent of policy and the use of higher education institutions to achieve social goals may continue, is it possible that the very process of carrying out these policies will fundamentally and dramatically change the relation of government to higher education?

QUALITY AND DIVERSITY: "RIGHT PERSON, RIGHT STUDY"

The title of this book includes the words "quality, diversity, and budgetary efficiency." They seem to me to admirably define the areas in which the carrying out of public policy might bring about change in the basic relationship, whatever the intent of particular legislation. I will focus on issues relating to quality and diversity with some reference to budgetary efficiency.

Quality: Consider first the word "quality," and one way (among many others) in which that word might be defined: the level of academic performance exhibited by students in higher education. There is little doubt that state governments in recent years have shown increasing interest in the topic. Peter T. Ewell and Carol M. Boyer in an article in the July/August 1988 issue of *Change* point out that a "growing number of states now require colleges and universities to undertake identifiable assessment programs. More significantly, growing numbers have signified their seriousness about the issue by linking an institution's response to eligibility for incentive funds or other tangible rewards." The authors embarked on visits to five states to make an intensive study of the development. One of their conclusions, which would not have surprised Jefferson and might even have pleased him, was stated in these words:

> One myth quickly put to rest as we travelled from state to state is that all state mandates are not alike. Not only do their actual contents differ, but each is played out in a unique economic and political context . . . Contrary to expectation, we found no substantial correlation between type of institution and response to state assessment initiative. Contrary to wide belief we found state leaders more than willing to listen to a range of local options in assessment—if intelligently sold. Harder for state leaders and policy makers to accept was institutional silence on the issue. (p. 4)

It is perhaps wise, at this stage of affairs, to assume that state governments will continue to press for action on assessing the quality of academic performance—and equally wise to expect that a variety of methods will be employed. Single, nationwide methods of testing students and of setting standards do not seem likely, and different states may react to different needs and set different priorities. Yet it would also seem prudent to assume that the piper will at least call for certain tunes, and thereby change the former relation between state government and higher education.

The situation of the federal government is at a very different stage of development. In *The Condition of Education*, the admirable report dealing with postsecondary education issued in 1988 by Commissioner Emerson J. Elliott of the National Center for Educational Statistics, it is stated on page three:

> National data comparing the knowledge and skills of students as they enter and then as they graduate from college are not available.

The report goes on to say on page nine:

> Several new periodic surveys are in progress at the National Center for Educational Statistics. These surveys will provide valuable baseline and trend data in a number of areas where little or no data exists.

Whether these surveys will add to our national knowledge about academic standards, student performance, and trends over time is not clear. There is, to put it mildly, hesitation in both political and educational circles to embark on a major national effort to assess the present state of what students are learning in higher education in our varied institutions, to record trend lines, or to make international comparisons. I cannot help but be reminded that a quarter century ago there was massive resistance by many leaders of the schools to the development of what has now become the accepted (and increasingly used) National Assessment of Educational Progress (NAEP). NAEP, indeed, will probably soon be used in making state-by-state comparisons of student performance, under state control. Perhaps higher education will travel a comparable path in the next quarter century. But in any case it seems unlikely that federal policy affecting higher education can soon be built on a solid data base, even if the federal government should decide for some reason to raise the academic quality of student performance in higher education. The present policy of providing student financial support without regard to which institution is attended by that student will, perhaps, continue largely unchanged.

Diversity: The second word in the title of this book, "diversity," leads me to two considerations that may change the federal role, perhaps even dramatically.

The first possibility may result from a combination of two developments in the last decade and a half: the nationwide concern with improving productivity and the rapid growth of student financial aid provided for those enrolled in proprietary schools. The attention now being given to the defaults on loans to students in some proprietary institutions to a degree both highlights and masks the underlying question: Does the quality of the result of the education and training, often in technical and service areas, justify the public investment? As the nation reevaluates the general federal program of vocational education, it is at least possible that the government will be urged to require some standards of student learning related to economic productivity. Since the federal government plays a considerable role in financing vocational education, such requirements may be seen as an exception to the general policies of staying away from controlling curricula and quality control that govern other student financial aid. The nonprofit sector in higher education, it is fair to say, does not generally regard proprietary institutions as members of its club and is less likely to resist some regulation and control. In any case, the issue of quality in proprietary institutions may arise at the federal level.

A second possibility, at least in my judgment, is even more speculative. We are observing nationally a hot competition among some colleges for academically talented students. This is not a new phenomenon, of course; nor are the ingredients that stimulate the competition: institutional desire to raise or maintain its reputation, faculty desire for talented and interested students, vigorous and increasingly sophisticated recruitment and retention (now entitled "enrollment management"), the use as an attraction to applicants of donated and institutional funds for merit scholarships in addition to aid based only on need (which the unkind may call Robin Hood grants since some of the funds come in part from charging higher tuition to those who can afford it), and the provision of amenities attractive to youth and, in some instances, to their elders as well.

Federal government policy has been built on the assumption that the competition for students, the market system, will work successfully to fit the student to the college for which he or she is qualified, which provides the program he or she needs, and which will stimulate his or her capacity to the fullest extent. Diversity of institutions is assumed to fit the needs of diversity of students.

When Lord Ashby of Clare College, Cambridge, was asked by the Carnegie Commission in 1971 to write an essay that "shall include a description and evaluation of American higher education," he chose the title *Any Person, Any Study*, which seems to me an accurate short description of underlying United States governmental policy for higher education. A free academic market, no fixed standards, and few external examinations are assumed to meet the nation's needs. But Lord Ashby, in speculating on some of the results of this policy, recorded one concern, which I venture to quote below, at some length:

> In the United States the traditional higher education and other kinds of postsecondary education are not segregated into different categories of institutions, and the distinction is correspondingly more difficult to define and maintain. Implicit in the plans for universal higher education is the assumption that this diverse mixture of disciplines and recipes, challenges which stretch the mind and codified techniques which merely stuff it, will accommodate the diversity of students who will come on the campus. And so it will, but the risk (as Martin Trow has observed) is that the popular functions of the university will swamp its autonomous functions.
>
> In America the thin stream of intellectual excellence is kept clear by two institutional devices: the highly selective university and the prestige graduate school. No one, however dedicated to egalitarianism, is likely to advocate open admission to the undergraduate college of Harvard or to graduate study in physics at Berkeley. But are these filters for excellence satisfactory? I venture to say no, they are not. (p. 31)
>
> All civilized countries . . . depend upon a thin stream of excellence to provide new ideas, new techniques, and the statesmanlike treatment of complex social and political problems. Without the renewal of this excellence, a nation can drop to mediocrity in a generation. The renewal of excellence is expensive: the highly gifted student needs informal instruction, intimate contact with other first-class minds, opportunities to learn the discipline of dissent from men who have themselves changed patterns of thought; in a word (it is one which has become a five-letter word of reproach) this sort of student needs to be treated as elite. De Tocqueville long ago predicted that this would be anathema in an egalitarian society. He was right: by a curious twist of reasoning, persons who enthusiastically agree to supernormal educational expenditure on the intellectually underprivileged, oppose supernormal expenditure on the intellectually overprivileged, who need it just as much. It is commonly assumed that America has to choose between one or other of two patterns of higher education:

mass or elite. I would deny this assumption. It is America's prime educational challenge to devise a coexistence of both patterns. There is already sufficient evidence to demonstrate that this could be done without dissolving and redesigning the whole system. (p. 101)

What can we say, almost twenty years later, about our nation's record in nourishing Lord Ashby's "thin, clear stream of excellence"? Is our record adequate in an era in which we are increasingly concerned about our ability to compete successfully in international scientific and economic affairs or, to use Ashby's phrase, in "the statesmanlike treatment of complex social and political problems"? Are we able to devise a "coexistence of both patterns . . . without dissolving and redesigning the whole system"?

As Commissioner Elliott has reported, we do not have much evidence available. What there is is not heartening. "Over the long term, from 1964–1987," the *Condition of Education* reports that on the basis of Graduate Record Examination (GRE) data, "only performance in mathematics shows a large degree of improvement, while scores for most other scientific and technical fields remained unchanged. Achievement declined . . . in the humanities and social sciences" (1988, p. 14). The GRE results can scarcely be considered a good measure of Ashby's thin, clear stream of excellence, but they at least raise a question in one's mind.

More directly related to federal programs of student financial aid (initiated in 1965 to raise the college participation rate of high ability yet disadvantaged students) are data from three national longitudinal data bases that have been collected over the past quarter century. The most recent study I have read, by Arthur Hauptman and Maureen McLaughlin, prepared for an Aspen conference in 1988, reports:

For students in the highest skills groups from the lower socio-economic status, there has been no appreciable change in their enrollment rates over the three studies. Students of high ability and low socio-economic status are still one third less likely to enroll than students of equal ability who come from the highest socio-economic status. (p. 15)

One source of the thin, clear stream seems to be partly blocked at the source.

Right Person, Right Study?: Just as important for the national interest is the answer to another question: are the students of high talent finding their way in adequate numbers to institutions and programs that are capable of nourishing that talent? To adapt Ashby's title, is the right person finding the right study? As far as I know, we do not have persuasive evidence on this second question. There is plenty of anecdotal and some institutional information that our successfully competing colleges enroll students of high quality, and that the still thinner and clearer stream that reaches a few graduate schools contains brilliant students. But is that the kind of information needed to persuade federal and state governments that our present system is meeting the new national and international needs? Is high talent finding the program best fitted to its potential? Do we not rather need data on both whether the proportion of high talent in the age group entering higher education is increasing and whether the "fit" between talent and program is even more effective and productive?

As Commissioner Elliott reported, "National data comparing the knowledge and skills of students as they enter and then graduate from college are not available." I assume this is true of students of high talent as well as other students.

We are, therefore, unable as a nation satisfactorily to answer the first question about the sources of the thin, clear stream entering higher education, and unable at all to answer the second question as to whether the right person finds the right study.

Is it reasonable to assume over the next decade or two that federal and state governments will be satisfied with what was described earlier as "the varying amounts of accountability by the institutions and individuals who benefit directly from these programs"? Earlier I suggested that it might be wise today to assume that state governments will continue to press for action on assessing the quality of academic performance in institutions under their governance. Given the national and international pressures for greater productivity, and the demands on the nation for increased international sophistication, it is possible to assume that the federal government will increasingly insist on better performance by higher education nationally in locating talent, especially high talent, and achieving an even better fit between that talent and the programs best designed to nurture it.

Lacking data on the present performance and trend lines to guide policy, I find it impossible to predict what the federal government either should or might do. I can only suggest that higher education should support greatly enlarged programs to identify talent in middle- and high-school years, and to encourage that talent to choose college-bound curricula, which probably means a major change in guidance and counselling services, especially in schools where the poor and minorities are clustered. It may also mean providing federal grants for such talent over and above the present system of meeting needs. The nation may have to decide that the "thin, clear stream of excellence" requires special treatment. And if indeed academic excellence is only one kind of excellence, other streams of high talent may need comparable stimulation as well.

If data show that the fit of talent to program is inadequate and higher education itself needs to adjust its programs, then the question will arise whether federal investment is being wisely spent. The larger public policy issue of whether the nation's human resources are being sufficiently developed to succeed in international competition will come to the point of decision at the federal level. Lacking data, we may well have to continue on our present path of assuming that the existing system of higher education is doing a satisfactory job of sorting and fitting. But what if data become available to raise doubts? Will the federal government stand still?

CONCLUSION

You will, of course, have noticed that I have wandered without invitation into the territory assigned to others in this book. I apologize to them though I fear that, knowing my habits, they will not be surprised. I can only plead that the title assigned to me, "The Role of Public Policy in Higher Education in the United States: Land Grants to Pell Grants and Beyond," was an invitation to a senior citizen to ramble. I welcome whatever comments and disagreements they might have. And I will benefit particularly, of course, from the responses and analyses of David Breneman and Maxine Greene. But as former dean of a faculty, you will understand if I am rather nervous at the reaction of a former college president and a professor to my work.

REFERENCES

ASHBY, ERIC. *Any Person, Any Study: An Essay on Higher Education in the United States.* New York: McGraw-Hill Book Co., 1971.

CREMIN, LAWRENCE A. *American Education: The National Experience, 1783-1876.* New York: Harper & Row, 1980.

ELLIOTT, EMERSON J. *The Condition of Education: Postsecondary Education*, Vol. 2. Washington, D.C.: National Center for Education Statistics, 1988.

EWELL, PETER T. and CAROL M. BOYER. *Change* 20, No. 4 (July/August 1988): 40–47.

HAUPTMAN, ARTHUR M., and MAUREEN MCLAUGHLIN. "Is the Goal of Access to Postsecondary Education Being Met?" A background paper prepared for the Education Policy Seminar, Aspen Institute, 1988.

2

IS THERE A FEDERAL POLICY TOWARD HIGHER EDUCATION?

DAVID W. BRENEMAN

It is a pleasure and an honor to have been asked to comment on the chapter by Francis Keppel, a man for whom I have the utmost respect. Mr. Keppel's distinguished career saw him involved as an active participant in many of the key education issues of the last twenty-five years or more, while I arrived on the Washington scene after most of the dramatic legislative enactments that marked Mr. Keppel's time had been achieved. His chapter serves as an excellent overview to the chapters that follow.

In reviewing the logic of the book it became apparent that this chapter was meant to provide an overview or historical context for the three following sections devoted to the themes of quality, diversity, and budgetary efficiency. In that spirit, Keppel's chapter opens with a challenge to the fundamental premise of the book that "the role of government in the higher education sector has changed dramatically over this nation's history," and he follows that discussion with observations on two of the themes—quality and diversity. In my chapter I will first discuss the arguments of his chapter with particular reference to his view about the role of government, and then emphasize certain topics or issues that were not covered in his chapter. I will restrict my remarks primarily to financial policies, as opposed to regulatory or qualitative discussions of education per se.

THE ROLE OF GOVERNMENT IN HIGHER EDUCATION

Has the Role Changed?: My first observation is that the bulk of Keppel's chapter is focused on federal, as opposed to state, policy in higher education. He begins by challenging the premise of this book by arguing that the fundamental role of the federal government in higher education has *not* changed in the last twenty-five years, or indeed

18

virtually since the beginning of the republic. His view, simply stated, is that the federal government has never really had a policy toward education, but rather has used the educational system as a means to accomplish other, more fundamental, federal ends, such as strengthening national defense, reducing unemployment, securing civil rights, reducing poverty, and spurring economic growth and development. Thus, when he argues that the federal role has not changed, he is interpreting that role in terms of the ultimate purposes served, not in terms of the nature, amount, or type of support provided to higher education.

In espousing this view, Keppel is in very good company, for over the years many observers of the Washington education scene have reached the same conclusion. Writing in 1961, for example, Alice Rivlin argued:

> The most important fact about federal policy toward higher education is that there has never been a clearly defined policy. Only rarely has Congress explicitly undertaken the support of higher education. Legislation affecting higher education has been a by-product of some other well-established federal concern, such as agriculture or public health or the disposal of public lands or military needs. This situation seems to be changing; the support of higher education as such is beginning to be recognized as an appropriate federal activity. (p. 118)

In my discussion I will draw heavily upon Rivlin's book, entitled *The Role of the Federal Government in Financing Higher Education*, because it was written at the beginning of the period under scrutiny in this book, and hence provides a valuable perspective on the thinking of that time. It is interesting to note, in the paragraph just cited, that Rivlin thought in 1961 that we were on the verge of a new era in which the federal government would take a positive and affirmative role in supporting higher education in its own right. Later in my remarks I will return to her analysis of the case for federal subsidies of higher education and evaluate the response to her arguments; for the time being, however, it is worth noting that she certainly would agree with Keppel's judgment on the federal role up to the early 1960s.

Having given that argument its due, it is surely true on another level that the theme of this volume is correct in suggesting that the role of government has changed significantly in the post-World War II era. Perhaps this debate is an example of the Hegelian concept that quantitative change can produce qualitative change, for the scale and nature of federal involvement has clearly expanded manifold. Once again, Rivlin's volume is instructive. In noting the increased support of university-based research, she writes, "Up to 1940 federal support of university research was largely confined to support of agricultural research in the land grant colleges" (1961, p. 24). After documenting the enormous increase in such support during World War II, she then notes that the federal government continues to support over 60 percent of the nation's research and development budget, up from 15 percent of the much smaller prewar budget (p. 34).

When we turn to student aid, which together with research support makes up the bulk of federal support for higher education today, Rivlin is able to describe only the post-World War II G.I. Bill and the newly enacted National Defense Education Act. Included in that latter act, of course, were graduate fellowships, an activity that received considerable federal support before being sharply reduced in the last years of the Johnson administration and in the Nixon administration. Rivlin's account of the federal role also includes the College Housing Loan Program, as well as some of the programs supporting academic facilities. In sum, when one looks back to 1961, one is struck by the limited amount of federal support available and by the tentative nature of the discussion regarding the future federal role. One is also struck, however, by a sense of excitement in Rivlin's book about bold new initiatives looming on the horizon.

In her chapter on the federal government's changing role, she writes:

> The National Defense Education Act may represent the beginning of a new era of explicit recognition of higher education as a legitimate area of federal concern. To be sure, the word "defense" is in the title and there is considerable verbiage about "national security" and the "present emergency." Nevertheless, the Act comes closer to being an out-and-out education measure than any previous legislation. (p. 119)

She goes on to note that the provision for a student loan program seems to indicate acceptance of the notion that helping undergraduates finance their education is a good thing in itself, and that the fellowship programs seem designed to increase the number and quality of college teachers, rather than simply producing more defense and health researchers.

In an effort to help clarify and formulate policy, Rivlin advances three arguments for federal subsidy of higher education—social justice, economic growth, and the national interest, by which she means the nonmarket benefits that we achieve through an educated citizenry. These arguments can be related to the opening chapter in the book, where she discusses the "crisis" in higher education (have we ever had a period when higher education was not in a crisis?). The crisis she foresaw in 1961 was the sharply growing demand for higher education (the baby boom), financing the rapidly increasing costs of higher education, and the plight of private colleges and universities. Behind her more abstract arguments for increased federal support was her judgment that federal aid would be needed to overcome the "crisis" facing colleges and universities in the 1960s. How would we evaluate her claims twenty-nine years later?

First, the argument for aid for low-income students (social justice) provided much of the rationale for expansion of federal programs in 1965 and 1972, giving us the current mix of grant, loan, and work programs that have helped millions of young people finance higher education. We have also witnessed the perhaps inevitable backsliding from the pure principle of aid to the needy in the move to provide aid to middle- and upper-income students in the late 1970s (Middle Income Student Assistance Act) and in the shift from grants to loans that marked the 1980s. Nonetheless, providing aid to low-income students seems to be well established as federal policy, coupled with steady pressure to extend that aid to middle- and upper-income families.

The argument for economic growth seems to have been accepted as a basis for both federal and state support of research and development efforts, as well as for student aid, viewed as investment in human capital. Certainly in recent years the emphasis on international competitiveness has produced much interest, particularly at the state level, in ways to use the university for increased productivity, technical innovation, and local economic development. Again, this argument seems to be well accepted as a basis for continuing federal financial support of higher education.

Only in one area did Rivlin's analysis go seriously awry; I refer to her notion that the federal government might focus specifically on the plight of private colleges and universities, providing institutional assistance in much the same way that state governments do for public institutions. The issue of direct institutional aid was the battleground of the Education Amendments of 1972, and was settled decisively on behalf of aid to students (basic educational opportunity grants) and against aid to institutions, whether private or public. Arguably, this historic decision put an end to the potential federal role of providing direct support to education, as opposed to students or to research projects. Had the decision gone the other way, and had funds for institutional aid been appropriated, we would not be arguing whether the federal role in higher education had changed dramatically, for clearly it would have. As it stands, one would have to say that Rivlin's vision has only been partly realized, and that Keppel's argument cannot be dismissed. One is forced to emphasize the growth in federal funding rather than any fundamental change in federal purpose in deciding the argument.

As a small footnote to history, it is worth noting that the Education Amendments of 1972 did create the State Student Incentive Grant (SSIG) program, which was designed in part to help private colleges by encouraging the growth of state programs of student aid. Had that program grown significantly, the competitive position of private colleges might have improved markedly, for the indirect effect would likely have been an increase in public university tuition levels. The federal government, however, has shied away from any attempt to influence state policy on the pricing of higher education, another bit of evidence favoring Keppel's position.

Quality: Let me turn briefly to Keppel's discussion of quality in higher education and the government's role (or lack thereof) in influencing it. Keppel is surely right in focusing on the state, as opposed to the federal, role in this area, although this area remains murky at best. We simply do not have any consensus on how to evaluate a multidimensional attribute such as quality, nor any clear notion how to measure it or improve it by state actions (other than by increased financial support). Quality is a bit like pornography—we cannot define it, but we know it when we see it. Nonetheless, efforts are being made primarily at the state, local, and institutional levels to improve it, and it may be that the current rage for assessment will produce positive results. I would have to state my preference, however, for private as opposed to public efforts in this area and would hope that private accrediting activities could be strengthened rather than have that function taken over by the state.

I must say I was somewhat surprised that Keppel did not mention the role that former Secretary of Education William Bennett has played in using his "bully pulpit" to lecture all of us on the need to improve educational quality. Regardless of one's views about Bennett's prescriptions or motivation, he demonstrated undeniably that the secretary of education can focus national attention on the educational agenda in a way that no one else can. Fortunately (or unfortunately, depending on one's philosophy) the secretary has little other than the power of persuasion, but then again, that is what we say about the presidency!

Diversity: Keppel's paper concludes with an interesting and thoughtful discussion of the nature and meaning of diversity, with particular reference to institutions and programs, as well as to the often neglected needs of the most talented segment of the student population. I found his critical treatment of the role of proprietary institutions welcome, for I consider it one of the shameful features of our era that these schools have amassed political power far in excess of their educational value. There is much unfinished business to be done in both evaluating the performance of these schools and excluding from eligibility for federal student aid those programs that merely exploit our most vulnerable citizens.

Similarly, I can do nothing but applaud Keppel's discussion of the educational needs of our most talented students and the failure of public policy for the last twenty years to concentrate on that group. It is easy to assume that the "best and the brightest" will take care of themselves, but we cannot afford to take this group of young people for granted. We have no way of knowing the amount of talent loss incurred in this country, but I cannot believe that it is negligible. Much of the damage is probably done, however, by the time students are of college age, and thus this matter would seem to be treated best at the earlier stages of education.

TAX POLICY AND HIGHER EDUCATION

A few words now on subjects not mentioned in Keppel's chapter. First, federal and state tax policy are of vital importance to the financial well-being of colleges and universities, and should not be overlooked. Emil Sunley, writing in a Brookings volume that I coedited twelve years ago, estimated federal tax expenditures on higher education in 1977 at nearly $4 billion, the sum of nine separate direct or indirect policies (1978, p. 284). Arguably, the most important federal legislation affecting higher education in recent times was the Tax Reform Act of 1986.

Related issues would include recent federal proposals for tax-favored treatment of savings for higher education and policy decisions on state savings plans, such as the tax ruling handed down on the Michigan Education Trust. Another hardy perennial in this area is the tuition tax credit, a proposal that has thus far been rejected at the federal level, but will not die. The exemption of institutions from state and local property taxes is also vital public policy, periodically subject to attack. And, in an era of monstrous federal budget deficits, we can hardly be surprised when proposals surface to tax endowment income, as they did in 1988. In short, at the federal level, the tax side of public policy is every bit as important as the expenditure side.

ISSUES IN STATE POLICY

State policies of support for higher education were also not discussed in much detail in the Keppel chapter. This omission is understandable because one would have to write fifty different stories to do justice to the topic. Let me simply note three areas of state policy that have exerted enormous influence on the shape and nature of higher education and that have undergone substantial change in recent decades.

First, the most significant institutional change in this era is the growth—in some states the wholesale creation—of community college systems. In 1956-57, the nation had 377 public two-year colleges; in 1986-87, 1,068. In 1956-57, public community colleges enrolled 776,000 students; in 1986-87, 4.7 million (American Council on Education, pp. 7-8). All of our talk in Washington about programs to guarantee access

to higher education would have been hollow had the states and locali-
ties not built this incredible system of "people's colleges." In our
lifetimes we will not see a comparable program of institutional expansion. The community college is America's one unique contribution to
the world's portfolio of educational institutions.

A second policy development of critical importance was the growth
in the 1970s of state programs of aid for students attending private
colleges and universities. It is interesting to speculate how many private colleges would have disappeared by now in the absence of these
programs. One side effect of these programs was the reduction of
interstate mobility of students, for now a private college costs a resident of the state less than it does an out-of-state student. Despite
heroic analytical efforts to devise incentives for states to make their
programs portable over state lines, with few exceptions, such aid is
limited to state residents who attend private institutions within the
state. The federal government could have used the SSIG program to
provide incentives for portability, but chose not to do so.

One reason that Washington avoided expanding SSIG into a large
federal student aid program was the probability that it would have
influenced state policies toward public tuition levels, the third issue I
wish to mention. The bulk of state aid to higher education comes in the
form of institutional subsidies, which can be thought of as non-need
based grants of many thousands of dollars each to students enrolled in
public colleges and universities. The share of educational costs to be
borne by students and their families versus the state is a crucial policy
issue decided annually in each of our states. One would like to think
that the division of costs is determined in a systematic and rational
manner, but most observers would not attribute economic rationality to
this quintessentially political decision.

THE FUTURE

Let me close with a few brief thoughts about the future, which, as the
pundits say, is *not* what it used to be. The overriding federal issue is
the budget deficit—for a particularly chilling vision of the problems we
have created for ourselves in this regard, I refer you to Ben Friedman's
book *Day of Reckoning* (1988). The Reagan fiscal policy of borrow and
spend, borrow and spend, must come to an end, leaving little room for
new federal spending on higher education. While I assume that Washington will continue to be an important partner in the total picture of
higher education support, I do not look for new initiatives of any great
interest from this sector in the next few years.

Instead, I see a continuation of interesting developments at the
state and private levels, much as we have had in recent years. Con-

cerns for economic development will continue to drive much of state policy, and higher education will benefit from that thrust. As Theodore W. Schultz has pointed out, "The decisive factors of production in improving the welfare of poor people are not space, energy, and cropland; the decisive factors are *the improvement in population quality and advances in knowledge*" (1981, p. 4). Thus, higher education will continue to flourish and receive support, not necessarily for its own sake, as Keppel has pointed out, but because it is the surest means to an improved quality of life. And, unlike so much of our manufacturing industry, higher education is not subject to foreign competition—Tokyo University is not likely to displace Harvard. Thus, I admit to considerable optimism about the future of higher education, unusual perhaps for a practitioner of the dismal science, but optimism that is reasonably based nonetheless. I hope that this volume sheds light on the path ahead.

REFERENCES

AMERICAN COUNCIL ON EDUCATION. *Community College Fact Book*. New York: Macmillan Publishing Co., 1988.

FRIEDMAN, BENJAMIN M. *Day of Reckoning*. New York: Random House, 1988.

RIVLIN, ALICE M. *The Role of the Federal Government in Financing Higher Education*. Washington, D.C.: Brookings Institution, 1961.

SCHULTZ, THEODORE W. *Investing in People*. Berkeley: University of California Press, 1981.

SUNLEY, EMIL. "Federal and State Tax Policies." In *Public Policy and Private Higher Education*, edited by David W. Breneman and Chester E. Finn, Jr., pp. 281–319. Washington, D.C.: Brookings Institution, 1978.

3

THE DEMANDS OF DIVERSITY: IMPLICATIONS FOR PUBLIC POLICY

MAXINE GREENE

This is a paper by someone who has never held a policy position, someone writing from the vantage points of the humanities and educational philosophy. It is also, in part, a response to the work of Francis Keppel, whose lifelong commitment to equity and excellence cannot but help keep alive a desire to contribute to more humane social change.

My closest contact with policymakers on the federal level occurred when I was president of the American Educational Research Association (AERA), at the time when Terrel Bell was secretary of education, and when there still existed a National Institute of Education. I certainly did have the impression at that moment that the federal government was playing and would continue to play a significant role, most especially in the support and maintenance of an educational research community with a strong involvement in research and development in a multiplicity of fields. Understandably, I no longer have quite so strong an impression, what with the recent preoccupation with statistics and assessment. I do acknowledge, along with Francis Keppel, that the most obvious contribution of the federal government since the Second World War has been in the areas of selected research and (lately, to a limited degree) the provision of increased equality of opportunity. In the present period, the federal government has been using whatever "bully pulpit" it finds available and whatever financial resources can be mustered to involve colleges and universities in the nation's search for productivity, technological innovation, and various contributions to "competitiveness." This is quite different, as can be easily seen, from a concentration on traditional humanistic aims, cultural renewal, or the cultivation of citizenship!

As Francis Keppel has reminded us, this does not signify a very dramatic break from the past, either in terms of veteran employment or the allaying of middle-class fears aroused by what seemed to be an

26

overemphasis on aid to minorities and the poor. Acknowledging as we must higher education's economic, scientific, and technical roles, calling (as I believe we must) for more deliberate action to promote fairness on all levels of the population, I am still convinced that fundamental to federal policy ought to be concern for language, citizenship, and commitment to community. For all the resounding talk about reclaiming our legacy and attaining cultural literacy, these concerns have been almost totally lacking in the rhetoric of public policy regarding higher education.

DIFFERENTIATION AND DIVERSITY

In current literature on higher education, there has been a great stress on the universal accessibility and openness of our educational system in comparison with others. Writers in the field call proper attention to what Burton Clark calls the "large, heavily differentiated open system of higher education" with its elite and its mass functions (1987, pp. 3-23). Commentators continue to remind us of the tension between credentialling and quality education; and almost everyone pays heed to the likelihood that diversity is American higher education's guiding vision. Martin Trow has recently said that our system is the best in the world, not only because of the great research universities in the United States, but even more "because of the numbers and diversity of our four-year and two-year colleges, their nearly 12.5 million students and hundreds of thousands of teaching faculty, and the vital functions these institutions perform for their students and for society as a whole" (1987, p. 414). This has not, of course, prevented critics (some of them at the federal level) from attacking higher education for the abandonment of some mythic Golden Age, for disarray, for relativism, indeed for a "closing of the American mind." And all this has been carried on in an impersonal language that tends to ignore the uniqueness of the various institutions and the facts of diversity themselves.

Struck by the lack of attention to what was once thought of as a literally "republican" interest in the citizen's virtuous responsibility to care for the res publica, I am continually reminded that it was that interest which underlay the founding of our postrevolutionary secular colleges. The fading of what is thought of as republicanism in the traditional sense has been traced by historians; and the articulation of what is involved in the creation—or the recreation—of a polis has been a concern, not among official policymakers or official critics, but among representatives of the humanistic and social disciplines, many of them now interested in the hermeneutic or interpretive approach to what is "real." Like Gary Quehl in his report *Higher Education and Public Interest* (1988), I should like to see a new social contract negotiated between higher education and the public: one that defines what the nature of their relationship should be in the years immediately ahead. Quehl believes that public understanding of the purposes of higher education "must strike a balance between short-term economic needs, both individual and societal, and long-term pursuit of knowledge and truth that is the lifeblood of the academy." In my view, this is unlikely to happen if we cannot educate what John Dewey once called an "articulate public" (1954, p. 184); and it seems to me equally unlikely that we will experience the changes presumed in this book if public policy statements do not respond to present calls for a restoration of community.

I think of the philosopher Alasdair MacIntyre ending *Beyond Virtue* with the stark reminder of the need to construct "local forms of community within which civility and the intellectual and moral life can be sustained through the dark ages which are already upon us" (1981, p. 245). I think of Richard Rorty speaking of himself as one of the "partisans of solidarity" in opposition to the "realist partisans of objectivity," one who thinks of his "sense of community as having no foundation except shared hope and the trust created by such sharing" (1985, p. 15). The crucial point is that this becomes an affirmation of belief in intelligence and rationality, as well as in liberal democracy; and that, in turn, becomes the kind of argument for higher education we might some day hear from a federal government interested in higher education for its own sake. Like Dewey, Hannah Arendt argued in her time for a public sphere or a public space (1958); Martha Nussbaum today speaks of "relational goods" in *The Fragility of Goodness* and reminds us that, for Aristotle, the main job of politics was to educate the young so that they would become capable of leading good lives according to their own choice (1986, pp. 252-63). Contemplating that, some of us might like to see a restoration of politics too.

Robert Bellah and his associates, in *Habits of the Heart*, put great stress on the loss of community in this country and the lack of attention to the public good. Some of this they attribute to the tension in the universities, where the hunger for common cultural meanings experienced by many persons is at odds with the emphasis on technique, which is encouraged by federal policy and which has, thus far, won out over the others. Bellah and his associates remind us of the focal transformation of the university in the late nineteenth century, as professional specialties developed and the so-called man of learning became the twentieth century "scientist" (1985, pp. 298-99). They go on to point to the many positive achievements in this transformation: "The new educational system prepared vastly larger numbers of people for employment in an industrial society, and it included as students those who, because of class, sex, or race, were almost completely excluded in the early nineteenth century." But they warn that we must be aware of the costs. "One of the major costs of the rise of the

research university and its accompanying professionalism and special-
ization was the impoverishment of the public sphere. As Thomas
Haskell has put it, the new man of science had to 'exchange general
citizenship in society for membership in the community of the competent' " (p. 299); and this has made it increasingly difficult to reconceive
public policy in the last decade.

FROM DISPERSION TO SOLIDARITY

Turning to Francis Keppel's interest in what can be done to encourage
talented poor and minority young people to choose college-bound
curricula and thereby to widen the "stream of excellence" (as well as to
expand the spheres of citizenship), I cannot but recall Robert Reich's
comment in *Tales of a New America* that a modern society "premised
solely upon the principle of selfish interest, even of the enlightened
variety, cannot summon the shared responsibility upon which any
scheme of social insurance or social investment must depend" (1987,
pp. 179-80). He reminds us of the way in which our discussions about
poor people are couched in terms of public charity or in terms of
guarding "them" against hardship while helping "them" gain independence. We must, he suggests, inculcate—or educate for—"mutual
responsibility and simultaneously celebrate the resulting mutual gain."
This goes back, for him, to a call for the value of "solidarity" reminis-
cent of Rorty and, yes, Franklin Delano Roosevelt, rather than philanthropy or altruism.

To ponder what solidarity and a public space might mean in these
times is to confront head-on what Burton Clark describes as "competitive disorder" among universities (1987, p. 46). Discussing the disper-
sion of initiative, and of the various master plans and mechanisms of
coordination to be found among the states, he writes that state officials
try to "specify jurisdictions, reduce overlap, and eliminate institutional
redundancies. But the competitive imprint has not been eradicated."
He says that if universities and colleges "find state guidance not to
their liking, they wriggle out from under the master plans and state
requirements as best as they can. And with public control always
divided among fifty states, with the national government more in the
background than up front, 'state coordination' ends up as much on the
side of interstate rivalry and competition as in the service of an imposed order" (p. 51). Public institutions reach towards private sources,
while private institutions widen their financial bases by extracting
support from public quarters. This includes the Pell grants and student
loans. A point frequently made is that, as tuitions rise to meet rising
costs, a larger part of those tuitions is designated as student aid to
subsidize those who cannot afford to pay the full cost. Uniform tuitions

must be high enough to support both the program and students who cannot themselves pay their expenses. The consequence is that tuition levels will rise to such an extent as to make it impossible for more and more families to receive the subsidies they need. At once, the diversifying responsibilities of higher education will continue requiring additional staff commitments, which will become more and more of a financial drain.

There is some irony in the prediction that higher education is likely to see increasing funding for student financial aid programs. As Keppel points out, accountability and performance measurement will be used more and more frequently to justify the acquisition and allocation of financial resources. The issue of authentic quality control over student aid remains unresolved. It appears that new policies will be devised when it comes to matters of access and choice, and that these will differ from state to state. Diane Yavorsky and Laurence Marcus, writing with a special emphasis upon New Jersey, discuss the reports recently issued by the National Commission of the States and the National Governors' Association, both of which emphasize the importance of undergraduate education for the sake of state economic development. These reports represent the views of governors, state officials, and higher education commissioners, those who "serve as the most powerful and practical potential source of outside influence over public institutions of higher education. In an era when policy leadership in education...has been shifting from the federal to the state level, this is clearly an audience of consequence" (1987, p. 446). The aim of both reports appears to be a transformation of the state role in bringing about desired improvements.

Yavorsky and Marcus also make the case that, in response to the establishment of incentives and the removal of constraints on the pursuit of excellence, "more rigorous assessment and accountability will be expected from institutions in exchange" (p. 447). Again, I find myself struck by and concerned about the emphasis on budgetary efficiency and the setting aside of the meanings of quality, the nature of governing norms. What comes to the forefront is the talk of trade-off and triage; and, given the state of the current dialogue, this is sadly understandable.

MULTIPLE PERSPECTIVES AND A PUBLIC

The spirit of apparent rigor and trade-off permeated the address given by then Assistant Education Secretary Chester Finn at the 1988 Annual Convention of AERA, especially when he complained about what he saw to be a domination of research centers by single research paradigms. What he viewed as "unconventional" in the way of scholarship was being discouraged, he said; and the very existence of such centers (presumably characterized by such practices) prevented the United States Department of Education from supporting research grants and field-initiated research. As we know, the Office of Educational Research and Improvement (OERI) replaced the National Institute of Education; and, with its compendia called "What Works" in the background, OERI has been translating and disseminating research findings rather than initiating new undertakings in those areas, or in the areas of equity. Finn has often made the point that the clientele for the dissemination of reliable data and pertinent research findings extends far beyond the profession itself, and that argues for a shift of resources from the conduct of new research to the explication of what is already on the "shelf" and to the eradication of (for whatever the reason) the complacency with regard to what is silenced, set aside, perhaps even lost.

What is silenced, it seems to me, is the swelling talk with regard to what Howard Gardner calls "multiple intelligences" (1983) and how they might be tapped to feed into the "stream of excellence," if excellence is conceived of in a more than monological way. What is set aside is what Clifford Geertz talks of as "a mutually reinforcing network of social understandings" (1983, p. 151). This notion derives from the view that today "thought is spectacularly multiple as product and wondrously singular as process," and that it has become important, as never before, to create a "disciplinary matrix" (p. 152). Then Geertz writes about what happens when the imagery gets political—"an uneasiness expressed in a number of not altogether concordant ways: as a fear of particularism, a fear of subjectivism, a fear of idealism, and, of course, summing them all into a sort of intellectualist Grande Peur, the fear of relativism" (p. 153). His affirmation of multiplicity and difference, along with his call for reciprocity among distinctive specialists and individuals, makes me see connections between his view and the idea of people coming together in speech and action to create a public space. As Hannah Arendt saw it, "The reality of the public realm relies on the simultaneous presence of innumerable perspectives and aspects in which the common world presents itself and for which no common measurement or denominator can ever be devised. . . . Being seen and heard by others derive their significance from the fact that everybody sees and hears from a different position. This is the meaning of public life" (1958, p. 57). If we do seriously acknowledge and respect diversity, if we are able to affirm the multiple and changing possibilities within institutions of higher learning, we may be able to think in terms of "innumerable perspectives" even as we try to make sense of the "common world," in our case the common world of higher learning. In any event, I should like to see the problem of the public kept in the foreground as we ponder new contracts between the federal government and the people, as we strive to reconceive the role of higher education with regard to an endangered polity.

REFERENCES

ARENDT, HANNAH. *The Human Condition*. Chicago: University of Chicago Press, 1958.

BELLAH, ROBERT N., Richard Masden, William M. Sullivan, Ann Swidler, and Steven M. Tipton. *Habits of the Heart*. Berkeley: University of California Press, 1985.

CLARK, BURTON R. *The Academic Life: Small Worlds, Different Worlds*. Princeton: Carnegie Foundation for the Advancement of Teaching, 1987.

DEWEY, JOHN. *The Public and Its Problems*. Athens, OH: Swallow Press, 1954.

GARDNER, HOWARD. *Frames of Mind: A Theory of Multiple Intelligences*. New York: Basic Books, 1983.

GEERTZ, CLIFFORD. *Local Knowledge*. New York: Basic Books, 1983.

MACINTYRE, ALASDAIR. *Beyond Virtue*. Notre Dame: Notre Dame University Press, 1981.

NUSSBAUM, MARTHA. *The Fragility of Goodness*. Cambridge: Cambridge University Press, 1986.

QUEHL, GARY. *Higher Education and Public Interest*. Washington, DC: CASE, 1988.

REICH, ROBERT B. *Tales of a New America*. New York: Times Books, 1987.

RORTY, RICHARD. "Solidarity of Objectivity?" In *Post-Analytic Philosophy*, edited by John Rajchman and Cornel West, pp. 3–16. New York: Columbia University Press, 1985.

TROW, MARTIN. "The National Reports on Higher Education: A Skeptical View." *Educational Policy* 1, No. 4 (1987): 413–425.

YAVORSKY, DIANE K. and LAURENCE R. MARCUS. "Converting Crises to Challenges: New Jersey's Effort to Promote State College Quality." *Educational Policy* 1, No. 4 (1987): 445–459.

SECTION II

The Tenuous Connection: Public Policy and Higher Education Quality

Aside from budgetary matters, quality is probably the primary education-related concern of public policymakers today. Years of declining SAT scores, publication of *A Nation at Risk* (1983) by the National Commission on Excellence in Education, and growing concern about America's ability to compete in a global market have sensitized government officials to the tenuous connection between public policy and education quality. In spite of numerous government programs and billions of dollars dedicated to strengthening our higher education system, a great deal of evidence suggests that America's colleges and universities are not producing enough of the highly skilled, creative talent the nation needs to prosper in a dynamic technological era.

Budget-minded politicians often argue that more money from Washington or the state capital will not automatically improve educational programs or students' performance. The chapters in this section reflect on the complex relationship between public policy and educational quality and lend support to this political platitude. However, the authors do not offer legislators and other government policymakers an easy exit from the educational quality arena. Rather, their chapters demonstrate that public policymaking is a highly skilled craft that requires the best efforts of both educational and government leaders.

In his chapter "The Influence of Public Policy on the Quality of Higher Education," Gordon Davies illuminates the difficulties and common shortcomings of public policymaking. He acknowledges that developing public policy that is good for everyone is very hard to do and often leads to undesirable homogenization rather than quality enhancement. From his perspective as head of a major government agency coordinating higher education, Davies speaks with the authority only years of front-line experience can provide. He writes candidly about the plethora of forces that make good public policy difficult to design as well as the unintended consequences that often result from well-meaning policy initiatives. His awareness that public policy frequently responds to fads and seeks simple solutions may account for Davies' flexible conception of educational excellence. Davies argues that educational quality is a relative phenomenon that varies in different settings and circumstances. In his opinion, institutions should be valued for the particular role they play in the educational system, not for their position on some rigid, idealized standard of excellence. Davies sees a relative definition of quality as a key element in the defenses of institutional autonomy and distinctiveness. He believes it is unwise to apply one standard to all institutions in a dynamic society with a diverse higher education system. A flexible standard can serve to protect higher education from what Davies describes as "the dubious craft of policymaking."

Amy Gutmann, in "What Counts as Quality in Higher Education?", concurs with Davies' belief that a pluralistic society must have a plurality of standards of quality. She is not comfortable with a single set of assessment criteria by which higher education should be judged. In contrast, Gutmann asserts that higher education quality is relative to an institution's purposes. What constitutes quality at a national research university does not necessarily constitute quality at the local community college. Yet Gutmann refuses to say that "anything goes," that colleges and universities should be totally free to "do their own thing." Instead she advocates a principle of pluralism in higher education. Institutions should be assessed according to their contributions to the "three significant social purposes" that higher education serves in the United States: as gatekeepers to the professions, as sanctuaries of free and critical inquiry, and as communities of students and scholars. Gutmann cautions against the "measurement mania" that appeals to some public policymakers. The purpose of public education policy, in her view, should be to foster principled pluralism, to preserve diversity in America's higher education system. The overall public policy challenge she identifies is "to avoid the problematic side effects without giving up the goods policies further." In sum, Gutmann offers a basis for assessing the quality of colleges and universities without resorting to the oversimplified number crunching that so perplexes many educators. Yet she leaves no doubt that the task of judging and preserving quality will not be easy for educators or policymakers.

Denis Doyle proposes a strategy radically different from the two other authors in his chapter, "Higher Education Quality: The Eye of the Beholder." Instead of advocating more sensitive and more enlightened public policy in support of education quality, Doyle suggests restoring market forces in higher education. He argues that as long as public money is involved, there is no escaping the hand of the public policy-maker. The conditions of the times, rather than political philosophies, seem to determine how and what public policy is made. Whether political liberals or conservatives are in office, if the opportunity arises, public policymakers will get involved with education for better or for worse. And because public policy tools are blunt instruments, more akin to a hammer than a scalpel, some negative consequences inevitably result. In spite of traditions and structures that buffer higher education institutions from meddling legislators and bureaucrats, Doyle believes that higher education quality cannot be completely protected from the vagaries of the public policy process. Hence, Doyle's strategy is to minimize government intrusion by reinforcing market strategies. By letting the beneficiary (the student) pay the bulk of the costs of education and by unleashing institutional competition, Doyle suggests that higher education will become more consumer oriented and more responsive. Enhanced educational quality should result as well. Whether Doyle's assessment of the steps needed to protect educational quality is on or off target, his provocative analysis is guaranteed to stimulate a lively dialogue among public servants charged with promoting educational excellence.

Concerns about the tenuous and controversial connection between public policy and educational quality are likely to persist through the 1990s. The chapters in this section offer substantial food for thought for individuals charged with maintaining educational quality through the complex alliance between education and public policy. Each author provides a distinctive philosophical perspective on an issue that is too easily and often erroneously reduced to simplistic political positions and methodological strategies. This section makes it abundantly clear that educational quality is not the responsibility solely of education professionals or government personnel. It is the shared responsibility of everyone who cares about the welfare and future prospects of a dynamic society.

4

THE INFLUENCE OF PUBLIC POLICY ON THE QUALITY OF HIGHER EDUCATION

GORDON K. DAVIES

My assigned topic is "The Influence of Public Policy on the Quality of Higher Education." I think that public policy does affect quality, although not always for the better, not always explicitly, and not always as intended. But we can control the effects of policy to some extent, and I shall propose an approach that we have used in Virginia higher education to do so.

There are at least three working definitions of quality left to us in a postmetaphysical age. 1) Quality is whatever is valued (and paid for) in a society. 2) Quality is whatever the prevailing cultural and economic hegemony defines it to be. 3) Quality is whatever we in higher education think it is. The three overlap and are in tension with one another. None of them is adequate, but I shall not try to come up with a better definition. Instead, I am interested in developing a way of dealing with quality questions that offers higher education some protection from errant public policy.

REFLECTIONS ON PUBLIC POLICY, POLICYMAKING, AND HIGHER EDUCATION

"Public policy" itself is a term that warrants consideration. I regard it in somewhat the same way St. Augustine must have regarded time. The venerable bishop of Hippo complained that he understood perfectly well what time was until he was asked to define it.

I take a broad view, considering public policy to be articulated in the law, in regulations and guidelines, in the budget (regarded by many as the most philosophical document published in Virginia), and in government practice. Public policy is the rules for official behavior and the behavior itself.

37

Someone once remarked that two things one doesn't want to watch being made are sausage and policy. Indeed, the process of policymaking often is neither sanitary nor reassuring. But its results can affect our lives in ways that are quite striking.

Public policy is generalized to cover some function of government. Whether it is explicit or, as it often is, implicit, judgments are made about what "the people" need, want, or will tolerate. "The greatest good for the greatest number" is a goal toward which policymakers in a democracy strive when they are conscious of goals at all. (There is, of course, a more operational view. "Public policy is whatever we can get away with," a politician once told me.)

But definitions of "the people" often exclude whole sets of individuals, not because the definitions are based on generalizations—we must generalize—but because our generalizations are drawn improperly. The people, as Alexander Hamilton observed without acknowledging his literary debts, "is a great beast." The "greatest number" often is not that at all, but rather a minority that is taken, erroneously, to represent the whole.

Thomas Jefferson laid before the General Assembly of Virginia the first piece of education legislation presented in the Western hemisphere. It provided that every child would have three years of education at the commonwealth's expense. The bill was defeated but set us on the way toward public education.

By "every child," of course, Jefferson meant no such thing. He did not mean to include the children of slaves and, while the bill is silent on this, probably also did not mean to include girls. But the fault lies not with Jefferson's proposal for public education. It lies with the inadequacy of his generalization about "every child." Such inadequacies are always with us.

In higher education, we have at one time or another worked from basic assumptions that were represented as generalizations about the needs and demands of the people but that actually excluded blacks, Hispanics, women, and others. A 1955 legislative study of Virginia higher education, for instance, included two sets of enrollment projections: one for whites and one for blacks. One year after the Brown decision, the authors of the Virginia report could not conceive of a unified system of higher education for students of all races. We still deal with the residual effects of assumptions about girls not wanting to become scientists and engineers and about blacks being best suited for manual trades. Schools and colleges have excluded nonresident aliens and students from other states, disabled persons, sick children, pregnant women, the poor, and young mothers with no place to leave their babies. In a fit of fiscal prudence, we even excluded white, middle-income families from financial aid programs.

These exclusionary generalizations persist, of course, and are far more subtle than most of us recognize. They are deeply embedded in policies that affect financial support, administration and governance, and the curricula of higher education.

Policymaking as an activity is inimical to particularity. Policymakers, in so far as they belong to a governing (though elected, appointed, or anointed) minority, tend to define the good of those with whom they are most familiar—or with whose needs they are most familiar—as the common good.

Yet we must make policy, we must generalize, in order to fulfill the normal functions of society (including speaking to one another). Even when we try to deal with each individual human being, or with each situation, we think in patterns. We draw analogies among similar persons or situations. We search for general rules to apply—especially when we are trying to be fair.

Many of us who have testified before legislative committees know that one good anecdote—especially a heart-tugger—can beat pages of careful analysis hands down when public policy decisions are being made. The well-timed anecdote is an occupational hazard of policymaking.

But the anecdote—or story—is also a powerful antidote to generalization, and that is why it is so effective. The story is concrete, particular, embedded in space and time. In stories we tell, as we cannot using abstractions, who we are, whence we have come, and whither we are going. Stories are about *this* woman rather than about humankind, *this* university rather than about institutions of higher education. Daniel Webster's famous defense of Dartmouth College was effective not so much because it was brilliant (though it may have been) as because it was intensely personal, intensely particular.

We cannot make adequate policy without both the concrete and the abstract. Tough-minded analysis should lead to generalizations that are tested against both personal and institutional stories. In Thomas Mann's *The Magic Mountain*, Hans Castorp describes Herr Settembrini's teaching method as proceeding "first by means of anecdotes, then by abstractions." This constant movement between the particular and the general is dialectic. If there is an aesthetic of public policy, it is an aesthetic of tension between the particular and the general. From it emerges the best possible public policy.

QUALITY IN HIGHER EDUCATION: THREE WORKING DEFINITIONS

Whatever is Valued (and Paid for) in a Society: Policy sometimes defines quality by allocating money to support certain behaviors rather than others. This definition is, often as not, implicit and may be at odds with political rhetoric. We say, for instance, that we value teachers and teaching as a profession, but a substantial amount of public policy implies that we do not. We do not give teachers the status of professionals in choosing the textbooks and setting the curriculum. We do not let them operate the schools, and we certainly refuse to let them control access to the profession, a privilege exercised by other professionals (for instance, lawyers, doctors, and engineers).

In our representative political system, policy often emerges from coalitions formed to advance special or common interests. The tendency of such coalitions is to be broad and egalitarian, at least insofar as necessary to produce a voting majority. In a relatively stable legislative body, these coalitions become structural and do not have to be formed anew on each issue.

The policies that emerge from coalitions will tend to spread governments' resources more or less equitably, if not equally, among participating interest groups. In higher education, this often results in money being spread around to the various institutions in ways that will tend to homogenize a state-supported system.

Public policy sometimes provides incentives that elicit behavior policymakers did not intend. For instance, funding formulae that are based exclusively on enrollment levels encourage institutions to grow in enrollment in order to get more staff, operating funds, and buildings.

While political and educational leaders alike may recognize that some funding policies provide incentives for undesirable behavior, they also may be reluctant to change them because formulae are a fairly simple and measurable system of resource allocation. They help to prevent open warfare among institutions and offer some assurance that the institutions with the most political power will not take home more than their share.

A classic example of a policy decision that elicited unintended behavior is the Middle Income Student Assistance Act. This piece of legislative largesse was intended to prevent the creation of an "educationally indigent middle class." It permitted students to take out federally subsidized Guaranteed Student Loans (GSLs) without regard to their financial need.

What happened is legendary. The GSLs were the cheapest money in the market. Thousands of families took out loans they did not need simply because it made more sense to pay the subsidized interest than to disturb savings and investments that were returning greater rates of interest. I shall not even guess how many loans were used for purposes that were not educational (unless buying and operating a motorcycle qualifies as experiential education), but I know of at least one. The federal government is still paying a frightful price in loan subsidies because of the unintended consequences of generous legislation. This has been at least one cause of the decrease in federal dollars actually available to students as financial aid in the last several years.

Public policy often focuses on short-range priorities because elected representatives must produce results before they stand for reelection and administrations before they end. (Happily, there are exceptions. Virginia's former governor, Gerald Baliles, set the transportation agenda for the next decade with planning and financing undertaken in the first two years of his four-year term. His predecessor, Charles Robb, backed the Higher Education Equipment Trust Fund, the nation's only debt-financed, self-perpetuating fund for purchasing instructional and research equipment, as he left office. Governor Baliles gave the trust fund his strong support during its first three years of operation, even though its full benefit would not be realized until after he was to leave office.)

Public policy also is apt to respond to the fad of the year (for example, one year we were concerned about the quality of mathematics and science teaching, another year we were concerned about geography and foreign languages) and to seek simple answers to complex questions. For instance, several states have responded to the vexing questions about how much college students are learning by mandating statewide testing. At both the state and federal levels, the passion to define education as the transmission of knowledge has led to the manufacture of lists and nostalgic marches backward into some idyllic past that never was. It is simpler to assess familiarity with items on a list than to assess ability to think, and there is no form of testing simpler than machine-graded, multiple-choice examinations.

Other forces in the culture influence the making of public policy. The United States Constitution and federal law, for instance, guarantee that those not in the defined majority or the dominant coalition of interest groups will have equal access to resources. This does something to ensure that policy is inclusive rather than exclusive. It also ensures that equal access is a theme to which all others must be related in this generation.

Even here, of course, we are beset by poorly drawn generalizations that exclude many from the benefits of public policies. Some of these generalizations are embedded in the Constitution itself and only activist courts and strong social movements have altered them. Unfortunately, the dominant political rhetoric of the eighties seems determined to redraw them only slightly and retain their exclusivity.

Whatever the Prevailing Cultural and Economic Hegemony Defines It to Be: A prevailing cultural hegemony creates and maintains the "tradition" as a standard of behavior that influences public policy. The tradition derives from the perceptions and values of the corporations, families, and others that have been economically and socially dominant in our culture. It is not imposed by conspiracy or even, necessarily, consciously. The prevailing cultural hegemony does not meet weekly at the Harvard Club. But the tradition is a pervasive influence in all that we do. It provides another definition of quality that is most often implicit. This definition appeals to a substantial portion of the citizenry but is accessible and useful only to a small number of them.

The tradition defines quality so as to preserve a hierarchy in which a few are taken to stand for or to be the whole. This definition tends to be based upon an understanding of education as the transmission of knowledge rather than as the process of learning how to think. Public policy, to the extent that it is influenced by the tradition, tends to have the same basis. Thus it is likely that public policy will seek to measure the quality of higher education by students' ability to master a list of items that the "educated man" (another exclusionary generalization) should know.

Matthew Arnold's famous definition of criticism, "a disinterested endeavor to learn and propagate the best that is known and thought in the world," fits very well the way the tradition understands education. From it follows logically Arnold's notion that the study of poetry should consist largely of meditation upon "touchstones": brief passages—nuggets, really—of poetry that say in the best possible way the best that has been known and thought.

Whatever We in Higher Education Think It Is: The third working definition of quality only adds to the complexity: it is what we in higher education say it is. To some considerable extent the intellectual life of the academy reflects the tradition, and to some extent it is shaped by competition for public funds. But we never are entirely comfortable either with the tradition or with the marketplace. Elements within the academy continue to question established truths and to value thinking above knowing. This, obviously, is a risky business, as history shows (Socrates, Duns Scotus, Galileo, Hobbes, Descartes, Spinoza, Kant, etc.).

PARTICULARITY, PUBLIC POLICY, AND HIGHER EDUCATION

There is no simple resolution of these issues. But I think there is a position that can be the basis for a tactical defense against public policy that is potentially damaging to higher education as an enterprise.

We might apply the notion of particularity, which I have introduced above in discussing the difficulty of generalizing in public policy, to institutions. The Greek concept *arete*, or excellence, places the scale not outside the individual as hierarchical, but within her or him. H. D. F. Kitto observes that when we come across the word *arete* in Plato, "we translate it 'Virtue' and consequently miss all the flavour of it. 'Virtue', at least in modern English, is almost entirely a moral word:

arete on the other hand is used indifferently in all categories and means simply 'excellence'. It may be limited of course by its context: the *arete* of a race-horse is speed, of a cart-horse strength. If it is used, in a general sense, of a man it will connote excellence in the ways in which a man can be excellent—morally, intellectually, physically, practically" (1964, pp. 171-72).

By applying this concept to colleges and universities, we create a situation in which each possesses its own possibility for excellence, its own potential to be what it is, rather than to be placed on some rationalized scale. We can help to create policies under which institutions are valued (assessed and supported) for the roles they play within a system not the extent to which they look like the ideal (be it Oxford, Harvard, or the Miami-Dade Community College).

Like individual women and men, institutions have their own stories. They are distinctive because of what each has done and is doing. The *arete* of each is different, just as the *arete* of the racehorse and the cart horse are different. They can be arranged hierarchically, of course; anyone can make a list. But the hierarchies are secondary and artificial. First and foremost, each is particular. Each lives, learns, changes, and dies in its own way.

This approach will be criticized as relativistic. It is, without apology. But what makes *arete* so interesting as a concept is its suggestion that particularity is epistemologically prior to other philosophical concepts with which we have burdened our thinking since Socrates routed the rest of the sophists. The boundaries of particularity are fundamental. The schemes of organization, monistic or dualistic, are not. They are secondary, contrived—imposed as we try to order (create) a world in which to live.

This is attractive to me as a participant in the dubious craft of policymaking because it helps to protect the autonomy and distinctiveness of individual institutions. If each has its own excellence (is excellent in its own way), collectively they are not amenable to being listed in rank order or divided into classes.

We are using this approach in assessing undergraduate student learning at Virginia's state-supported colleges and universities. In 1986, the General Assembly directed the Council of Higher Education to propose an approach to assessment. We studied what was going on around the country and funded a pilot project at one of Virginia's universities.

What we found was not especially surprising. Virginia has worked for years to develop a diverse system of higher education, within which there are institutions that can meet the needs of virtually every conceivable student. It simply made no sense to recommend imposing upon that diversity—intentionally supported for decades—an assessment examination administered statewide across all institutions.

The university conducting the pilot project, moreover, found that different curricula of study yielded to different methods of assessment. It ended up recommending that an array of assessment methods be adapted to the various curricula, the numbers of students enrolled in them, and the articulated goals of the institution. Like the personal stories we tell to identify ourselves to others, the institutional stories turned out to be fundamental in determining how each would assess what its students were learning.

We have built upon the culture, distinctiveness, and behavior of each college and university. In so doing, we have invited each institution to assess student learning against the collective understanding of its unique accomplishments. If we are successful in tapping into the institutional story, we shall have systems of assessment that flow as part of the deepest streams of institutional identity. Assessment will not be something mandated to be done to colleges and universities, but something that is part of their stories. It is an unusual approach to public policy, but hardly unique.

The assessment effort, then, led to the most difficult tasks of all: articulating goals and agreeing about the institutional story. But the rewards of self-examination, while painfully gained, and the prospects for change have made the entire undertaking very exciting. This public policy does not (or need not: an institution can if it so chooses) conceive of education as merely the transmission of knowledge. There is ample leeway to consider assessing the process of learning how to think or even the far more problematic process of learning how to be a morally responsible citizen of the state, the nation, and the world. The important point here is that this public policy is grounded upon the priority of particularity.

The protection offered by the particularist approach is neither absolute nor guaranteed. We need and love our lists, rankings, and labels. We cannot think and certainly cannot make public policy without generalization. But to some extent, each college and university is protected against the inevitable generalizations. We admit and even use their similarities in various ways, but we insist that they are first of all particular.

REFERENCES

Kitto, H. D. F. *The Greeks*. Chicago: Aldine Publishing Co., 1964.

5

WHAT COUNTS AS QUALITY IN HIGHER EDUCATION?

AMY GUTMANN

Quality in higher education cannot be counted. Many public officials who fund higher education understandably wish that quality could be measured in such a way as to rationalize limits on public spending for higher education. As the national deficit mounts, so too does the pressure to decrease public spending on higher education. Whatever we think of the pressure, we should recognize that some standards of assessment are likely to do more harm than good as bases for guiding public funding decisions and public assessments of educational quality more generally. Gordon Davies considers three standards in his chapter in this volume: the subjective standard, the market standard, and the hegemonic standard. Each is an example of a standard that we would do well to avoid either in assessing the quality of higher education or in justifying limits on public funding.

The quality of higher education is not merely in the eyes of the beholder (or the consumer), any more than is the quality of a diamond. We should therefore resist the temptation of the purely subjective standard. People who confuse "diploma mills" with good colleges are just as confused as people who confuse zircons with high-quality diamonds. Both may be fooled into believing they have the real thing. They may even be happy in their ignorance. While ignorance may sometimes be bliss, it is never knowledge.

Second, we must reject the market standard. The quality of higher education (unlike that of diamonds) is not well measured by what people are willing to pay for it. The "market" in higher education is necessarily imperfect for many reasons. The costs and benefits of higher education do not fall primarily on the same people who pay for it. Because the benefits of higher education are significantly social as well as individual, even if individuals did not want to pay for higher education, there would be good reason for a society, especially a democratic society, to value and therefore to fund higher education.

This point was appreciated by Thomas Jefferson, and it is no less true for the United States today than it was at our founding. If anything, the social value of higher education has grown with the increasing complexity of the issues arising for democratic government to resolve.

Third, we must also reject the "hegemonic" standard. The quality of higher education is not whatever the dominant cultural and economic groups say it is. In a pluralistic society like the United States (and most other Western democracies), there is no single hegemonic view of what constitutes quality in higher education. There are a plurality of competing standards of quality, about which we can and do argue (as the chapters in this book amply and admirably indicate). Continuing public argument and deliberation about what constitutes quality in higher education is our greatest hope for arriving at a national consensus. It is our only hope for arriving at a consensus that does not neglect the interests of all citizens of a liberal democracy in higher education.

So much for how the standard of quality in higher education should *not* be defined. How should we determine the standards of quality in higher education? Let me preface the answer that I develop briefly below with a disclaimer. There is no single "we" to fall back upon in judging the quality of higher education. There is far less consensus among Americans on what constitutes quality in higher education than there is on what constitutes quality in diamonds. But our lack of consensus is not a good reason to be skeptical about the value of higher education, any more than the lack of consensus on religion is a good reason to be an atheist. (Skepticism on either issue must find other sources.) The comparison of how much many wealthy Americans are willing to spend on diamonds for themselves and how much they are willing to spend on higher education for their children is legitimate cause for skepticism about what the market is capable of accurately valuing. Although many Americans seem willing to spend more money for diamonds, vacations, and summer cottages than for higher education (and spend it more happily), few would say that diamonds, vacations, and summer cottages are more valuable than higher education.

Like any test, the market measures only a limited range of values (and then only imperfectly), and higher education is not one of the values that the market is best at measuring. Like the consumers of medical care, the consumers of higher education are often not the same people who pay for it. Even if students paid for their own education, they would fall far short of having the full information that is necessary (but not even sufficient) for policymakers to measure the value of higher education by what students were willing to pay. A perfect market requires consumers to have close to complete information *before* they decide what goods to consume. Paradoxically, higher education (or its equivalent) is a prerequisite to satisfying the free market standard of measuring value by consumers' willingness to pay. High school students have very limited knowledge relative to what would be necessary to assess the quality of their future education *before* "consuming" it. A small but relevant example taken from my experience at Princeton University is the mandatory senior thesis, which is not the reason most students decide to come to Princeton. Yet the overwhelming majority of Princeton graduates report that writing their senior thesis was the single most valuable educational experience of their college years (and they value it very highly). It is inherent in the nature of higher education (as of medical care) that an adequately informed assessment of its value can only come after the experience. And then it is, of course, too late to get one's money back. Or, more accurately, getting one's money back is not a solution to the problem of making the wrong choice either of how to spend four years of your life or of whether to entrust one's health to a particular physician.

In addition to these inherent shortcomings of the market model with regard to higher education, it is also mistaken to presume that limiting *governmental* subsidies of higher education would create an accurate market measure of its value. The price of higher education would be highly subsidized by third parties even if the government ceases to be a major subsidizer.

Rather than leading us to skepticism about what constitutes quality in higher education, the lack of an obvious consensus in the United States today should drive us to developing standards. We can then publicly articulate those standards both to defend what is good in our present system of higher education and to develop a better system for the future.

JUDGING QUALITY RELATIVE TO THE PURPOSES OF HIGHER EDUCATION

The first positive step in developing a set of standards is to recognize that the quality of higher education, like that of other goods, is relative to its purposes. The system of higher education in the United States—of which every college and university is a part—legitimately serves three significant social purposes.[1]

First and probably foremost in the minds of college students, parents, and policymakers today: colleges and universities serve as *gatekeepers to the professions* and most other highly valued jobs in our

[1] I provide a more extensive account of these three purposes of higher education in *Democratic Education*, Princeton, NJ: Princeton University Press, 1987.

society. To serve this gatekeeping function well, it is essential that colleges and universities impart to students the knowledge and understandings that are necessary to becoming well-educated professionals and that are least likely to be imparted to them through professional education or on-the-job training. It is equally essential that colleges and universities not discriminate in their recruitment, admissions, or student aid policies against potential applicants on grounds that are irrelevant to their ability.

Second and perhaps most essential to the social purposes of higher education (certainly foremost in the case that Jefferson made for public subsidy of higher education): colleges and universities serve as *sanctuaries for free and critical scholarly inquiry.* They are bulwarks against the repression of ideas by governments and all powerful groups in society. This essential purpose of higher education is often overlooked in contemporary policy discussions, which tend to focus on the gatekeeping function of higher education and therefore upon how governmental policies can influence the content of the curriculum and regulate admissions so as to ensure equal access to higher education. It is surely important that colleges and universities are equitable and efficient in serving their gatekeeping functions. But it is no less important that they continue to be bulwarks against the threat of majority or minority tyranny. Any adequate public policy toward higher education must therefore seek ways of encouraging higher education to live up to the moral demands of its gatekeeping function without sacrificing the substantial social good to democracy that comes of its academic freedom.

The third significant social purpose served by higher education is the role played by colleges and universities as *communities of scholars, students, administrators, and alumni* who enjoy freely associating with each other and identifying with an institution that they can in some small but meaningful sense call their own. Although colleges and universities are not truly voluntary communities since so many careers today require a college degree, most students (and some faculty) choose among institutions of higher education not merely on academic but also on social grounds. Here is yet another reason why the standard of quality in higher education must be pluralistic: there is no single kind of community that can possibly satisfy the diverse associational preferences of college-bound students. Preserving diversity in the American system of higher education—between large and small, urban and rural, religious and secular, research and teaching oriented institutions, and so on—would be valuable if for no other reason than to satisfy the associational preferences of students. But there are other reasons as well, rooted in the more academic purposes of higher education, which are best served by a system that accommodates competing conceptions of excellence in scholarship and teaching.

A high-quality system of higher education would be one that served each of these three purposes well. Only a *pluralistic* system of higher education could possibly serve these purposes well, but a pluralistic system must be *principled* if it is to avoid the standardlessness of subjectivism, the value distortions of the market, and the tyranny that results from blind acceptance of prevailing, "hegemonic" authorities.

There are three principled parts to a pluralistic system of higher education corresponding to the three significant social purposes that higher education serves in the United States and other liberal democratic societies. As gatekeepers to the professions, colleges and universities must uphold the principle of *nondiscrimination*. They must not discriminate against potential applicants on grounds that are irrelevant to the three social purposes served by the system of higher education. As sanctuaries of free and critical inquiry, they must be accorded the right of *academic freedom* and live up to the responsibilities of that right. As communities of students, scholars, administrators, and alumni, colleges and universities should be granted the greatest degree of *freedom of association* that is consistent with their academic purposes.

HOW PUBLIC POLICY CAN FURTHER A PRINCIPLED PLURALISM

Gordon Davies is surely correct in casting suspicion upon any simple generalization to the effect that public policy operates for better—or for worse—in subsidizing and regulating higher education. The question of how public policy can help or hinder the achievement of a principled pluralism in higher education is best answered by assessing the potential influence of public policy on the achievement of each purpose. My assessment here is necessarily incomplete, sorely so. A brief foray into this territory can at most highlight a method of inquiry and a few substantive areas of special concern that deserve further investigation.

With regard to colleges and universities as gatekeepers to the professions, public policy has played and should continue to play a crucial role in furthering nondiscrimination. Title VII of the Civil Rights Act of 1964 and Executive Order 11246, as amended to require affirmative action to correct past discriminations in employment, decreased racial and sexual discrimination by many academic institutions. Although the pressure against discrimination from the federal government has diminished in recent years, the legislation set many procedures in place that are still useful in furthering nondiscrimination. The paperwork requirements that accompanied affirmative action regulations also placed real burdens on academic administrations and departments and interfered to some degree with their ability to carry out their other academic responsibilities. Administrative time and money spent complying with state regulations is often time and money not spent on improving an academic department or responding to the concerns of faculty and students. The administrative side effects of the legislation did not justify the charge by some universities that the federal government was violating their right to academic freedom, but the burdens were sufficiently onerous to caution future policymakers against erecting unnecessary bureaucratic hurdles on top of otherwise sound policy directives.

Ostensibly good public policy often creates serious problems in its wake. The debate over the policy typically follows the form taken by the controversy over affirmative action regulations: should we keep the policy or scrap it? But the real challenge to policymakers is to find ways of designing policies that avoid the problematic side effects without giving up the goods that the policies actually further. This reasonable middle ground is of course sometimes undiscoverable, or politically unrealizable after some policymaker discovers it. But the potential benefits surely justify greater efforts along these lines.

Consider the potential benefits of such thinking with regard to a recent policy initiative. In the name of greater access and diversity, several states are pressuring small colleges to become bigger. "If you take more students," the statehouse says to the small liberal arts college, "we'll give you more money. If you don't, we'll lower your quota of out-of-state students." Here is a genuine tension between the value of increasing access to higher education and the value of preserving college communities with distinctive academic and social cultures. As is often the case, the conflict does not take the form of a "High Noon" showdown. If the policy goes forward, there is likely to be a slow but steady erosion of the academic and cultural pluralism that contributes to the quality of higher education in the United States. State policymakers should ask themselves whether it is possible to obtain the benefits of increased access without the sacrifice to academic and cultural pluralism.

To serve their social function as sanctuaries of nonrepression, colleges and universities need academic freedom. They must protect themselves and be protected from those private and public pressures that ask them to sacrifice scholarly standards to other worldly goods. But colleges and universities also need money, which public as well as private patrons supply. In subsidizing higher education, governments (like most private industries and some private patrons) have a tendency to demand useful, if possible *immediately* useful, research and teaching. (They also often want colleges and universities to show immediate results in research and teaching.) Immediately useful research and teaching is not without value, but it is often in conflict with the distinctive social purposes that institutions of higher education serve better than any other institutions in democratic societies: pursuing knowledge and learning that is useful in the long run and safeguarding unpopular ideas against unscholarly standards.

Governments understandably want to show evidence of value-added for their money, but the best way of securing the value of higher education is not to succumb to the kind of valued-added thinking that has led to "measurement mania" in education: If you can't measure it, it's not worth funding. Testing is not the only form of accountability, and certainly not the best form for higher education (although minimal competency tests may serve some useful function even at the level of higher education, where many students still perform at shockingly low levels of literacy and numeracy).

The only kind of accountability that is worth defending for higher education is one that is consistent with the primary social purpose of higher education: to secure for a democratic society substantial realms of free, creative, and critical inquiry that can serve as sanctuaries for nonrepression. It is not utopian to believe that there are standards of accountability that are compatible with this role. The executive director of the Middle States Association of Colleges and Schools has championed one such standard, greater openness in developing and applying accrediting standards for colleges and universities. He has met with both external and internal resistance because many colleges do not want their academic weaknesses to be publicly exposed and many accreditors do not want to hold their standards up to public scrutiny. Nonetheless, his policy of publicizing accrediting standards is precisely the kind of accountability that makes sense for higher education. The educated public can then discuss whether the official standards live up to their best, publicly defensible understanding of the purposes of higher education. The recent more public discussions of the policies of colleges and universities with regard to student athletes is just one example that highlights the potential for improving our understanding of the defensible purposes of higher education along with improving our actual practices. The policy of greater openness in accrediting standards is compatible with academic freedom, indeed conducive to it. In the long run, higher education will be better served if our standards of academic excellence are more openly discussed and more responsibly applied.

CONCLUSION

In conclusion, I want to emphasize that the quality of higher education will be better served, in both the short and the long run, if the case for (or against) public subsidies and regulations is not couched purely or even primarily in economic terms. The value of the system of higher education in this country is not best judged by the sum of the economic advantages gained by college graduates over high-school graduates (either in the short or the long run). The three social purposes of higher education discussed above take us far beyond this relatively narrow (although undoubtedly important) realm of economic value.

Higher education contributes to furthering political freedom in a democracy in a way unmeasurable by money. It is no paradox that some goods—such as political freedom—whose public worth is not measurable by money require a great deal of public money to prosper. Without substantial governmental support, colleges and universities might not survive, and certainly would not flourish in our society. Even as gatekeepers to the professions, colleges and universities are valued for significantly more than the added income they provide.

Each of the purposes of universities, properly pursued, is in significant part a public good. The pursuit of knowledge for its own sake contributes to preserving our cultural heritage and also to discovering socially useful knowledge. The broad liberal arts education available to future professionals contributes to our welfare in a way that money cannot measure, as does the establishment of academic communities that serve—among other things—as sanctuaries for nonconformists.

We need not place a price on all the parts of higher education to answer some of the central questions concerning the role of public policy in higher education. There are good reasons for a democratic government to support a mixed system, consisting of both public and private universities. Private universities have generally been better able to resist political sources of repression, such as McCarthyism, while public universities have been better able to resist private sources of discrimination, such as resistance by trustees and alumni to admitting qualified Jews, blacks, and women (there are of course significant exceptions to both rules). Democratic governments have good reason to support a system of higher education where both private and public universities flourish. Since private universities serve as gatekeepers to many of the most prized offices in this country, democratic governments should also ensure that their subsidies do not support economic, racial, sexual, or religious discrimination in the distribution of higher education.

Public policy must not merely respect, it must also further, a principled pluralism in higher education. A principled pluralism leaves room for a variety of college and university communities to flourish at the same time that it ensures that the system of higher education, taken as a whole, fosters equity in the distribution of opportunities for higher education and for access to highly valued and highly paid professions and other jobs that require a college diploma. The quality of higher education depends both on the forbearance of policymakers when regulation and subsidy threaten the pursuit of excellence and on their positive aid when the lack of regulation or subsidy threatens the pursuit of equity. The achievement of equity is ultimately essential to the achievement of excellence at all levels of education.

6

HIGHER EDUCATION QUALITY: THE EYE OF THE BEHOLDER

DENIS P. DOYLE

ETERNAL VERITIES

All public policy questions can ultimately be reduced to the two eternal verities, death and taxes. In the arcane world of public policy, of course, they are not ordinarily referred to in so vulgar a fashion. Rather they are referred to as people and resources. But in the final analysis that is what it is all about. Higher education does not escape this simple truism.

The impact of public policy on higher education, then, has first to do with public expenditures for higher education; the more independent, that is to say the more "private," is higher education, the less note public policy is likely to take of it.

Put the other way round, "he who pays the piper calls the tune." The more public money that finds its way to higher education, the more intense the interest of public policymakers. As I will try to suggest, it makes some difference how that money is spent—allocated to students rather than institutions, for example—but there is no escaping the heavy hand of the policymaker if public monies are involved.

(Not even purely private higher education could entirely escape the reach of public policy, particularly in the modern world. Higher education impinges on public policy in numerous ways, and is itself the primary means by which wealth and status are created and allocated in the modern world. In short, higher education would be of interest to public policymakers even were it completely private. It would be a lot less interesting, however, which makes a difference.)

The question, then, is not whether higher education might escape the reach and tender mercies of public policy but under what terms and conditions it shall be subject to public policy strictures.

> *Just give me a one-armed economist.*
> —Harry Truman

The question of public policy goals for higher education—quality, access, efficiency—simply embodies two broad streams of public policy analysis, most vividly rendered in the prose of the true social scientist: "on the one hand; and on the other hand."

The underlying question is, of course, to what extent public policy has a negative or deleterious effect on quality, access, and efficiency. Alternately, to what extent does it have a positive effect? These broad themes are themselves reflected in ideological views of the world, though they are not necessarily related in linear fashion. That is to say, one broad stream of public policy experience is interventionist and active, based on assumptions (both explicit and implicit) about the need to intervene—a problem exists; policymakers can successfully intervene (they caused the problem to begin with, no doubt); "it's broken and we can fix it."

The other broad stream of public policy is the impulse to leave well enough alone. Although this is the perfectly reasonable extension of the Founders' view that he who governs least governs best, ever since Pat Moynihan got burned with his "benign neglect" statement, few people are willing to propose this as a strategy—at least in public.

One public policy framework, then, is a public policy of commission, one a public policy of omission. But both are designed to secure public policy objectives; this is not a case of one set of actors being responsible, the others irresponsible. Rather, it is a case of very different views of responsibility.

Unfortunately, this conceptual division, while reasonably accurate, does not provide much help in identifying who will behave in what way. Indeed, role reversals are not infrequent. If a problem appears to be amenable to public policy intervention, actors who had previously espoused a "hands-off" policy may propose forms of intervention. Alternately, policy "activists" may in certain circumstances deliberately refuse to intervene—itself a form of intervention, no doubt—to achieve their objectives.

Let me offer three illustrations of this general point:

- When Sputnik went up, the National Defense Education Act (NDEA) followed, a product of Republican inventiveness. The first version out of the Eisenhower administration was grants for college study, to which the Democrats rejoined, "no giveaways." Loans are the American way.
- With the "feeding frenzy" of 1981 the biggest federal higher education program in history, Social Security payments to orphans and children of disabled workers, was terminated. (Remember who controlled each house of Congress? It just goes to show you that orphans make poor lobbyists.)
- The original "principled" opposition to federal aid to higher edu-

cation was not Hillsdale College but Oberlin and other private colleges that refused the "price of the gift": loyalty oaths.

(It hardly needs noting that one of the great pleasures of modern "policy watching" is that you can't identify the actors without a program.)

The questions to consider, then, should be of two kinds. One should be a set of empirical issues about "what works"; what have been the circumstances conducive to high-quality higher education? What are the trends affecting higher education? In particular, what are the trends that suggest more (or less) intervention by policymakers as they attempt to influence higher education quality?

(The one issue guaranteed to attract the attention of policymakers in Congress is "waste, fraud and abuse," or its perception. When enough people think quality is falling, something will be done about it. That is surely the lesson of the National Commision on Excellence in Education's *A Nation at Risk* (1983): it did not precipitate the "excellence movement," it simply confirmed everyone's worst suspicions about the quality of elementary and secondary education.)

The second set of questions should be conceptual, albeit informed by experience. What should be done to preserve the best of what we have and encourage quality in the future? This is by far the more interesting question, and as a consequence less likely to get asked and even less likely to get acted upon.

To think of the issues this way is useful, however, because of the extraordinary nature of American higher education. To use that much overworked word, it is unique.

AMERICAN HIGHER EDUCATION: A REPRISE

Because we take American higher education so much for granted, it is worthwhile to remind ourselves just how unusual our system is. It is unusual in two dramatic ways, both of which sharply distinguish it from the other industrialized democracies.

First, we have a mixed system of provision, public and private (and for cognoscenti of such things, we have hybrids or blends in some states, part public, part private). No other industrialized nation has anything remotely like this. Abroad, if you go to school at all it is to a government school.

This has a powerful impact on life chances; in the industrialized nations—other than America—you have only one chance. Attend a government college or university or go to work. (There are modest exceptions to be sure, but I am talking about prevailing practice.)

Second, only in America can you (and/or your family) *invest in your own human capital*. That's what tuition is all about, in both the public and private sectors. In unitary higher education systems sponsored by government, government not only decides whether or not you go, government pays the freight. Wonderful for winners. Not so wonderful for second place finishers.

GENEROSITY AND THE PRICE OF A GIFT

What does all this have to do with the issue of quality? In centralized, government controlled systems, the question of quality is almost by definition one of regulation. It need not be in the American system, though that is clearly the way it will go if the issue is cast in terms of the interest of the funding parties. This is so because of the kind of funding that is at issue: it is one kind of subsidy or another, whether it is Pell Grants, or GSLs, or College Work Study. And subsidizers want to know how their subsidies are being used. What other choice do they have?

By the way of illustration, look at the issue of defaults on GSLs. (Unfortunately the policy issue is clouded by race because of the default rate among blacks and at black institutions; for purposes of discussion, hold that issue to one side and think simply of the "default" problem.) What is a fiscally concerned lender likely to do? Clamp down.

Conceptually, the issue is no different as one moves "up" the quality scale; what about loans to students who don't do badly but don't do very well either? What about institutions that have low standards and induce students to attend them using GSLs, Pells, and the like?

Particularly in a period of budget difficulties, it is possible to imagine a fairly severe ratchet effect, in which the public sector lender—to protect the integrity of the program—expects more and more of some kind of compliance on the part of borrowers and the institutions they attend. The details of the expected compliance system, and the details of the standards to which people and institutions would have to conform, would boggle the mind. No one would know how to design let alone implement such a system; it would be invented on the run, imposed bureaucratically, and at least in the first instance, shamelessly manipulated by the cleverer institutions. That is probably the best one could hope for.

Not to put too fine a point on it, the reason for this dismal scenario is the great god Mamon: the principal reason and the principal justification for public policymakers getting involved in questions of higher education quality is public funding.

Were it not for public money, the impulse to regulate higher education quality could be easily overcome. As it happens there are

some safety valves. First is the long tradition of private higher education that can be expected to resist government efforts to regulate
quality. (It bears repeating that during the McCarthy era private schools
were the last line of defense against loyalty oaths. It was institutions
like Oberlin College that refused federal funds, not public institutions.)
Now, of course, massive federal funding of higher education is a
settled matter.

In addition to private institutions that might expect to be a bulwark
against undue government intervention, the great majority of public
institutions are organized in such a way as to protect their organiza-
tional integrity, at least for a while. That is, public colleges and universities have historically been organized along the lines of the private
sector; they have independent boards of trustees, enjoy some fairly
substantial insulation from the vagaries of transient political processes,
and have their own traditions. But they are obviously much more
vulnerable to public policy pressure—over both the short and long
haul—than private institutions are.

THE PUBLIC POLICY TOOL KIT

Problems arise in the public policy realm because of the discontinuity
between policy objectives and the tools available to the policymaker.
The instruments are blunt and not well suited for fine tuning. They
are principally statutes, rules, regulations, dollars given and dollars
withheld. On occasion moral suasion works, but not often. The name
of the game is power and money, not surprising in America. If there
is an analogy, it is early surgery in the mid-nineteenth century; a
pretty messy business, particularly when antisepsis is not understood
and anesthesia barely exists. It may beat the alternative, but just
barely.

Trying to assess higher education quality will almost of necessity
sink to a lowest common denominator, particularly as the pressure to
quantify what is largely unquantifiable goes forward. Using quantity as
a proxy for quality is an old technique, particularly in education, but is
no less unappealing for its familiarity.

Moreover, it is a path down which there is little hope of success,
but equally, once taken, little hope of retreat.

This, in turn, is a function of program design. A subsidy program
of the kind in place is a program waiting to be regulated. It is expensive, confusing, complex—indeed, it is virtually unintelligible. You
have to be an expert to understand it; the programs invite abuse and
eventually contempt.

Which puts the ideas Gordon Davies discusses in this volume
squarely before us. *Arete*, excellence, and autonomy are not only desir-

able, they are commendable. Indeed, if higher education is to survive over the long haul, the ideas are necessary.

Davies is exactly on target with his three definitions of quality in a public policy context. The most pertinent, of course, is the first: "quality is whatever is valued (and paid for) in a society." That, indeed, is what budgets are all about—they are expressions of preference. They are numeric statements of value.

He is also on target when he expresses concern with protecting "higher education . . . from errant public policy" because it is entirely possible that the budget will ride roughshod over more sophisticated and sensitive definitions of "quality" once it becomes subject to the budget process.

And there is the rub. Can higher education "quality" be protected from the vagaries of the public policy process? Not likely. As we have seen already, "loyalty oaths" are easily imposed in times of high anxiety; orphans are easily "cut" in periods of real or imagined budget scarcity. What's next?

As Davies suggests, perhaps the best that can be hoped for is "a tactical defense against public policy that is potentially damaging."

He concludes with a defense of the "particular," one that I find attractive but romantic. That is, I have a hard time putting it in public policy terms short of constitutional guarantees about pluralism, diversity, variety, and the like. But college attendance is not a "civil right." It is not constitutionally protected. (The logic is found in *Pierce v. Society of Sisters*, 1925; the state cannot compel you to attend a particular school—that is, you are free to go where you like, but no obligation is imposed on the state to send you where you like. It is up to you.)

What happens when your "entitlement" becomes more and more narrowly circumscribed? You are eligible for a GSL *so long as* you register for the draft, get tested for AIDS, don't use dope, and the like. These may be perfectly sensible public policies; the fact that they are attached as riders to higher education financing shows how popular they are and how seriously policymakers take higher education.

So too are other policies—Senator Bradley's Truth in Sports, for example. Student athletes aren't being told the whole story; student athletics is only one step from professionalism anyway; by regulation, we can require the nation's colleges and universities to tell all. And we will protect would-be athletes from themselves (and their institutions). That this policy change is being debated at all is a sign of just how far we have come.

Without being harsh, it is almost certainly the case that many institutions have lost their intellectual and ethical moorings; how else could student athletics come to be what they are? But is regulation the answer?

SO MANY PROBLEMS, SO LITTLE TIME

The policy fire is fueled, as it were, by four other issues. First is the "education excellence movement" generally. While it has focused on elementary and secondary education, it will inevitably enlarge its focus to include higher education. Education in this country may not comprise a formal system as it does in some industrialized nations, but it is a "system" none the less. The criticisms of William Bennett, former secretary of the United States Department of Education, while not popular, have a strong resonance.

Second, and perhaps more important, it is becoming abundantly clear to everyone—the man in the street and not just policymakers and analysts—that education is the key to status and income in the postindustrial economy. The Jeffersonian vision of a natural aristocracy of talent is being operationalized in the modern meritocracy.

Third, there is an increasing perception—justified or not—that higher education is getting more and more expensive, without a corresponding increase in "value."

Fourth, the funding programs that are leading to increased oversight were designed in the first instance because the private sector could not underwrite the costs of educating large numbers of youngsters who were "poor risks." That, ultimately, is the justification for federal grant and loan programs. Thanks to the Thirteenth Amendment, human capital cannot be collateralized, which made it tricky for even "good risks" to get loans until only recently. Private sector, unsubsidized loans, such as the Parent Loan Program (PLP), have grown dramatically over the past two decades, in tandem with the growth of GSLs.

A MODEST PROPOSAL

If, as I have suggested, the problem is a direct consequence of government funding as it is now practiced, perhaps the solution is simpler than we might otherwise think: change the funding so policymakers are no longer inclined to regulate higher education quality.

I am not proposing that the federal government stop funding higher education; rather, we should reexamine the basis for it. I have made proposals along these lines in a number of places, most recently for Dartmouth College in "The Federal Government and Education in the Next Decade: The 1988 Presidential Sweepstakes" (1987). Without going into unnecessary detail, let me briefly recapitulate.

The established reason for a federal higher education program is to increase access and equity yielding, Pell Grants, GSLs, and the rest. I have proposed that we reemphasize those original objectives and take into account who is the beneficiary of higher education. The evidence, of course, demonstrates overwhelmingly that the immediate beneficiary is the student who becomes educated. His lifetime earnings stream is very significantly increased over his less well-educated counterpart. (There are, to be sure, significant social benefits to diffusing education widely, but society derives those benefits even if the individual pays for his own education.)

Indeed, the increase in lifetime earnings is much greater than the cost of the education. The return is very large. As a consequence there is no compelling *economic* reason for the federal government—any government—to subsidize the cost of that person's education.

One solution is to increase the size of the Pell Grant to compensate for inflation; limit its duration to two years (to put all students on their own after the sophomore year or the A.A. degree); eliminate interest subsidies on student loans; make Uncle Sam the guarantor of those loans; and provide for repayment through the IRS over the lender's working life.

A number of fine tuning elements can be added depending on preference: make the loan's income contingent if there is some compelling reason to subsidize some students; require Pell Grant and or Student Loan recipients to perform some form of public service; provide a public service opportunity to "work off" part or all of the loan; and so on.

The point is to restore market forces in higher education financing by letting the beneficiary pay. We are all familiar with the problems created by third-party payment schemes; neither the provider nor the beneficiary has any strong incentive to control cost, and the provider's incentive to maintain quality is attenuated.

In higher education, the consequence should be a more responsive market, one that attends to the questions of cost and quality in a way that will be useful to "investors," in this case, students. If there are compelling reasons to subsidize that person's education they are noneconomic; they are social. We subsidize them because without the subsidy the individual might not have the wit, luck, or energy to take advantage of the opportunity higher education affords, and there are potential social benefits.

This issue, however, is empirical and its solution is technical. If there is a large number of youngsters who would profit from higher education but who would not take out unsubsidized loans because they are fearful or suspicious about assuming large, long-term debt, give them Pell Grants to introduce them to higher education, and let them take out loans for the long haul.

Finally, the logic of this proposal would be complete if public institutions would forego their direct subsidies and enter a higher education "market," with tuition paid by students enrolled as a principal source of income. This, of course, would solemnize the end of intergenerational income transfer in higher education, a process that is already well under way. Even if the end of intergenerational transfer payments is unappealing, we should recognize that it is over.

The likelihood of this occurring spontaneously is, to say the least, not great; public institutions are not going to march on their state capitols requesting an end to their subsidies. But, if the fiscal squeeze at all levels of government continues, and the need to increase tuition continues—as it surely will, the principal having been firmly established— the drift in this direction will continue.

In closing, it is clear to me that the pressure to regulate higher education "quality" will continue to build so long as the existing structures are left in place. Indeed, they are an irresistible invitation to such meddling. He who pays the piper calls the tune. If anyone doubts it, witness developments in England. The most venerable of venerable institutions, Oxford and Cambridge, are reaping the whirlwind of public support of higher education. Unfortunately for us, in this country, it is as fickle as loyalty oaths, aid to orphans, and "truth in sports."

REFERENCES

DOYLE, DENIS P. "The Federal Government and Education in the Next Decade: The 1988 Presidential Sweepstakes." An essay prepared for the Nelson Rockefeller Center for the Social Sciences at Dartmouth College, Hanover, NH, August 1987.

———. *American Higher Education: Understanding The Puzzle*. Washington, D.C.: Council for International Exchange of Scholars, 1987.

DOYLE, DENIS P. and TERRY W. HARTLE. "Student Aid Muddle." *The Atlantic* 257 (February 1986): 30–34. Reprinted in *Education Digest*, April 1986: 54–57.

———. "Facing the Fiscal Chopping Block: It's Time to Rethink Student Aid." *Change* (July/August 1985): 8–10, 54–56.

NATIONAL COMMISSION ON EXCELLENCE IN EDUCATION. *A Nation at Risk: The Imperative for Educational Reform*. Washington, D.C.: United States Department of Education, 1983.

SECTION III

The Goal of Diversity in Higher Education

Diversity in higher education brings to mind both the notions of access to higher education and choice of options within the higher education sector. This side of the uneasy triangle is one that often leads to explosive debates in the public policy arena. How accessible is higher education to various groups in society—whites and minorities, men and women, disadvantaged and advantaged, rural and urban? To what extent does participation and successful completion of higher education vary with an individual's circumstances? Have college participation and completion rates changed over time? To what extent are participation and completion rates, especially for minorities and the economically disadvantaged, positively affected by government programs, and can these programs be altered to improve performance? These are difficult questions and as will be evident from the three chapters in this section, there is little agreement as to the primary causes of unequal educational outcomes or the public policy solutions.

In his provocative chapter "The Goal of Diversity: Access and Choice in Academia," Robert Zemsky initially focuses on patterns and trends in college participation rates. He chooses samples from the Current Population Survey by the Bureau of the Census to gauge the college participation rates of whites and blacks in the United States over the years 1973 to 1986. He finds that over this fourteen year period: (1) the college participation rate of black females has risen and led to some narrowing in the racial gap for females and (2) college participation rates for black males age nineteen to twenty-one remained unchanged and continued to lag behind those of white males. These lead Zemsky to what he calls the critical question as to when exclusion takes place. Have colleges and universities failed to reach out or are there "larger patterns of educational exclusion and disenfranchisement" responsible for the college participation gap?

To gain some insights into the problem, Zemsky examines the high school completion rate and finds there is no significant rise in that rate for black males and therefore no increase in the supply of educationally qualified black males upon which American colleges and universities can draw. On the other hand, Zemsky does find a statistically significant increase in high school completion rates for black females that runs parallel to the rise in college participation rates. He also finds there has been no substantial increase in the college participation rate for white males from lower-income families; therefore there is no narrowing of the approximately 20 percentage point gap between high- and low-income white males. There has been a gradual rise in the participation rate for white females from lower-income families, paralleling the rise in participation rate for white females from higher-income families, leaving in tact the more than 25 percentage point gap.

Zemsky argues that the issue is not access, but rather social and economic enfranchisement, on which educational attainment depends. He concludes that colleges and universities cannot be expected to solve the broad social and economic problems of the poor and disadvantaged. Zemsky also says that in designing policy to increase the inclusiveness of education in America, we should consider shifting funds from higher education toward improving primary and secondary schools. Finally, Zemsky notes the homogenization of higher education in terms of sorting of students and how this leads to spending more on the more advantaged and less on the less advantaged.

Reginald Wilson, in "Barriers to Diversity and the Myth of Equal Access," questions Zemsky's conclusions in terms of their "grounding in historical reality and the incompleteness of his data." First, Wilson questions America's "commitment to educational diversity and equal access." Taking issue with how much higher education has done for minorities, Wilson notes that, historically, "the academy has restricted access and excluded minorities, and only grudgingly, under the sanctions of Congress and the courts, opened its doors." He acknowledges that there has been some progress in access over the past twenty years, but such progress must be viewed "in a context of real historical and continuing barriers." Wilson therefore argues that American higher education must continue to view equality of opportunity as a mandate.

Wilson also questions the data used by Zemsky. Zemsky develops a statistical definition of the college participation rate in terms of youth aged nineteen to twenty-one years. The restriction of the data to this age cohort is an attempt to "include all youths who completed high school in the expected length of time" and avoids including "many who have already earned their baccalaureate degree." Wilson suggests that the focus on this age cohort, as opposed to the broader group of eighteen- to twenty-four year-olds, tells only part of the story and ignores those who delay going on to postsecondary education for a few years and dropouts who later earn their General Equivalency Degree (GED) and then head toward postsecondary education. Analyzing this broader age cohort, Wilson finds that black males and females significantly *increased* their high school graduate rates and *both* groups declined in college participation rates (between 1976 and 1986).

Wilson also takes issue with Zemsky's suggestion regarding the shifting of existing Pell Grant funds to primary and secondary public school budgets by arguing that such a shift would have little impact on the primary and secondary education sector and a very large negative impact on the higher education sector. Finally, Wilson suggests that "it is not the lack of a larger pool of prepared minority students that has contributed to the declining participation rates, but the concurrent raising of admission standards in many public university systems, in the name of 'excellence,' that has resulted in the rejection of many ordinarily eligible students."

The chapter by Alan Ginsburg and Maureen McLaughlin, entitled "Improving Minority Postsecondary Outcomes: The Need for a Comprehensive Approach," contains a slightly less negative message. They examine the twenty- to twenty-one year-old cohort to account for completion of high school at slightly older ages. Using this older age cohort they find the following: (1) the overall graduation rate for black twenty- to twenty-one year-olds rose substantially from 1969 to 1985, improving more for black females than for black males; (2) the high school completion rate for blacks has risen since 1969, while that for whites has remained relatively constant over that same period. Thus the gap has narrowed, although whites are still more likely to complete high school than blacks; (3) the proportion of black males attending college (among twenty- to twenty-one year-olds) rose from 1969 to 1985. Most of these gains were due to increases in high school graduation rather than increases in the rate of college attendance; (4) the gap in college participation rates between black and white females declined over the 1969 to 1985 period, and for black women (twenty- to twenty-one year-olds), unlike black men, college participation gains are attributable to improvements in both high school graduation and college participation rates; and (5) using the age cohort twenty-five to twenty-nine year-olds (since the younger cohort would not have had the opportunity to complete four years of college), Ginsburg and McLaughlin found that patterns of college completion for blacks did not match the improvements in their college attendance. There was a decline in college completion rates for those ever attending college. Over this same time period, white males who had ever attended college experienced an increase in their college graduation rate, while the rate for white females remained constant.

Ginsburg and McLaughlin conclude that student aid has had positive effects on college enrollment for low-income students although it does not appear to increase enrollment for persons from higher-income families. They also argue that while student aid has been the primary federal policy tool for encouraging economically disadvantaged youth to attend college, such instruments must be combined with approaches that improve academic achievement. They conclude their discussion with a useful and thought-provoking outline of ways to improve the efficacy of student aid programs and policies to improve the academic preparation and motivation of students.

Perhaps the most notable findings in this section are the areas of disagreement—in measurement, historical perspective, and likely efficacy of the policy alternatives. These three chapters provide interesting and enlightening debate, but it is clear that the debate will continue.

7

THE GOAL OF DIVERSITY: ACCESS AND CHOICE IN ACADEMIA

ROBERT ZEMSKY

As a nation, we have made our mixed beginnings a cause for celebration. For us there is no sense of insularity, but rather Emma Lazarus's lyric beckoning of others to a land of immigrants:

> Give me your tired, your poor,
> Your huddled masses yearning to breathe free,
> The wretched refuse of your teeming shore.
> Send these, the homeless, tempest-tost to me,
> I lift my lamp beside the golden door!

In this America the melting pot is a national symbol, a reminder to all that our strength derives directly from the amalgam of peoples who made this land their own.

We also celebrate diversity in our sense of America as a nation of handcrafted communities, each distinctive in its combination of different people attending to the needs of that community. In part, these values reflect an agrarian past, though champions of the modern worker have adapted the same themes and metaphors. The paintings of Thomas Hart Benton express this strong lyrical vision of a nation gathering strength from its individual citizens—people of different backgrounds engaging in different trades and occupations—with the composite effect exceeding what any one group might have achieved separately. The songwriters Lewis Allan and Earl Robinson evoked a similar vision in the 1940s in their song, "The House I Live In." In an unintended affirmation of American diversity, this song was recorded by both Paul Robeson and Frank Sinatra.

These images—America as melting pot, America as community—prefigure much of our commitment to educational diversity and equal access. We seek at all levels, but particularly from our colleges and universities, a broadly inclusive system, one truly open to all and truly representative of the demographic profile of the nation. Historically, we have measured inclusion according to the college participation rate. What we want to see is an America in which everyone benefits from access to postsecondary education and lifelong learning. We want no one excluded. We are uncomfortable when our institutions draw their students from too narrow a socioeconomic band, when the gap in college participation between rich and poor, men and women, whites and racial minorities is sustained and substantial. We expect that, in the aggregate, the institutions among which these students choose will also be representative of the diversity of the nation. We want our colleges and universities to be handcrafted communities that, despite their size and complexity, represent America's highest academic aspirations as well as its cultural and ethnic heritage.

During the decades immediately following the Second World War, that promise seemed within our grasp. It was a time of extraordinary expansion—those energizing years between 1945 and 1970 when college ceased to be the preserve of the privileged, when there was a genuine reaching out to the poor, to minorities, to the children of families who had never before thought that college was for them, when new institutions were founded and old ones transformed. The generation of scholars now in charge of America's colleges and universities are themselves the product of that time, having begun their careers convinced that both individuals and institutions could make a difference in the educational life of the nation.

What troubles us today is the sense of stalled promise and lost momentum. Much of the current criticism of higher education derives from the realization that there remains an America substantially beyond higher education's reach. Despite the federal government's unprecedented investment in student financial aid and the adoption by most institutions of nondiscriminatory admissions, the educational gap between advantaged and disadvantaged has not narrowed. Most institutions remain stratified largely along socioeconomic lines; and there is a growing suspicion that the degree of stratification may be increasing rather than decreasing. We have also come to understand that higher education can no longer be said to be handcrafted. Our colleges and universities are now less unique, less a product of their origins, less a reflection of their geographic and cultural settings.

We are already in the midst of a national debate over the purposes and responsibilities of the nation's system of postsecondary institutions. As always, the stakes are enormous, with institutions, political leaders, and public advocates all measuring carefully what effect any changes in the status quo will have on their constituencies. It is not likely to be a pretty or an uplifting debate—too many jobs, too much money, too much of the nation's sense of self-efficacy is at stake. For these reasons, it is unlikely that the discussion will begin with a frank admission that what we have tried thus far has not worked. Nevertheless, I would like to broach just such a theme.

COLLEGE PARTICIPATION

As a nation we continue to seek a broadly inclusive system of postsecondary education. Our celebration of educational opportunity is genuine, reflecting a long-standing national commitment to equal opportunity and the notion that all citizens have a direct stake in the social and economic well-being of the country. While we need not insist that everyone go to college, we understand that equal access means both adequate preparation for lifelong learning and access to the financial means to make enrollment possible.

Traditionally we have measured the inclusiveness of American higher education by focusing on the college participation rate. What proportion of any specific cohort—defined by gender, economic circumstance, ethnic or racial background, region of the country, or some combination of attributes—has actually attended an accredited two- or four-year college, if only for a semester? The explicit goal of much federal and state policy in conjunction with institutional practice over the last two decades has been to increase that college participation rate for all groups in general and for women, minorities, and low-income groups in particular.

The most consistent data for estimating college participation rates derive from the October Current Population Survey (CPS), conducted by the Bureau of the Census. The Bureau interviews a sample of more than fifty thousand households to discover the employment status, age, and educational level of each member of the household, the racial and ethnic groups to which the household belongs, and the household's aggregate income. As long as the basic rules underlying the probability sample are observed, remarkably accurate estimates of the basic demographics of the American population are possible.

My analysis of the CPS and related data is drawn from a pair of larger studies, the first funded by the College Board, the second by the Higher Education Research Program sponsored by The Pew Charitable Trusts. In the former, my colleague Michael Tierney and I focus on how black students in general and those attending historically black colleges in particular currently finance their educations, and what alternate means of financing might provide greater resources for the institutions historically responsible for college education of blacks in America.

The second study is a broad examination of what we have called the "sorting function" in American higher education—that combination of social values, economic incentives, and institutional practices that discourages some students from attending college and channels those who are college bound into particular sets of institutions. In this endeavor I have drawn on the efforts of Timothy Warner, Lewis Solmon, Arturo Madrid, Dolph Norton, and Arthur Levine, who are members of the roundtable that oversees the Pew Higher Education Research Program.

For both these projects, Tierney and I took the October CPS for each year from 1973—the year the draft ended—through 1986, the most recent year for which data are available. From these samples we estimated the proportion of nineteen to twenty-one year-olds who reported having received at least some college education. We chose this age cohort because it would include all youths who completed high school in the expected length of time and would not include many students who had already earned their baccalaureate degrees. The sample of each cohort was also sufficiently large to reduce the probability of statistical error. Because of the relatively small size of the Hispanic sample, however, our analyses were able to focus only on blacks as a minority population.

Figure 7.1 plots the percentage of white males, black males, white females, and black females, aged nineteen to twenty-one, who were estimated to have had some college education prior to the date of the survey. As tracked by the CPS, it is clear that during these fourteen years:

- there was a sustained increase in the college participation rate for black females, leading to some narrowing of the gap between blacks and whites;
- the college participation rate for black males aged nineteen to twenty-one remained unchanged, continuing to lag behind the participation rate for white males by more than 15 percentage points.

The critical question becomes one of determining when the exclusion takes place. Have colleges and universities failed to reach out to eligible blacks or, worse, created institutional climates that effectively deny substantial numbers of blacks unfettered access to a college education? Or, is there a larger pattern of educational exclusion and disenfranchisement responsible for the lower college participation rates for blacks in general and black males in particular?

To a large extent, the answer lies in understanding whether there has been a real increase in the number of young blacks in the pool of potential students. Again, the most consistent way to answer this question is to focus on high school graduation rates as reported to the

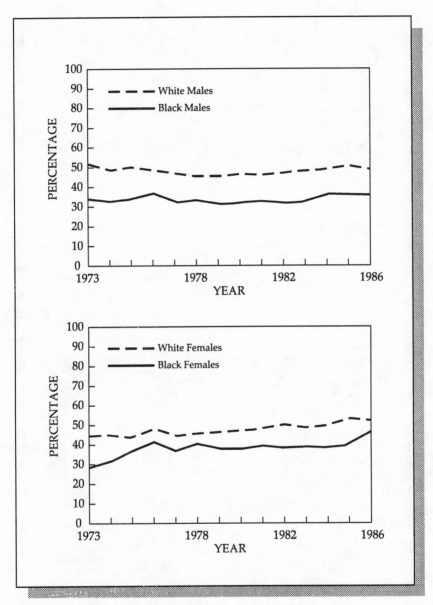

FIGURE 7.1. College Participation, 19- to 21-Year-Olds

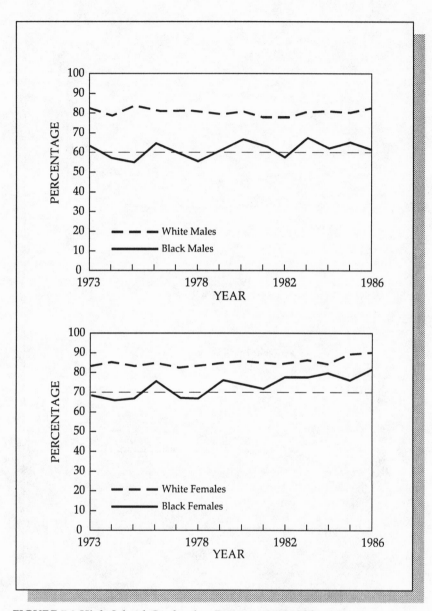

FIGURE 7.2 High School Graduation Rates, 19-Year-Olds

CPS. Figure 7.2 plots the percentages of nineteen-year-old black males and females reported to have graduated from high school. For black males the fourteen-year mean (represented by the dashed line) constitutes as good a statistical estimate of the graduation rate as the actual data points (represented by the unbroken line), leading us to conclude that:

- there has been no significant increase in the high school completion rate for black males, or in other words, no increase in the supply of educationally qualified black males for American colleges and universities to draw upon.

For black females, on the other hand, the fourteen-year mean (again represented by the dashed line) understates the actual experience over the last half of the period, indicating that:

- there has been a statistically significant increase in the high school completion rates for black females, one that parallels their increased college participation rates.

These data largely measure the rate at which blacks graduate from high school in the expected amount of time; they do not necessarily include the number of blacks who later gain a high-school diploma or its equivalent. Alan Ginsburg, in his commentary on an earlier draft of this paper, noted that the high school completion rate for blacks aged twenty and twenty-one has increased over the last fifteen years. Most colleges and universities, however, are unaware of the substantial number of blacks and other minorities who, often at considerable cost to themselves, complete their high school educations as young adults through special programs preparing them for the general equivalency exam. These successful learners are not likely to take the SAT or see a college counselor or appear on the mailing lists that colleges and universities assemble. The task is to develop both recruiting methods that seek out these nontraditional students and financial aid policies that recognize that these learners are more likely to attend college part-time than those who proceed directly from high school to college.

We also wanted to know whether there has been any significant change in the college participation rates for young whites from lower-income families. Using the same CPS data, we split the samples of white males and white females into two groups: those from households reporting an aggregate income greater than $24,999 in 1986 constant dollars; and those reporting a household income less than or equal to $24,999, again in 1986 constant dollars. Because substantial numbers of twenty and twenty-one year-olds in the sample reported themselves to be the head of the household, we limited the analysis to nineteen year-olds, of whom less than 10 percent reported themselves

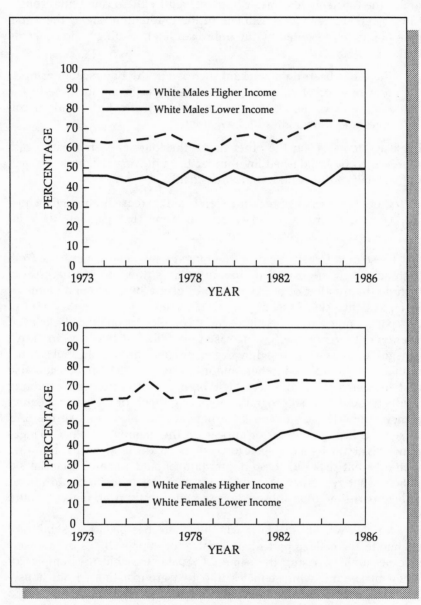

FIGURE 7.3. College Participation, 19-Year-Old High-School Graduates

as being heads of household. Figure 7.3 illustrates the results of our analysis, which suggest that the experience of lower-income white students parallels the experience of blacks:

- there has been no substantial increase in college participation rates for white males from lower-income families and hence no narrowing of the nearly 20 percentage point gap separating their college participation rates from those of white males from higher-income families;
- there has been a gradual increase in participation rates for white females from lower-income families, paralleling the increase in participation rates for white females from higher-income families and leaving unchanged the more than 25 percentage point gap separating the participation rates of the two groups.

What these results suggest to us is that the issue is not access, but rather the social and economic enfranchisement on which educational attainment depends. Colleges and universities cannot be expected to solve the problems of the poor and disadvantaged—to end illiteracy, provide gainful employment, or develop effective health and welfare programs. Indeed it is not even clear (and here I know I speak heresy) that colleges and universities are the best place to invest national funds designed to increase the educational inclusiveness of American society. Unless we are prepared to change fundamentally what college is about, the best way to increase college participation may in fact be to shift current investments from student aid to programs that will improve primary and secondary schools and the environmental supports on which educational attainment depends.

THE HOMOGENIZATION OF HIGHER EDUCATION

Where the practices and environments of colleges and universities do make a difference is in the sorting into particular institutions of those prepared to participate. Here the concern is that higher education restricts access by effectively limiting the collegiate options of minority students and, more generally, of young high-school graduates from families with lower incomes or with no tradition of college attendance.

For nearly a decade, my colleagues at the Institute for Research on Higher Education and I have monitored the patterns of college choice as reflected in the kinds of institutions to which individual students send their SAT scores. Those data, drawn from the College Board's Admissions Testing Program (ATP) and reported through the College Board's Enrollment Planning Service, provide a remarkably detailed picture of how more than a million high-school seniors annually go about the business of choosing a college. What we find each spring, as we process another year's transactions, is that while the American higher education system is one of the most pluralistic in the world, it is also one of the most stratified; one knows a great deal about a student's social, family, and economic circumstances simply by knowing the names of the colleges and universities to which that student sends an SAT score.

Black and Hispanic SAT takers exhibit much the same behavior as their white counterparts in organizing their college choices. The same social and academic attributes—parents with college educations, above-average family income, higher SAT scores, more focused academic aspirations—propel SAT takers from each group toward more selective institutions, public as well as private.

For the most part, these patterns derive from the importance more advantaged families have historically placed on securing college educations for their children. They are not, however, accidental remnants of past patterns of social and economic discrimination. They are inherent in a public policy that has sought to balance the need for an inclusive system of higher education with national aspirations for a system that rewards merit and academic determination. Robert Birnbaum summarized this policy perspective in his 1983 report, *Maintaining Diversity in Higher Education:*

> If quality and access can be considered two of the major ideological commitments of the American system of higher education, the development of institutions serving an elite student body, as well as those providing opportunities for serving the need of mass higher education, provides the operational means by which these two apparently conflicting values can be accommodated within a single system. This in turn requires a commitment to the concept of institutional diversity, thus permitting what Clark [in "The Insulated Americans"] (1981) called the capacity to face simultaneously in different directions. (p. 15; Clark, p. 317)

One example of a statewide system that very consciously seeks to face simultaneously in different directions is California's, with the University of California system at its apex. Most California high-school graduates are expected to enroll in the California State University system. The eight campuses with undergraduate programs in the University of California system are reserved for the state's best-prepared students, roughly the top 15 percent of each graduating class. One of the more troubling aspects of the California scheme is that community colleges are assigned the role of serving as educational institutions of last resort. While many believe that community colleges deliver unique and sorely needed services, others contend that students who attend two-year colleges are less likely to complete the baccalaureate degree and more likely to get lower-status jobs. Too many students are channeled from the start into vocational rather than liberal arts curricula, thus diminishing their chances of transferring to four-year colleges.

At its core this is an argument about resources. Those institutions with fewer financial resources per student now have principal responsibility for educating those students who are less advantaged in terms of educational preparation, family custom, and financial resources. Conversely, the nation's more advantaged students are concentrated in less than a hundred colleges and universities, public as well as private, with better-paid faculty, better endowments and access to private philanthropy, more extensive physical plants, major science and library facilities and, in the case of the universities, major reputations as national research centers. These institutions, which set the standard for American higher education, are far more likely to graduate their students in four or five years; and these graduates are most likely to dominate national and regional institutions and economies.

One of the arguments for accelerating the homogenization of American higher education is that it would offset the contrary correlation between the number of disadvantaged students and institutional resources. Both friends and critics alike, from Tom Hayden and Sandy Astin to Christopher Jencks and David Riesman to David Stockman, have worried aloud about the fairness and efficiency of an educational system that is both stratified and inherently more costly at the top than the bottom. Stockman, for example, was offended by the success of high-priced institutions in defending federal student aid programs that inadvertently rewarded them for charging higher tuitions. In *The Triumph of Politics* he vents his spleen at student aid entitlements "so lavish that a $100,000 per year family can get thousands of dollars in subsidies to send its children to Harvard" (1986, pp. 406-7). This is not the way it was supposed to work out:

> We had come up with a $5,000 annual cap on college student aid that saved billions, but Bob Stafford, chairman of the Higher Education Subcommittee, regretted that he couldn't go along. Someone might need $8,000 or $10,000 from Uncle Sam to go to Harvard or Middlebury College in Vermont. We gratefully took his vote and a token cut in lieu of real reform and moved on. (p. 389)

In only slightly more measured terms, Jencks and Riesman (1968) make the same point:

> The question . . . is not whether a dollar spent on a talented undergraduate has more effect than a dollar spent on a mediocre undergraduate, but whether the three thousandth dollar spent on a talented undergraduate has more effect than the first (or perhaps the five hundredth) dollar spent on a mediocre one. Does an Ivy League

college that spends $20 a day on able undergraduates really achieve
five times as much as an overgrown teachers' college which spends $4
a day on less gifted young people? (p. 128)

For Jencks and Riesman, the answer is clear: "Resources going to
colleges with very expensive instructional programs for talented students are being misallocated. The payoff would be higher if these colleges
admitted more students and spread their resources thinner" (p. 129).

As Jencks and Riesman point out, however, resource-rich institutions are not likely to adopt strategies that in their view dilute their
talent pools and thus threaten their reputations as prestigious institutions. This is as true of the great public flagships—the Michigans,
Wisconsins, UCLAs, and Berkeleys—as it is of the high-cost, highly
selective private colleges and universities that belong to the Consortium
on Financing Higher Education (COFHE). The alternative is to redis-
tribute resources, particularly those that derive from public agencies,
concentrating more of them in what have been too easily described as
"overgrown teachers' colleges." To respond to a question by Jencks
and Riesman, it may indeed make more sense "to augment Los Angeles
State's budget by $600 per student, increasing its resources by 100
per cent," than "to augment Cal-Tech's budget by another $600 per
student, increasing its resources by perhaps 10 per cent" (p. 128).

For nonselective liberal arts colleges, which still account for between 15 and 20 percent of all enrollments in four-year institutions,
that redistribution has already begun, but not in ways that were intended or beneficial. Indeed, for these institutions the diminishing
value of federal student aid programs is already having a telling impact
on institutional finances and educational programs. The most detailed
analysis of how decreased federal student aid programs have affected
educational investments is Timothy Warner's study of private colleges
in California. In the case of small, largely nonselective institutions with
limited endowments (all designated as Carnegie Classification Liberal
Arts Colleges II), Warner found average rates of real expense growth
between 2 and 3 percent per year between 1976 and 1986, compared
with the 4 to 8 percent real growth rates of California's larger, more
selective institutions. Across the state over the same period of time,
funds derived from Pell Grants and the federal campus-based programs declined in real terms by 3 percent per year, for both sets
of institutions. State of California scholarship funds to both sets of
institutions declined even faster, at an average rate of 3.4 percent per
year.

The result, of course, was an increase in the use of institutional
funds for student aid. Among the colleges in Warner's sample, institutional aid budgets rose, in real terms, at an average of 18 percent per
year. Expenditures on physical plant grew at roughly the rate of infla-

tion, thus leaving untended the damage done by more than a decade of deferred maintenance. Significantly, student service costs increased an average of 6 percent per year. Low on the expenditure priority list were the faculty and the instructional budget, which rose at just 1.5 percent per year.

Based on these data, as well as on interviews with the presidents of the institutions, Warner's conclusion was that discretionary funds, coming primarily in the form of increased tuition revenues, were being invested primarily in financial aid and recruitment. In effect, these nonselective, tuition-dependent colleges were replacing lost federal and state aid with their own funds in order to reduce costs to students, thereby maintaining their competitiveness in a state dominated by low-priced public institutions.

The implication is clear: further cuts in publicly funded student aid programs will accelerate the rate at which these and similar institutions fall behind the rest of the industry. We have ample evidence that these institutions will not close, but rather will continue to make those internal adjustments necessary for them to remain competitively priced. Monies that might otherwise be invested in new programs and faculty development will be diverted to the financial aid budget and to better marketing of what must inevitably become a diluted product. Given that these institutions educate a substantial number of youngsters, many of considerable talent who shy away from the competitive pressures of the elite schools, it is just as inevitable that there will be a net loss of educational assets to the nation.

IN THE PUBLIC INTEREST

By now the central theme of this essay should be clear. In the cold, practical world of public policy, any examination of how educational diversity can best be achieved means focusing on the efficacy of current federal student aid programs. In the title to his provocative publication for the College Board, Michael McPherson asks, "How can we tell if federal student aid is working?" The answer, he suggests, lies in determining whether current practices and policies: (a) promote "wider opportunity for post-secondary education"; (b) distribute "the burden of college costs fairly"; and (c) contribute to "the general institutional health of colleges and universities" (1988, p. 17).

Current practices and policies seem to fall short of meeting at least two of these criteria. It is long past time to conclude that current programs have not succeeded in further expanding educational opportunity for minorities or for young people from lower-income families. One has simply to look at the unchanging graphs of college participation rates over the last fifteen years to conclude that federal and state programs have made no difference for black or lower-income males. The sustained increase for females, on the other hand, is true for all groups, suggesting that the increase is largely a function of the recent redefinition of roles and opportunities for women in American society. These observations are not new. Lee Hansen has persistently argued that financial aid programs were not having the intended effect. The response was to quarrel with his methodology, his way of dividing groups, and his reluctance to consider other explanations for the trends he described. His critics ultimately argued that time would tell—that as federal financial aid diminished in value, participation rates for the disadvantaged would fall. We must now admit that time has told. The trends continue unchanged, demonstrating their imperviousness to changes in federal financial aid programs.

It is also clear to me that current federal and state student aid programs are not a very efficient way of investing in the "general institutional health of colleges and universities." Baccalaureate institutions are coming to understand, somewhat belatedly, that distributing federal funds through student choices—in essence, a voucher system—has its drawbacks, particularly when students use the program for income maintenance rather than educational investment.

The alternatives we might consider are as potentially dangerous as they are stark. Indeed, many will argue that frank discussion is in itself too dangerous, too likely to be used by those who would lessen the importance of colleges and universities to American life. Yet the defects in the systems we use are now so apparent that to defend current policy and practice does certain damage to the future of higher education in America.

REFERENCES

BIRNBAUM, ROBERT. *Maintaining Diversity in Higher Education*. San Francisco: Jossey-Bass Publishers, 1983.

CLARK, BURTON R. "The Insulated Americans: Five Lessons from Abroad." In *Higher Education in American Society*, edited by P.G. Altbach and R.O. Berdahl, pp. 315–326. Buffalo, NY: Prometheus Books, 1981.

HANSEN, W. LEE. "Economic Growth and Equal Opportunity: Conflicting or Complementary Goals in Higher Education?" In *Education and Economic Productivity*, edited by Edwin Dean, pp. 57–93. Cambridge, MA: Ballinger Publishing Co., 1984.

JENCKS, CHRISTOPHER, and DAVID RIESMAN. *The Academic Revolution*. New York: Doubleday & Co., 1968.

LITTEN, LARRY. *Some Further Evidence on How the Costs of College May Affect Students' Application Decisions*. The COFHE Market Research Project, Project Report III. Cambridge, MA: COFHE, 1987.

McPHERSON, MICHAEL S. *How Can We Tell if Federal Student Aid is Working?* New York: College Board Publications, 1988.

STOCKMAN, DAVID, A. *The Triumph of Politics: How the Reagan Revolution Failed.* New York: Harper & Row, 1986.

WARNER, TIMOTHY. *Maintaining Balances: The Relationship Between Student Financial Aid and Institutional Finance.* Sacramento: The Eureka Project, 1988.

8

BARRIERS TO DIVERSITY AND THE MYTH OF EQUAL ACCESS

REGINALD WILSON

Mr. Zemsky's paper is a useful contribution to the discussion of the future of access and choice in higher education. He raises important issues and asks hard questions about educational policy and financing to achieve equity. And that is a necessary and important corrective. During the Reagan-Bennett years, the higher education establishment was so busy protecting what it had that it could not take the time to examine if what it had was worth protecting.

Now Mr. Zemsky properly asks questions that we should be compelled to answer. Are we getting the maximum effectiveness from our federal financial aid policies? Are institutions that educate the neediest students getting the least resources? Do student aid formulas reward high-priced institutions? Does not the limited environment of elite institutions create barriers to the achievement of minority students?

HISTORICAL REALITY OF HIGHER EDUCATION

Nevertheless, despite the cogency of these questions and the importance of his argument, the conclusions and policy implications he draws from his analysis are disturbing and, I believe, ultimately flawed for two substantial reasons: the lack of sufficient grounding in historical reality and the incompleteness of his data. I am reminded by Mr. Zemsky's paper of a novel I read many years ago by the Nigerian author Amos Tutuola called *The Palm-Wine Drinkard*. It begins as a pleasant fantasy that describes the adventures of a native who discovers that the oil coming from the palm trees in the forest is really wine, and he goes from tree to tree tapping and drinking joyously the palm wine emanating from these trees. It is a pleasant fantasy, but a fantasy nevertheless. Similarly, Mr. Zemsky describes an America in which "our celebration of educational opportunity is genuine, reflecting a long-standing national commitment to equal opportunity." Indeed, he says, higher education is characterized by "our commitment to educational diversity and equal access." Mr. Zemsky even describes Paul Robeson recording the song "The House I Live In," which ends with a stirring description of America as a home for every race and religion. Like the country of the palm-wine drinkard, Mr. Zemsky describes an America that I have never visited, a country that is essentially a fantasy.

The United States has not historically had a "long-standing national commitment to equal opportunity." In fact, the very nature of higher education has been elitist and exclusionary. The first universities established in this country were private and primarily intended for the sons of the affluent white upper class. They were not for poor men, any women, and certainly not slaves. Not until the middle of the nineteenth century, with the passage of the Justin Morrill Land Grant Act, were public, land-grant institutions established for the education of ordinary white people. And not until the second Morrill Act of 1890 were public, segregated colleges established for black citizens. Even so, it was not until 1973, seventeen years ago, that this legal higher education segregation was declared in violation of the law by the *Adams* case decision of Judge John H. Pratt in the United States District Court.

For example, in Virginia, desegregating public education was met with "massive resistance." Indeed, I spent two summers in Virginia in 1963 and 1964, helping to establish "Freedom Schools" for young black children who had their public schools closed by the state, which preferred shutting schools down to integrating them. Twenty years ago we would not even have been able to hold a racially integrated meeting at most white colleges. The access to higher education for minorities was not brought about by a commitment to equal opportunity, but by Title VI of the 1964 Civil Rights Act, which said institutions that segregated would be denied federal funds, and by Executive Order 11246, which mandated affirmative action policies in hiring. Nor during this time did institutions of higher education have largely open admission policies. In fact, during the past twelve years, over thirty states have raised entrance requirements to attend public colleges and universities.

When I last heard Paul Robeson sing "The House I Live In," it was in a black Detroit church—Hartford Avenue Baptist Church—in the 1960s. At that time he was vilified for allegedly being a communist sympathizer: his passport had been taken from him, and he was barred from every concert hall in America. Certainly, the America he was describing in his song was not the America he lived in, but an ideal America of the future that he hoped would some day come about.

These are not trivial matters. Statistical data not grounded in historical context can, however accurate in themselves, lead to unsound conclusions. Mr. Zemsky's paper essentially implies, "Well, higher education has done everything for minorities that it can and they still don't do very well; so, the problem must not be us, it must lie elsewhere." The historical reality is that the academy has restricted access and excluded minorities, and only grudgingly, under the sanctions of Congress and the courts, opened its doors. Certainly some progress in access has occurred in the past twenty years, but only in a context of real historical and continuing barriers. Thus, the considerable responsibility of the academy to make maximum equal opportunity in higher education remains a continuing mandate.

RESTRICTIONS ON MINORITY ACCESS

The second area where I question Mr. Zemsky's conclusions is related to the narrowness of his data source. He chooses for his study the college participation rate of college-attending youth, aged nineteen to twenty-one years, between the years 1973 and 1986. He chooses this cohort because it "include[s] all youths who completed high school in the expected length of time" and does not "include many students who had already earned their baccalaureate degrees." Examining the participation of this cohort, Mr. Zemsky finds, after desegregating by sex, that there has been an increase in the college participation of black females that parallels an increase in their high school graduation rates. Black male college participation, on the other hand, is unchanged, as is the high school graduation rate for this cohort. Mr. Zemsky sees these rates as essentially reflecting a class phenomenon since he finds the same disparate graduation and participation rates for lower-class white males and females.

However, the behavior of blacks who "completed high school in the expected length of time" is only one part of the traditional college-age cohort of eighteen to twenty-four year-olds. Why eighteen to twenty-four? Official data-gathering and analyzing agencies find this cohort more representative of the range of college-going behavior: the on-time high-school graduate who immediately goes on to college; the graduate who delays going on for a few years; the dropout who later gets a GED and decides to go to college, etc. In looking at this entire cohort, the American Council on Education (ACE), in its *Sixth Annual Status Report: Minorities in Higher Education*, found that black males *and* females significantly increased their high school graduation rate and *both* declined in college participation between 1976 and 1986 (see figures 8.1–8.4). Mr. Zemsky dismisses GED test takers as individuals of whom "colleges and universities . . . are unaware." That is not the point. Over 30 percent of GED test takers pursue the equivalency in order to go to college; however, restrictive admission policies requiring

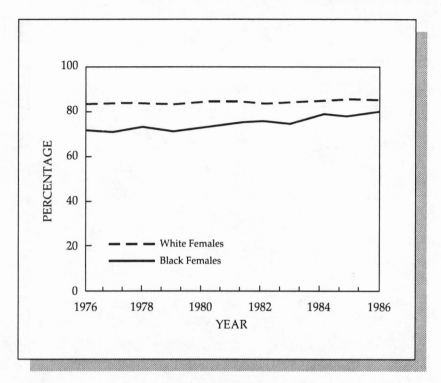

FIGURE 8.1. High School Completion Rates for 18- to 24-Year-Old Women, by Race, 1976 to 1986
Source: Bureau of Census, *Current Population Reports,* various years.

certain high-school course sequences bar many blacks from college even with the GED. Nevertheless, many of these GED takers do enroll in "open door" community colleges and eventually transfer to four-year colleges and universities.

DEFINING THE COLLEGE-GOING COHORT

All of the official and widely used data-gathering sources arrive at the same conclusions as ACE. For example, the Bureau of the Census, *Current Population Reports,* August 1988, found that: "For Blacks . . . the proportion (of eighteen to twenty-four year-olds enrolled in college) declined to 28.6 percent in 1986 from 33.5 percent ten years earlier. Much of the decrease for Blacks can be attributed to the increase in the proportion of youths completing high school but not a concurrent rise in the proportion of the age group attending college." The 1985 publication of the College Board, *Equality and Excellence,* also found that "after 1975 the number of Black youth eligible for college increased by 20

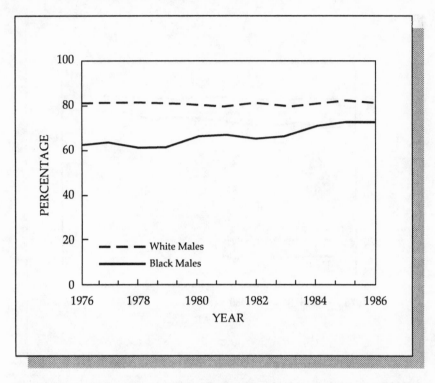

FIGURE 8.2. High School Completion Rates for 18- to 24-Year-Old Men, by Race, 1976 to 1986
Source: Bureau of the Census, *Current Population Reports,* various years.

percent. . . . Higher education participation of Blacks . . . increased during the first part of the 1970s when Federal Policies aimed at reducing barriers were enacted or expanded. However, these gains were eroded during the last half-decade when Federal Aid leveled and economic recession set in."

These data-gathering sources all agree with the ACE findings because the traditional college-going cohort, eighteen to twenty-four year-olds, is more representative of the complexity of motives, times, and intentions of college-going behavior. Moreover, their conclusions are grounded in historical realities, such as economic recession and changes in financial aid policies. For example, Hansen and Stampen conclude "the long term gains from efforts to improve both quality and equity are unlikely unless progress toward removing financial barriers is maintained and unless non-student sources of funding (Federal, state, private) increase to finance improvements in quality" (1988, p. 17).

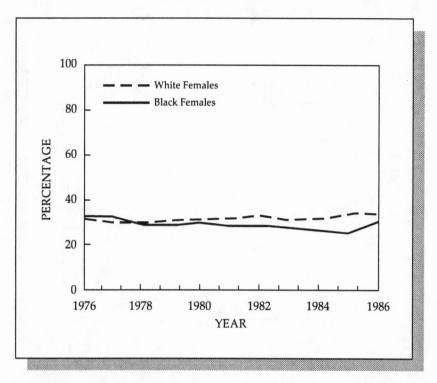

FIGURE 8.3. College Participation Rates for 18- to 24-Year-Old Women, by Race, 1976 to 1986
Source: Bureau of the Census, *Current Population Reports*, various years.

FINANCIAL AID AND EQUITY

Lacking a historical foundation, Mr. Zemsky's conclusion that "colleges and universities cannot be expected to solve the problems of the poor and disadvantaged" erroneously attributes a passive, neutral role to higher education in equity decisions rather than the active, conscious one it has often played historically in restricting access and perpetuating societal bias. Having justified the academy's lack of blame, Mr. Zemsky then, inevitably, concludes that "it is not . . . clear . . . that colleges and universities are the best place to invest national funds designed to increase . . . inclusiveness." He goes on to recommend that the government should "shift current investments from student aid to programs that will improve primary and secondary schools and . . . environmental supports."

Both Mr. Zemsky's conclusions and his policy recommendations are counterproductive to the achievement of educational equity for black students. What would be the consequences of adopting his policy

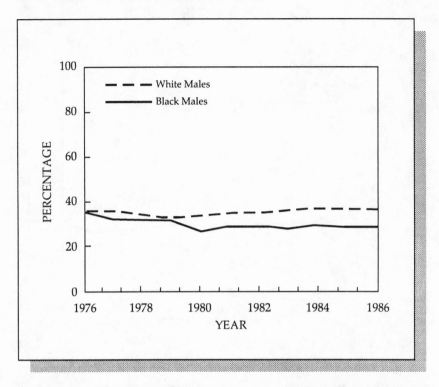

FIGURE 8.4. College Participation Rates for 18- to 24-Year-Old Men, by Race, 1976 to 1986
Source: Bureau of the Census, *Current Population Reports*, various years.

recommendations? First, if one were to shift all of the currently appropriated Pell Grant funds—$4.2 billion—to the elementary and secondary public education budget—$161 billion—the contribution would be less than 1 percent of that budget, an amount negligible in its ability to make any substantial contribution to the improvement of primary education unless it were targeted to a few specified school systems and designated for particular demonstration programs. The effect would be similar to that of current federally funded TRIO programs (or, Special Programs for Students from Disadvantaged Backgrounds), which have been very successful, but have impacted only a fraction of the youngsters eligible for and needing their services. Second, the withdrawal of Pell Grants would be devastating to the support of black students currently in college, of whom some 85 percent depend on financial aid. The result would be to grievously harm one sector of educational equity while making no appreciable contribution to ameliorating another. We cannot play a zero-sum game with educational equity. There is no question of the need to improve primary education, particularly in the big city school systems where most black students are educated;

and we should insist that states be held responsible for such improvement. However, we must equally provide efficient financial aid programs for needy college students. And if current aid programs "have not succeeded in further expanding educational opportunity for minorities," as Mr. Zemsky contends, then let us critically examine those programs in order to improve them where possible, or replace them where necessary. In the "kinder, gentler" presidential administration of Mr. Bush, the higher education community has found a more reasonable secretary of education with whom it can constructively dialogue; however, no significant changes have been made in federal financial aid programs to make them more effective for the needy or to create an expanded federal role in the improvement of elementary and secondary education for minority and low income students.

CONCLUSION

As part of his argument that colleges are not implicated in the lack of increase in the number of black students, Mr. Zemsky asserts that there has been "no increase in the supply of educationally qualified black males" in recent years. Again this conclusion is not supported by the evidence. For the past ten years, the most significant improvement in standardized test scores—SAT, ACT, and NAEP—has been among black and Hispanic high-school students. Their scores do continue to lag behind those of white students, and this is cause for concern and the reason for continued pressure on states to improve the quality of primary education offered to minority students. Nevertheless, given the test score improvements and greater high school graduation rates of blacks and Hispanics, they represent a significant increase in competitive students. It is not the lack of a larger pool of prepared minority students that has contributed to the declining participation rates, but the concurrent raising of admission standards in many public university systems, in the name of "excellence," that has resulted in the rejection of many ordinarily eligible students. Indeed, over thirty states have raised entrance requirements, as previously stated, for undergraduate admissions; and, as reported in the *Chronicle of Higher Education*, some minority students are now being denied admission to medical school with MCAT scores that would have gotten them in ten years ago. Conscious policy decisions that restrict access cannot then be turned around to assert that the reason there are fewer minorities in the university is because they are academically underprepared.

Let me summarize by again recognizing Mr. Zemsky's salutary contribution to serious higher education policy discussions by raising hard questions that the academy will have to deal with substantively, in coming years, with the Bush administration and the Congress. Since

Mr. Bush characterizes himself as the "education president" and has held a well-publicized Education Summit with the governors of all fifty states, it is hoped that there will be a more positive working relationship between the administration and the higher education community to tackle some of the knotty problems Mr. Zemsky has identified. For example, Senator Paul Simon's address suggesting that Pell Grants might be made an entitlement is a beginning of considered alternatives to current federal financial aid policies.

Mr. Zemsky's own policy recommendations are, I believe, flawed because they are insufficiently grounded in a historical and societal context and are supported by too narrow a statistical data base. That does not detract, however, from the importance of the questions he asks, and we are indebted to him for the seriousness and clarity of the issues he raises.

REFERENCES

AMERICAN COUNCIL ON EDUCATION. *Sixth Annual Status Report: Minorities in Higher Education.* Washington, DC: ACE, 1987.

HANSEN, W. LEE, and JACOB O. STAMPEN. "Economics and Financing of Higher Education: The Tension Between Quality and Equity" College Board. 29 April 1987.

WILSON, REGINALD. "Developing Leadership: Blacks in Graduate and Professional School." *Journal of Black Studies* 19, no. 2 (December 1988): 163–173.

9

IMPROVING MINORITY POSTSECONDARY OUTCOMES: THE NEED FOR A COMPREHENSIVE APPROACH

ALAN L. GINSBURG AND
MAUREEN A. MCLAUGHLIN

This paper presents a more optimistic picture of improvements in minority participation in college than Bob Zemsky's paper. Moreover, our analyses indicate that student aid does have positive effects on decisions of lower-income persons to enroll in college. Financial assistance is not enough, however. Improving academic achievement is essential.

- Our analysis suggests that Zemsky's analytic procedures understated progress in high school completion and college enrollment among minorities, although sizeable disparities in educational attainment still separate disadvantaged groups from the more advantaged. The college graduation rate of minorities is of particular concern.
- Econometric studies indicate that student aid increases college participation for low-income persons but does not increase enrollments for more affluent students. Student aid influences enrollment decisions by lowering the price students must pay for college.
- Poor academic preparation limits the benefits that students can derive from postsecondary education. These students are also less likely to complete their education than better prepared students.

These analyses indicate that highly targeted financial assistance coupled with better academic preparation and achievement would help

Views expressed in this paper are those of the authors and do not necessarily reflect positions of the United States Department of Education.

to improve college participation for disadvantaged groups. More money alone will not improve the preparation of disadvantaged students, however. What is required is a substantially restructured education program that exposes minority children to a rich and challenging college preparatory curriculum that students from economically advantaged families are now more likely to receive.

ROBERT ZEMSKY'S "THE GOAL OF DIVERSITY: ACCESS AND CHOICE IN ACADEMIA"

Bob Zemsky's paper analyzes the degree to which access to postsecondary education has improved for disadvantaged populations during the past two decades. He reaches generally disheartening conclusions with respect to the openness of the system and the success of financial aid policies in encouraging greater diversity.

Using data from the Current Population Survey (CPS), Zemsky analyzes educational progress by race and family income for nineteen year-olds over the period 1973 to 1986. His central findings are:

- Black males have failed to improve their high school graduation rate, although black females have narrowed the gap with white females.
- Black males are substantially less likely than white males to go on to postsecondary education, and this difference is not diminishing. Black females have generally boosted their college participation rates, however, and have lessened the disparity with white females.
- Lower-income males have not improved their college attendance rates, while lower- and higher-income females made roughly equal improvements. As a result, the differences between lower- and higher-income groups are undiminished for males, as well as females.

Zemsky also discusses how low-income and black students continue to be underrepresented at elite postsecondary institutions. Since these institutions tend to have the highest per-pupil expenditures, postsecondary education resources are distributed regressively with respect to economic need. He condemns diminished diversity among elite institutions as they increasingly compete for a common pool of academically select students. It is hard to see, however, how such competition could be stopped and, even if it could, whether it is not in society's best interest to inform its preeminent students of their choices.

Zemsky concludes that financial aid programs have failed to improve the situation for the disadvantaged. "The trends [in college participation] continue unchanged, demonstrating their imperviousness to changes in federal financial aid programs." He is rather unsure, however, as to how to increase participation among disadvantaged groups. He warns that we must consider new methods because "the defects in the systems we use are now so apparent that to defend current policy and practice does certain damage to the future of higher education in America." He also suggests that "the best way to increase college participation may in fact be to shift current investments from student aid to programs that will improve primary and secondary schools and the environmental supports on which educational attainment depends."

In summary, Zemsky's paper indicates a real quandary in which present student aid policies seem to have failed to promote access to postsecondary education, but alternatives are unclear. These conclusions and the analyses on which they are based warrant careful probing and further examination.

REEXAMINATION OF MINORITY PARTICIPATION

To provide additional insights into minority progress in higher education, this paper expands upon Zemsky's analyses in several important respects. This section expands the analysis of CPS trends to:

- Examine a slightly older age group to account for students who complete high school at an older age.
- Use three-year moving averages of participation rates rather than focusing on actual annual rates because the CPS is subject to sampling error, particularly for population subgroups.
- Begin with the late 1960s rather than 1973 in order to develop a longer-term perspective on trends in college attendance.
- Examine the educational progress of Hispanics, who represent the fastest growing minority group, as well as analyze black college participation.
- Examine educational attainment along with college enrollment to determine the extent to which those starting college complete their education.

The analysis based on these refinements and expansions suggests that Zemsky's analytic procedures understated progress in high school completion and college enrollment among minorities, although sizeable disparities in educational attainment still separate disadvantaged groups from the more advantaged. Of particular concern is the continuing low representation of minorities among four-year college graduates. Apparently, minorities are not translating increased access into baccalaureate degrees.

High School Graduation: The potential pool of college students comes from high school completers. To better adjust for delayed graduation, this study examines the high school graduation rate for twenty to twenty-one year-olds (see table 9.1) instead of nineteen year-olds as Zemsky did. The proportion of nineteen year-olds who graduate from high school understates the rate of high school completion, particularly for disadvantaged populations who tend to graduate at a later age. Some nineteen-year-old youths who are not reported as high-school graduates are still enrolled in school and eventually graduate, albeit at an older than typical age. In addition, as many as 50 percent of the high school dropouts return to school and about 38 percent of these go on to receive a diploma or its equivalency within four years after their class finishes high school. (Kolstad and Owings, 1986).

TABLE 9.1. **High School Graduation Rates for 20- to 21-Year-Olds by Race/ Ethnicity and Sex, 1969-1985**

	WHITE			BLACK			HISPANIC			ALL
YEAR	*Male*	*Female*	*All*	*Male*	*Female*	*All*	*Male*	*Female*	*All*	
1969	84	83	84	65	67	66	NA	NA	NA	82
1970	85	84	85	67	68	68	NA	NA	NA	82
1971	85	85	85	67	72	70	NA	NA	NA	83
1972	86	86	86	69	71	70	NA	NA	NA	83
1973	86	87	87	72	71	71	59	61	60	83
1974	87	87	87	72	70	71	62	65	64	84
1975	87	87	87	69	74	72	64	62	63	84
1976	86	87	87	68	76	72	63	62	62	84
1977	87	88	87	69	78	74	58	61	59	84
1978	86	88	87	69	77	73	55	65	60	84
1979	86	88	87	68	78	73	55	62	59	84
1980	86	89	87	70	77	74	56	63	60	84
1981	86	88	87	71	79	75	60	62	61	84
1982	86	88	87	74	79	76	59	66	62	84
1983	86	88	87	75	82	79	59	65	62	84
1984	87	88	88	78	83	81	60	70	65	85
1985	87	89	88	79	84	82	62	71	67	85

Source: Three-year moving averages based on data from the October Current Population Survey. 1969 is the average of 1968, 1969, and 1970.

NA—not available.

Blacks. Based on nineteen year-olds, Zemsky concludes that although the proportion of black females completing high school increased, no similar improvement occurred for black males. According to our analysis of twenty to twenty-one year-olds, both black males and females have made progress in finishing high school.

- The overall graduation rate for black twenty to twenty-one year-olds rose substantially from 66 percent in 1969 to 82 percent in 1985. Graduation rates for black females improved more since 1969 than for black males (17 and 14 percentage points, respectively).
- Although blacks are still less likely to complete high school than whites, the difference has narrowed substantially since 1969 because black high school completion increased while white completion rates remained relatively stable.

Hispanics. Information on Hispanic educational attainment is available from the CPS only since the early 1970s. It is apparent that Hispanics have not achieved the same degree of improvement in educational attainment as blacks and that their lower rate of high school graduation is a major contributor to continuing disparities.

- Hispanics are still much less likely to complete high school than either whites or blacks—67 percent for Hispanics in 1985 compared with 88 and 82 percent, respectively, for whites and blacks.
- Hispanic males are even less likely to complete high school than Hispanic females—62 percent versus 71 percent in 1985. Hispanic females have achieved some progress in high school completion increasing from 61 percent in 1973 to 71 percent in 1985—whereas approximately the same percentage of Hispanic males finished high school in 1985 as was the case in the early 1970s.
- Because the white graduation rate has remained fairly stable, the difference in high school completion between Hispanics and whites has narrowed since 1969 for females, but not for males.

College Attendance: This section examines college attendance by looking at whether twenty to twenty-one year-olds are currently enrolled in college or had been at any time in the past. Zemsky looked only at current enrollment status, thus understating college participation.

We also present two indicators of college attendance. The first measure, college attendance rates as a percentage of the total twenty- to twenty-one-year-old population, combines changes in high school graduation and college attendance (see table 9.2). Second, since high school graduates form the pool of potential college enrollees, data on the proportion of high school graduates ever attending college are also presented (see table 9.3). This measure isolates the effects of changes in

TABLE 9.2. 20- to 21-Year-Olds Ever Enrolled in College as Percent of Age Group by Race/Ethnicity and Sex, 1969-1985

	WHITE			BLACK			HISPANIC			ALL
YEAR	Male	Female	All	Male	Female	All	Male	Female	All	
1969	61	42	50	33	26	29	NA	NA	NA	48
1970	60	43	50	36	28	32	NA	NA	NA	48
1971	59	45	51	35	30	33	NA	NA	NA	48
1972	56	46	51	36	32	34	NA	NA	NA	48
1973	55	46	51	35	33	34	31	25	27	47
1974	53	45	49	36	33	34	35	31	33	46
1975	51	46	49	37	37	36	34	31	32	46
1976	51	46	48	37	38	37	33	31	32	46
1977	49	47	48	36	40	38	26	29	28	46
1978	48	47	48	35	39	37	27	29	29	45
1979	47	47	48	34	39	37	29	28	28	45
1980	47	48	48	34	39	37	32	28	30	45
1981	48	49	49	34	40	37	31	29	30	46
1982	49	49	49	35	40	38	30	33	31	47
1983	50	50	50	37	40	39	31	36	33	48
1984	50	51	50	40	41	41	32	39	36	48
1985	50	52	51	41	42	42	31	37	34	49

Source: Three-year moving averages based on data from the October Current Population Survey. 1969 is the average of 1968, 1969, and 1970.

NA—not available.

college participation because it does not consider the effects of changing high school graduation rates.

Blacks. The fraction of black males attending college among all twenty to twenty-one year-olds rose from 33 percent in 1969 to 41 percent in 1985. Attendance increased through the mid 1970s, declined until the early 1980s, and has since risen. Most of this improvement for black males was due to increases in high school graduation rather than increases in the college attendance rate. The same percentage of high school graduates went on to college in 1985 as did in 1969—51 percent. College attendance rates fluctuated somewhat during the period, being a bit higher during the early 1970s and somewhat lower during the early 1980s.

The trend for white males is quite different and seems to be dominated by their response to the Vietnam War. In 1969, 73 percent of white male high school graduates went on to college. This fraction

TABLE 9.3. 20- to 21-Year-Olds Ever Enrolled in College as Percent of High School Graduates by Race/Ethnicity and Sex, 1969-1985

	WHITE			BLACK			HISPANIC			ALL
YEAR	Male	Female	All	Male	Female	All	Male	Female	All	
1969	73	50	59	51	39	44	NA	NA	NA	58
1970	71	51	60	54	41	46	NA	NA	NA	59
1971	69	53	60	53	42	46	NA	NA	NA	59
1972	66	53	59	52	45	48	NA	NA	NA	58
1973	63	53	58	49	46	47	52	40	46	57
1974	61	52	56	50	47	48	56	47	51	55
1975	59	53	56	53	49	51	54	50	51	55
1976	59	53	55	53	50	52	52	51	51	55
1977	57	54	55	53	51	51	45	48	47	55
1978	56	54	55	50	50	50	50	45	47	54
1979	55	54	54	50	51	50	52	44	48	54
1980	55	54	55	48	50	49	57	44	50	54
1981	56	56	56	47	51	49	52	47	50	55
1982	57	56	57	47	50	49	51	50	50	56
1983	58	57	58	50	49	49	52	55	53	57
1984	58	57	58	51	49	50	54	55	55	57
1985	58	59	58	51	51	51	49	53	51	57

Source: Three-year moving averages based on data from the October Current Population Survey. 1969 is the average of 1968, 1969, and 1970.

NA—not available.

declined for a decade, bottoming out at 55 percent in 1979-80. Since then, rates have turned up slightly. The net effect of these trends is to drive black/white disparities among males to an all-time low. For male twenty to twenty-one year-olds having some college education, 9 percentage points separate blacks from whites in 1985 compared with 28 percentage points in 1969.

Although college attendance increased substantially for both white and black females since the late 1960s, blacks are still less likely to go to college than whites—42 percent of black females in 1985 compared with 52 percent for whites. Among twenty- to twenty-one-year-old high-school graduates in 1985, 51 percent of black females and 59 percent of whites had enrolled in college at some time.

The gap between black and white females has narrowed because participation rates rose more quickly for black females than for whites. For twenty to twenty-one year-olds, as a whole, the difference between participation rates for black and white females declined from 16 percentage points in 1969 to l0 percentage points in 1985. For black women, unlike black men, increases in both high school graduation and college participation contributed to higher college attendance. Increased high school graduation rates contributed more, however, than higher college participation rates.

Hispanics. As a percent of the total age group, twenty- to twenty-one year-old Hispanics are much less likely to attend college than either whites or blacks—34 percent for Hispanics in 1985 compared with 51 and 42 percent for whites and blacks, respectively. These differences are larger for males—whose participation rates in 1985 are roughly equal to their rates in the early 1970s—than for females, whose participation has improved.

TABLE 9.4. 25- to 29-Year-Olds with Four or More Years of College as Percent of Age Group by Race/Ethnicity and Sex, 1969-1985

	WHITE			BLACK			HISPANIC			ALL
YEAR	*Male*	*Female*	*All*	*Male*	*Female*	*All*	*Male*	*Female*	*All*	
1969	20	14	17	04	07	05	NA	NA	NA	16
1970	21	15	18	04	07	06	NA	NA	NA	17
1971	23	17	20	06	07	07	NA	NA	NA	18
1972	25	18	21	09	07	08	NA	NA	NA	20
1973	27	19	23	10	08	09	09	04	07	21
1974	28	20	24	10	09	10	10	05	07	22
1975	28	22	25	11	10	10	09	04	07	23
1976	29	22	26	12	11	11	10	05	08	23
1977	29	23	26	12	11	11	09	06	08	23
1978	29	23	26	11	12	12	09	07	08	23
1979	28	23	26	12	12	12	08	07	08	23
1980	27	23	25	13	13	13	09	08	09	23
1981	26	23	25	14	13	13	09	09	09	23
1982	26	23	24	12	14	13	10	09	09	22
1983	25	23	24	12	14	13	09	09	09	22
1984	25	24	24	11	13	12	11	09	10	22
1985	25	24	24	11	13	12	10	09	09	22

Source: Three-year moving averages based on data from the October Current Population Survey. 1969 is the average of 1968, 1969, and 1970.
NA—not available.

Most of the lower participation is due to substantially lower high-school completion rates rather than lower college enrollment rates. Among high school graduates, Hispanic college participation rates are roughly equal to blacks and below whites. The situation has worsened for males but improved for females.

College Graduation: Simply looking at college attendance without examining college graduation does not provide a very complete picture of educational attainment. Because the CPS does not have data on college graduation, we considered completing four years of college as a reasonable proxy for graduation. We focused on twenty-five to twenty-nine year-olds because twenty to twenty-one year-olds would not have had the opportunity to complete four years of college (see tables 9.4 and 9.5).

TABLE 9.5. 25- to 29-Year-Olds with Four or More Years of College as Percent of Age Group Ever Enrolled in College by Race/Ethnicity and Sex, 1969-1985

	WHITE			BLACK			HISPANIC			ALL
YEAR	Male	Female	All	Male	Female	All	Male	Female	All	
1969	47	46	46	23	33	29	NA	NA	NA	46
1970	47	47	47	21	33	28	NA	NA	NA	46
1971	49	48	48	26	31	29	NA	NA	NA	47
1972	50	48	49	32	32	32	NA	NA	NA	48
1973	51	48	50	34	33	33	34	31	33	48
1974	50	48	49	32	33	33	34	30	33	48
1975	50	49	49	32	33	32	30	22	27	48
1976	49	48	49	32	31	31	30	22	26	47
1977	49	48	49	31	31	31	27	24	26	47
1978	49	48	49	31	33	32	28	29	28	47
1979	50	47	49	31	33	32	28	30	29	46
1980	50	47	48	34	34	34	33	31	32	47
1981	49	47	48	33	34	34	33	32	33	46
1982	49	47	48	30	34	33	35	32	34	46
1983	49	47	48	29	34	32	32	32	32	46
1984	49	47	48	29	33	31	35	29	32	46
1985	50	47	49	29	32	31	32	29	31	46

Source: Three-year moving averages based on data from the October Current Population Survey. 1969 is the average of 1968, 1969, and 1970.

NA—not available.

Blacks. College completion rates for blacks are still significantly below whites. For the full twenty-five- to twenty-nine-year-old age group, including noncollege attendees, a quarter of white males completed four or more years of college in 1985 compared with only 11 percent for black males. The comparable female rates are 24 percent for whites and

13 percent for blacks. Completion rates for this group have increased more quickly for blacks since 1969 than for whites. For both whites and blacks, however, most of the improvement is due to higher completion rates among those who enroll. For twenty-five to twenty-nine year-olds who had ever enrolled in college, 49 percent of whites completed at least four years compared with 31 percent for blacks. These rates have remained fairly constant since 1969.

Hispanics. As with blacks, college completion for Hispanics is relatively low. Hispanic twenty-five to twenty-nine year-olds with some college education are only 60 percent as likely as whites to attain a four-year degree. For twenty-five to twenty-nine year-olds as a whole, the Hispanic completion rate is only 40 percent of the white rate.

In summary, while the picture of minority educational attainment is not as bleak as Zemsky maintains, neither have minorities achieved access to postsecondary education in proportions equal to those of whites. Moreover, minority enrollment gains are not matched by increases in college graduation rates.

EFFECTS OF STUDENT PERFORMANCE AND FINANCIAL ABILITY ON COLLEGE ENROLLMENT

This section examines the underlying factors influencing college enrollment decisions, especially the effects of high school achievement, ability to pay, and student financial assistance. Increases in need-based student financial assistance and improvements in the academic program of minorities while in high school are two policies frequently mentioned to promote greater minority access to higher education. Judgments differ about the potential impact of each policy, and solid empirical information on the importance of financial and academic factors is essential to assess their policy importance.

In contrast to Zemsky's conclusions, our analyses indicate that student aid does increase college enrollment for disadvantaged groups. Econometric analyses suggest that price changes affect college participation for low-income groups, indicating that expanded federal student aid in the late 1970s did expand access to college.

Our analyses also suggest that raising the academic achievement of minorities to diminish differences with whites would reduce disparities in college attendance. While this is consistent with Zemsky's suggestion that investments in elementary and secondary education would improve college participation, his implication that greater spending for elementary and secondary education is the cure-all for improving minority attendance is false. Spending improvements must be coupled with a restructured education program that increases the rigor of minority precollege preparation.

Financial Assistance: Costs—both actual school charges and foregone earnings—weigh more heavily for low-income persons than for others in considering whether to attend college because students from lower-income families have fewer funds available from family resources to pay for their education. Federal student financial assistance, particularly the Pell Grant program established in 1972, has provided much aid to low-income students in order to ease the difficulties low-income students have because of limited financial resources.

Zemsky concludes that aggregate college enrollment trends, particularly for minorities, have not increased as would have been expected if student aid had been an important determinant of college going. On this evidence, he rejects the viability of student aid policies.

Our reanalyses of enrollment trends suggest that student aid may have positive effects on enrollment of low-income students. Federal Pell Grants for low-income students were phased in between 1973 when eligibility was limited to freshmen and 1976 when eligibility was extended to all undergraduates meeting income requirements. Over this period, black and Hispanic college going increased, although females experienced greater improvements than males. This suggests that grants for lower-income students equalize access to college.

During the mid-1970s, large student aid increases combined with slowly rising college costs worked to reduce the net cost of attendance (Hauptman and McLaughlin, 1988). Since then, the rapid increase in college costs and the expansion of eligibility to less needy students have worked to offset the effects of student aid, especially for the lowest income. Enrollment trends are roughly consistent with these changes in net price. The mid-1970s was a period of increased minority enrollment while the 1980s brought a leveling off of minority enrollments despite an overall increase in student financial assistance.

One must be cautious in drawing conclusions about student aid effects from aggregate CPS trend analyses, however, because rates of college going may have changed for reasons other than student aid availability. It is conceivable, for example, that total enrollment would have declined in the absence of student aid, in which case observed enrollment changes would understate true impacts. To identify relationships underlying college attendance, individual student data should be examined to assess how college attendance among low- and high-income groups has responded to changes in student aid, controlling for other relevant variables.

A number of econometric studies have examined the determinants of college going by exploring student-level data. A recent study used meta-analysis to synthesize twenty-five empirical studies of the student price response to higher education (Leslie and Brinkman 1988). It found that a student's college going was price-sensitive—a one hundred dollar increase in college tuition (in 1982 dollars) was associated with a 1.8

percent decline in the college participation rate among eighteen to twenty-four year-olds. The effects of grant aid were found to approximate those of price changes.

The findings of these studies are subject to several qualifications. First, virtually all studies included in the synthesis were based on data from the early 1970s or before and included only grant aid. This is the period prior to massive federal aid increases, including enactment of Pell Grants. Whether the synthesis results from this earlier period are applicable to one of expanded student aid is uncertain. Second, the studies included in the synthesis were almost entirely cross-sectional, comparing at one point in time the responsiveness of different students to the availability of different student aid packages. Differences in responses across students may be poor predictors of how individual students would respond over time to changes in aid levels.

McPherson and Schapiro (1990) address some of these flaws in their recent time series analysis of enrollment rates between 1974 and 1984. Enrollment trends for several income groups from the CPS are coupled with time series data on college costs of attendance and student aid, also adjusted by income groups. They conclude that enrollment responsiveness to costs depends on family income. For low-income students, each one hundred dollar increase in net prices (costs of attendance minus student aid) caused about a 2.2 percent decline in enrollment. For more affluent students, net price did not affect enrollments.

These findings indicate that student aid does influence college going by reducing the net cost of attendance. As would be expected, individuals from lower-income families are most sensitive to price changes. These findings, as well as previous econometric studies, support the case for targeting student aid on lower-income students.

Academic Achievement: Although student assistance has been the principal federal policy instrument for encouraging economically disadvantaged youth to attend college, it is clear that it alone will not increase college participation of disadvantaged groups. Improving academic achievement is essential. Poor academic preparation limits the benefits students derive from continuing their education past high school. Those that do go on are also at significantly increased risk of failing to complete their degree.

The role of academic achievement along with family income in influencing college enrollment is demonstrated using longitudinal data drawn from a nationally representative sample of 1980 high-school seniors (Chaikind 1987). When both achievement and income factors are controlled, blacks attend college in proportions about equal to or greater than whites. Within the lower and middle two-thirds of the academic achievement rankings, black attendance is particularly high compared with whites. It is these students who are the least prepared for college and experience higher rates of college noncompletion.

Since the 1970s, black and Hispanic students have made some inroads toward diminishing their achievement gap with whites. However, improvements have come primarily in the basic skills, rather than in the higher-order skills that students need to succeed in college. This performance gap is evidenced on the mathematics component of the National Assessment of Educational Progress (NAEP), the federal government's major national test. The percentage of seventeen-year-old blacks and Hispanics who were proficient in basic mathematical operations and problem solving increased by 16 and 13 percentile points between 1978 and 1986, to come near the white attainment rate of 98 percent. On the next higher proficiency level, the ability to perform moderately complex procedures and reasoning in mathematics, the percentage of black (22 percent) and Hispanic (27 percent) seventeen year-olds attaining this level changed little over the period, remaining at about only half the white percentage (58 percent).

Recent results on the NAEP test of writing skills of seventeen year-olds yield stark evidence of a higher-order skills gap in writing. Black seventeen year-olds are writing only at about the fourth grade level of their white peers, and the Hispanic performance level is not much higher.

Students who bring to college this degree of poor academic preparation will face difficult academic hurdles in college, and many fail to overcome these difficulties. Among 1980 high-school seniors, those at the highest quartile on an achievement test were almost three times as likely to complete their bachelors degree within five years after high school graduation than those at the middle 50 percent of performance (United States Department of Education 1989).

IMPROVING COLLEGE PARTICIPATION
AMONG DISADVANTAGED GROUPS

Justified efforts to obtain further parity in college-going rates of minorities should not diminish past progress. Refined empirical analyses presented above suggest that student aid contributed to these gains. They also suggest the need for substantially improved academic preparation.

Changes in Financial Assistance: Maintaining a sound student aid system that directs subsidies to low-income populations needs to remain an essential element of any strategy to equalize minority educational prospects. Zemsky's uncertain alternatives that would totally dismantle aid are unsubstantiated.

To improve the efficacy of student aid in improving college participation and completion among disadvantaged groups, further targeting
of aid on low-income students is essential.

> • *Improved Targeting of Aid.* Pell Grants, the foundation of aid for the
> neediest, are not sufficiently targeted on low-income students.
> Moreover, participation in Pell Grants of students attending trade
> and technical institutions has increased substantially in the past
> decade, thereby limiting increases in aid for the most needy stu-
> dents in collegiate institutions.
>
> Increased targeting of Pell Grants on the most disadvantaged
> would focus resources on those who would benefit most from
> such aid. There are numerous ways of doing this, including tight-
> ening need analysis and changing award rules.
>
> Changes in other aid programs, including subsidized loans,
> could also help to focus aid where it is most likely to increase
> enrollment. As with Pell Grants, loan subsidies could be further
> targeted. Loans—both subsidized and unsubsidized—help to pro-
> vide students with the ability to choose among institutions, in
> addition to influencing their decisions on whether to enroll.
>
> • *Early Awareness of Financial Aid.* Students should know early what
> aid they will be eligible to receive in order to motivate them to
> take the necessary courses for college and to perform well in high
> school. Aid alone is not sufficient, but early notification of eligibil-
> ity would help to make all youngsters—especially disadvantaged
> ones—view college as a real option for them. Along with this
> financial commitment, students need counseling, tutoring, and
> mentoring. Programs that have used this intensive approach have
> generally been quite successful.

Currently student aid does not have provisions that offer incentives to students to do better or provisions that penalize them for not
doing well. Our analysis indicates clearly the importance of financial
and academic factors in improving college-going rates. In addition to
improved targeting of aid, changes in the aid system should be considered that would encourage better academic preparation. Specifics on
how to improve achievement and preparation in the early years are
discussed in the following section, but some changes could be tied to
the financial aid system.

> • *Required Preparation for Postsecondary Education.* At the present time
> student aid is provided to students who do not have high-school
> diplomas. Requiring a high-school diploma or its equivalent would
> increase the likelihood that students would benefit from post-
> secondary education and would help to improve the quality of
> postsecondary options. Having a higher performance standard

than just a high-school diploma or not covering remedial courses are two other possibilities. Opponents of these types of changes argue that they would restrict access for the disadvantaged, who are less likely to have adequate preparation for postsecondary education.

- *Achievement Scholarships for Needy Students.* Extra aid for needy high-performing students would encourage better performance. A highly visible program of national achievement scholarships for high-performing needy high-school students is one such idea. Given limited federal funds and the importance of improving access to postsecondary education, this aid should be highly targeted by income and should supplement Pell Grants.

Changes in Academic Preparation and Motivation: In addition to student aid, improvement strategies must focus explicitly on academics. A combination of policies to address this end includes:

- *Increased Rigor in Minority Academic Preparation.* Although some nay-sayers argue that higher academic standards discourage the disadvantaged from succeeding, research suggests that at-risk students are fully capable of meeting greater academic challenges. In one study of six states that toughened elementary and secondary requirements, no evidence was found of increased high school failure and dropping out (Clune 1989). Instead, the researchers concluded that it was the lower-performing students who benefited most from rigorous requirements, as they were exposed to advanced courses that formerly were provided to only high-performing students. The researchers did find, however, that school administrators and teachers often expected the at-risk populations to fail.

  Additional support for more classroom rigor comes from noted researcher James Coleman's (1987) highly publicized findings that Catholic schools are more effective than public schools for educating low-income and minority populations, even after controlling for their initial achievement level. Coleman concluded that one reason for the Catholic schools' success is that they permit much less variation in exposure to advanced courses between at-risk and other populations. Because of their improved preparation, disadvantaged students attending Catholic schools were more likely to graduate high school and to attend college.

- *New Paradigms for Approaching the Education of At-risk Populations* are needed if the disadvantaged are to receive the same quality education available to advantaged students. Too often, low expectations for disadvantaged populations become self-fulfilling prophesies. Traditional approaches to educating the disadvantaged have emphasized the learners' deficits, long-term ability groupings, and a curriculum that moves in "fixed sequence" from basic to higher-order skills. Recent theory and experience are pointing to promising alternatives to "conventional wisdom" that emphasize the knowledge and experiences students do bring to school, expose them to appropriate higher-order tasks, and use mixed ability or more flexible grouping strategies.

· *Implementation of the National Educational Goals.* The president and the governors in their historic Charlottesville meeting produced an unprecedented agreement on educational performance targets for American schools to achieve by the year 2000. Although these targets were motivated by concern over the inadequate performance of American students in general, many of the targets focus on improving the performance of at-risk populations. One objective looks toward eliminating "the gap in high school graduation rates between American students from minority backgrounds and their nonminority counterparts." Another aims to increase significantly the academic performance of elementary and secondary students "in every quartile" and to achieve a "distribution of minority students in each level" that more closely reflects the student population as a whole. Still a third objective states that "the proportion of those qualified students, especially minorities, who enter college; who complete at least two years; and who complete their degree programs will increase substantially."

These objectives are not achievable without radical alterations to correct the deficient exposure of minorities to college preparatory coursework in high school. Although the proportion of minorities exposed to higher-level courses has improved somewhat in response to educational reforms, a black high-school graduate in 1987 was only two-thirds as likely to take a second course in algebra, half as likely to take a physics course, and 40 percent as likely to receive exposure to calculus as a white high-school graduate (Educational Testing Service, 1989).

Translating these national aims into concrete improvement targets at state, local, and institutional levels is essential if these goals are to produce improved outcomes. Many governmental organizations will not willingly hold themselves accountable by specifying their own performance targets to fulfill the national goals. To make the goals an effective system for public accountability will require widespread support from those outside the governing establishment, including parents, community, and businesses.

REFERENCES

CHAIKIND, STEPHEN. *College Enrollment Patterns of Black and White Students.* Prepared for Office of Planning, Budget, and Evaluation. Washington, D.C.: United States Department of Education, 1987.

CLUNE, WILLIAM, JANICE PATTERSON, and PAULA WHITE. *The Implementation and Effects of High School Graduation Requirements: First Steps Toward Curricular Reform.* New Brunswick, NJ: Center for Policy Research in Education, 1989.

COLEMAN, JAMES, and THOMAS HOFFER. *Public and Private High Schools.* New York: Basic Books, 1987.

EDUCATIONAL TESTING SERVICE. *What Americans Study.* Princeton, NJ: Educational Testing Service, 1989.

HAUPTMAN, ARTHUR, and MAUREEN MCLAUGHLIN. "Is the Goal of Access to Postsecondary Education Being Met?" A background paper prepared for the Education Policy Seminar, Aspen Institute, 1988.

KOLSTAD, ANDREW J., and JEFFREY A. OWINGS. *High School Dropouts Who Change Their Minds About School.* Washington, D.C.: United States Department of Education, Center for Statistics, 1986.

LESLIE, LARRY L., and PAUL T. BRINKMAN. *The Economic Value of Higher Education.* New York: Macmillan Publishing Co., 1988.

MCPHERSON, MICHAEL S., and MORTON O. SCHAPIRO. *Measuring the Effects of Federal Student Aid: New Evidence from a Study of Enrollment Patterns over Time.* Prepared for Office of Planning, Budget, and Evaluation. Washington, D.C.: U.S. Department of Education, (forthcoming) 1990.

UNITED STATES DEPARTMENT OF EDUCATION. *Digest of Education Statistics 1989.* Washington, D.C.: United States Government Printing Office, 1989.

SECTION IV

Budgetary Efficiency: The Federal and State Commitment in the Face of Severe Federal Budget Deficits

The term "budgetary efficiency" may bring to mind images of budget cuts by bureaucrats wearing green visors and having little understanding of the programs being cut. In the context of higher education, this side of the uneasy triangle is the most dismal to analyze, especially in the context of the current public budgetary climate. The federal government is facing nearly overwhelming deficits annually. In addition, many states are facing severe fiscal constraints due to such factors as increased responsibility given to them during the 1980s by the federal government and the continuing political difficulties elected officials face whenever they entertain the idea of raising taxes. These government budget realities spill over to the higher education sector (public and private) in the form of such trends as less (growth in) student financial assistance, less (growth in) research dollars going to universities, and less (growth in) money available for capital expenditures by colleges and universities. This section examines several dimensions of the budgetary efficiency question from the point of view of the public policymaker and the education policymaker.

In his chapter "Trends in the Federal and State Financial Commitment to Higher Education," Arthur Hauptman covers four major areas of inquiry. First, he reviews the federal and state roles in providing financial support for higher education, including a brief sketch of the history of these roles.

Second, Hauptman examines trends over the past two decades of public support for higher education. His focus on the last three federal administrations (Nixon/Ford, Carter, and Reagan) is quite illuminating and surprising. For a variety of reasons, the administration kindest to higher education was that of the Nixon/Ford era, next was the Reagan administration, and last was the Carter administration. The relatively generous support in the Reagan years (compared to the immediate predecessor) seemed to be due to some special factors and was in spite of, not because of, President Reagan's budget and programmatic proposals.

Third, Hauptman develops definitions and indicators of effectiveness (i.e., are the funds having the desired impact?) and efficiency (i.e., are the funds spent on those who can use the help the most?). He finds that the four categories of government support—federal student aid, federal support to university research and development, state support to institutions, and state student grant programs—vary greatly in terms of their achievement of effectiveness and efficiency.

From the analysis of trends in public support and effectiveness and efficiency considerations, Hauptman develops strategies to improve effectiveness and efficiency of what appears to be the relatively static amount of resources available to higher education. He suggests improvements in targeting, diversification, experimentation, and evaluation.

In his chapter "Federal Support for Higher Education in the '90s: Boom, Bust, or Something in Between?", Terry Hartle analyzes changes in federal support for higher education in the decade of the 1980s. He states, "Despite the Reagan administration's best efforts, federal student aid spending, in real terms, increased by 33 percent in the last decade." Hartle looks at trends in federal research dollars over time and compares the United States experience with four other industrialized nations. He suggests that a key question for the future is whether federal support will continue to increase, and if so, will it be in the form of defense R&D or nondefense R&D? He emphasizes that the federal deficit will be the most important public policy consideration in determining the future vitality of institutions of higher education.

Hartle then speculates on what to expect from the Bush administration in regard to support for higher education. He states, "Educators should not underestimate the value of a president with a strong personal commitment to education—neither should they overestimate spending options in the current environment." He also notes that President Bush's Education Summit focused on elementary and secondary, and not higher, education. Hartle suggests that in the face of severe federal budget problems and the apparent education focus not being on higher education, federal policymakers will tackle the issue, leaving little for colleges and universities to do but to wait and see.

Walter McMahon, in "Improving Higher Education Through Increased Efficiency," focuses on a broader concept of (economic) efficiency that emphasizes educational resource allocation. Using the underlying premise that the public budget problems are likely to continue in the foreseeable future and therefore it is important to search for ways to improve the (resource) efficiency in the higher education sector, McMahon develops the concept of efficiency in terms of internal and external efficiency of institutions and efficient investment strategies. He then elaborates on the efficiency properties of the United States higher education system by examining trends in social rates of return to educational investments over time and relative to other investments and by comparing the United States educational structure to that of a variety of countries with different systems. Some of his conclusions are that we have not overinvested in education in the United States and instead have, if anything, underinvested, and that the United States higher education system has certain efficiency benefits accruing to it as a result of the integration of graduate teaching and research. He considers several other efficiency issues and offers some potential for improvement in resource efficiency in the United States higher education sector.

The overall message from these three chapters is mixed. One cannot be terribly optimistic that large amounts of additional public monies will be flowing into the higher education sector in the foreseeable future. There may be some hope in terms of some tinkering with some of our public policy approaches (as suggested by Hauptman) and with some of our education policy approaches (as McMahon suggested), and/or we can "stay tuned" as was suggested by Hartle. In any case, this side of the triangle offers little hope for less uneasiness vis-à-vis the quality and diversity goals.

10

TRENDS IN THE FEDERAL AND STATE FINANCIAL COMMITMENT TO HIGHER EDUCATION

ARTHUR M. HAUPTMAN

This paper examines changes from 1969 to 1989 in the level of financial commitment by federal and state governments to higher education. The *two* principal components of the federal role in higher education are discussed: financial aid to students attending postsecondary education, and the support of scientific and other research conducted on campus or by organizations affiliated with universities. The state role in higher education also covers *two* principal activities: support of institutions, primarily those in the public sector, and student financial aid programs in the form of grants.

This paper also addresses *two* issues with regard to the federal and state role in higher education: First, what have been the patterns of federal and state support over the past *two* decades, spanning the Nixon/Ford, Carter, and Reagan administrations? Second, how do the federal and state programs for higher education of direct support to institutions, student aid, and research measure up on the *two* economic criteria of efficiency and effectiveness?

The paper is (surprisingly) divided into four sections. First, the evolution of the federal and state roles in providing financial support for higher education is briefly described. The second section examines trends over the past two decades in the amount of support provided by federal and state governments for institutional support, student aid, and research conducted on campus. The third section assesses how the major federal and state higher education efforts rate on the two economic criteria of effectiveness and efficiency. Finally, there is a discussion of what kinds of strategies might be employed to bring about greater efficiency and effectiveness in the expenditure of public funds for higher education.

THE PRINCIPAL FEDERAL AND STATE
ROLES IN HIGHER EDUCATION

The Federal Responsibilities: The federal role in higher education extends back at least to the Civil War with the Morrill Act of 1862, which provided the principal impetus for the creation of public land-grant universities in the states. But the substantial aspect of federal involvement in higher education during this century can be traced to the Second World War in both student aid and research activities.

The modern federal role in student aid stretches back over forty years to the establishment of the first GI Bill at the end of World War II. It was over thirty years ago that the launching of Sputnik spurred the passage of the National Defense Education Act of 1958 with its fellowship and loan programs. Twenty-five years ago the Higher Education Act of 1965 was enacted as part of Lyndon Johnson's Great Society; it included programs of grants for low-income students and loans of convenience for middle-income students, as well as enlargement of the college work-study program. Over fifteen years ago the Basic (now Pell) Grants program was created to serve as a floor of assistance for any individual who sought a postsecondary education. And over ten years ago there was the Middle Income Student Assistance Act, which expanded eligibility for both grants and loans to students from middle-income families.

Funding for all federal student aid programs in fiscal 1989 equalled roughly $10 billion. The value of federal student assistance, including the amount of federally guaranteed loans, is roughly $20 billion, equalling three-fourths or more of the total amount of student aid that is available from all sources. In this paper, the student aid category includes student support services as provided under the TRIO programs such as Upward Bound.

The federal role in campus-based research also goes back to World War II as universities were enlisted in the effort to advance the Allied cause. Since the end of the war, the National Science Foundation was created in 1950, the National Institutes of Health have become an indispensable national resource, and the federal role in promoting research has greatly expanded in a number of other areas such as space, agriculture, and education itself.

Federal funding for university research in fiscal 1989 was over $10 billion, or nearly $12 billion if federally funded research and development centers (FFRDCs) are also included. These federal funds represent over 60 percent of total funding for academic research and development efforts, which are highly focused on basic research. Over half of basic research conducted in this country occurs on university campuses. The proportion of all applied research and development performed by university personnel is much smaller.

There is a third federal role in higher education that could be described as everything else that could not be described as relating to student aid or research. This category includes: institutional support programs under Title III of the Higher Education Act; support for specific institutions such as Howard University or Galludet; programs for teachers and libraries; and research in higher education as well as demonstration projects supported by the Fund for the Improvement of Postsecondary Education (FIPSE) and others.

The State Role in Institutional Support and Student Aid: The principal state role in higher education—the support of public sector colleges and universities—dates back to the creation of these institutions beginning in the nineteenth century spurred by the Morrill Act. State appropriations for the purpose of supporting the operation of public institutions remain by far the largest form of any governmental support for higher education. Another, much smaller form of state support for institutions is what a handful of states do in making payments to private institutions. Total state institutional support in fiscal year 1989 was an estimated $35 billion, with less than $1 billion provided to private institutions.

State student grant aid programs date back at least a quarter century, predating federal efforts. But the funding for state efforts collectively has been much smaller than the federal grant funds, certainly since 1972 when the Basic Grants program was created. In the same 1972 legislation, Congress established the State Student Incentive Grant (SSIG) program to stimulate the creation and growth of state grant programs. Today, all the states have at least one grant program, and many states have several programs of grant assistance. States collectively in 1988-89 spent in excess of $1.6 billion for programs of need-based grant assistance for undergraduates as well as graduate and professional school students.

TRENDS IN FEDERAL AND STATE
FUNDING OVER THE PAST TWO DECADES

Figure 10.1 indicates the dollar growth in federal and state support for higher education between 1969 and 1989. Total federal and state spending grew from $8 billion in 1969 to over $50 billion in 1989. This represents a growth of six-fold, or an annual compound rate of growth of nearly 10 percent. When adjusted for inflation, the growth of federal and state support combined has been about 3 percent per year.

Between the federal and state governments, however, the rate of growth has not been the same over the past two decades, as Figure 10.1 clearly indicates. At the end of the 1960s, total state support was roughly a third more than the level of total federal support for higher

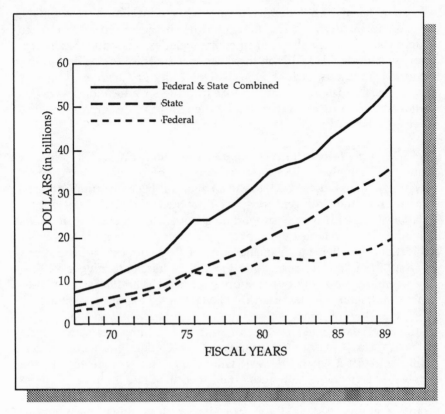

FIGURE 10.1. Federal and State Spending for Higher Education

education, $4.8 billion for the states compared to $3.5 billion in federal support. In 1989, state support of higher education was two-thirds higher than the amount of federal funding, $35 billion for the states compared to $21 billion at the federal level.

Thus, state funding of higher education has grown at a faster rate than federal levels. State funds for higher education grew at an annual rate of over 10 percent, and when adjusted for inflation, a real increase of 3.7 percent per year. During that time, the annual growth for federal funding for higher education was about 9 percent, or a real rate of increase of 2.2 percent.

The patterns of growth have also varied during different time intervals. Figure 10.2 indicates the annual real rates of growth in federal and state spending for time intervals that relate to three federal administrations: 1969 to 1977 for the Nixon/Ford years; 1977 to 1981 for the Carter administration; and 1981 to 1989 for President Reagan's tenure in office.

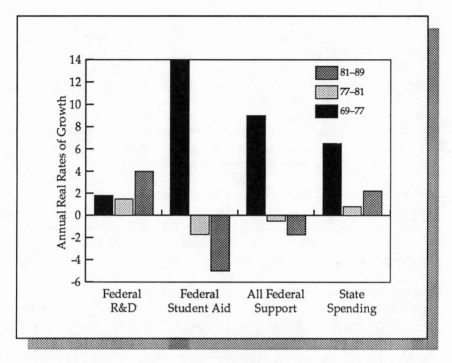

FIGURE 10.2. Trends in Federal and State Support for Higher Education

Federal Support Patterns: For federal R&D, the real rate of growth under Nixon/Ford and under Carter was less than 2 percent per year. Under Reagan, the annual real rate of growth was over 4 percent. In the area of federal support of university research, Reagan was as supportive as Jimmy Carter, especially over the last several years. Congress adopted much of what Reagan proposed and then added on to it. As a result, federal support of R&D at universities nearly doubled during the Reagan years, or over 35 percent in real terms. This is much faster than the growth during the Carter years, when federal R&D support to universities grew less than 10 percent in real terms.

Federal appropriations for nonentitlement student aid programs grew slightly in real terms during the Reagan years, contrary to most press reports, as Congress largely rejected the Reagan proposals. Total funding for federal student aid declined in real terms, however, because of developments in three entitlement programs. GI Bill spending fell as fewer veterans were eligible to use the benefits. The phaseout of Social Security benefits resulted in a $2 billion drop in federal student aid spending from 1980. And declines in market interest rates caused GSL interest subsidies to fall.

Overall, federal student aid expenditures grew fastest in real terms during the Nixon/Ford years, at an annual real rate of increase of 14 percent. Student aid spending fell by 2 percent per year in real terms during the Carter years and by nearly 5 percent per year under the Reagan administration.

Total federal funds for higher education grew fastest under Nixon/Ford, at an annual real rate of increase of over 9 percent, mostly as a result of the rapid increase in student aid fueled by the growth in GI Bill benefits. By contrast, under Carter, federal higher education funds fell slightly in real terms as veterans benefits began to decline, and under Reagan, overall federal spending for higher education declined by about 2 percent per year when adjusted for inflation.

State Patterns of Support: There has been much discussion recently about a slowdown in the growth of state support for public institutions in the 1980s and its impact in the form of increased public tuitions to make up for lost state revenues. When looked at in nominal terms, this impression about state funding is correct: the growth in state funding for higher education in the 1980s was slower than it was in the 1970s. But when adjusted for inflation, a different pattern emerges. State funds in real terms grew more in the 1980s than in the late 1970s. When adjusted for inflation, state funding grew about 2.5 percent per year in the 1980s, compared to 1 percent in the late 1970s. State funding grew faster earlier in the 1970s; between 1969 and 1977, state funding grew by over 6 percent per year in real terms.

In terms of state student grant programs, funding increased in real terms in the 1980s at a rate of nearly 5 percent per year. But the state funding of these programs is still relatively small (about 5 percent) compared to funds provided directly to public institutions. Moreover, in most states, there is no explicit policy that links public sector funding levels and tuitions with state student grant policies and formulas.

Trends in Federal Support for Higher Education: With the publicity over the Reagan budget cuts, much has been written about the cutbacks in federal support of higher education in the 1980s. Is this true? The answer is not really. But to understand this issue, it is necessary to look at the different components of federal support.

Figure 10.3 indicates federal spending for higher education as a percentage of total federal outlays. It peaked at slightly over 3 percent in 1977, and fell back to about 1.7 percent in the late 1980s. What is most interesting is that federal R&D funding for universities maintained a relatively level proportion of support throughout the period of between .7 and .8 of 1 percent of total federal outlays. By contrast, student aid jumped as a proportion of total federal funds from less than 1 percent in the 1960s to nearly 2.5 percent in the late 1970s, and then fell back to less than one percent of total federal spending in the late 1980s.

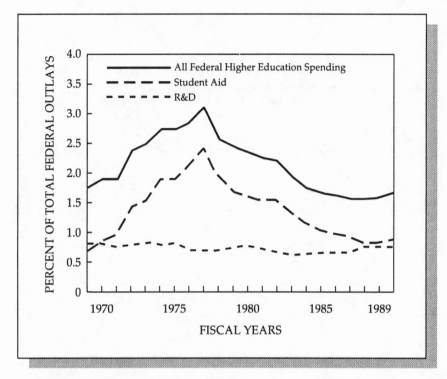

FIGURE 10.3 Federal Spending for Higher Education as a Percentage of Total Federal Outlays

These figures can be deceiving, however, in that they combine federal entitlements, where spending is affected by a variety of external factors, with discretionary programs that are dependent on annual appropriations and that more accurately reflect annual congressional decisions. Figure 10.4 indicates the trend in funding for nonentitlement federal higher education programs as a proportion of all federal discretionary spending. As the chart indicates, higher education programs captured an increasing share of the federal discretionary budget during the Reagan years. Federal university R&D support grew from less than 3 percent of the discretionary budget in 1980 to nearly 5 percent in the late 1980s. After a dip in the early 1980s, student aid programs grew from 2 percent in 1980 to 3 percent in the late 1980s. Higher education at the end of the 1980s claimed nearly 8 percent of the federal discretionary budget, up from 5 percent at the beginning of the decade. So while many domestic programs in fields such as transportation or housing suffered substantial cutbacks during the Reagan years, higher education increased its share of domestic discretionary spending.

Figure 10.5 indicates the difference in the growth of the different

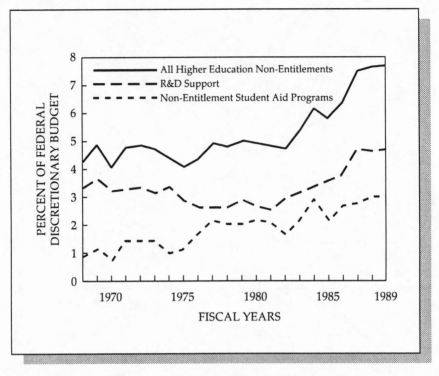

FIGURE 10.4. Federal Non-entitlement Programs for Higher Education as a Percentage of Total Federal Discretionary Budget

components of federal spending under the Nixon/Ford, Carter, and Reagan administrations:

- Surprisingly, DOD support of university R&D grew faster under Carter than under Reagan, while nondefense R&D grew faster under Reagan. Since nondefense R&D represents over 80 percent of federal support for university R&D, federal support for campus R&D grew more under Reagan than under Carter.
- Department of Education support for higher education exclusive of the entitlement GSL program grew at roughly the same rate under Carter and Reagan. GSL spending, however, grew by over 40 percent per year in real terms under Carter as eligibility for loans was expanded to all students regardless of family income in 1978. With the increase in interest rates in the late 1970s, the removal in 1979 of the previous cap on interest payments to lenders also greatly contributed to a sharp increase in federal GSL interest payments. The real increase in GSL spending came to a halt in the Reagan years as loan eligibility was once again restricted and lower interest rates reduced the amount of interest payments to lenders.

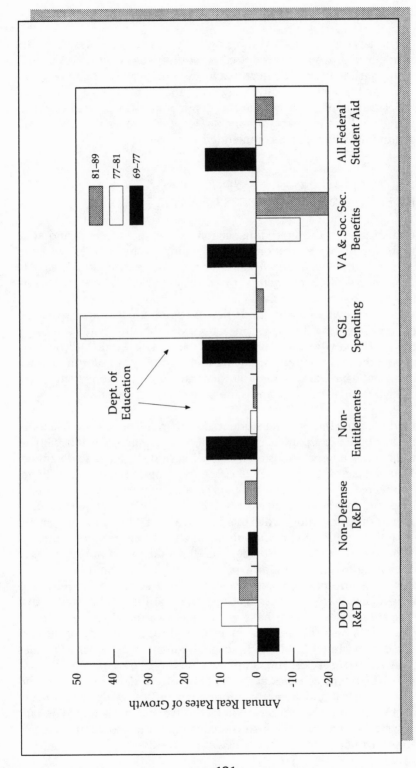

FIGURE 10.5. Trends in Sources of Federal Support for Higher Education

· The largest decreases during both the Carter and Reagan years occurred in VA and Social Security educational benefits. VA spending declined with the decrease in the number of veterans eligible to use these benefits after the end of the Vietnam War. The Social Security benefit for college-age dependents was phased out during the Reagan years, although it is worth noting that the Carter administration also recommended this action.

RATING FEDERAL AND STATE SUPPORT ON EFFICIENCY AND EFFECTIVENESS GROUNDS

The discussion in the preceding section on trends in federal and state funding for higher education does not address the issue of whether these funds are well spent. To answer this question, it is necessary to discuss how well government support of higher education does when graded on two economic criteria: effectiveness and efficiency. Effectiveness measures whether the funds that are spent are having the desired impact on behavior. Efficiency measures whether the funds are being spent on those who can use the most help. This section focuses on how well these two criteria are being met through each of four government activities: federal student aid; federal support of university R&D; state institutional support; and state student grant programs.

Federal Student Aid: Federal student aid programs have historically not been distributed in a particularly efficient way. Congressional inability or unwillingness to target funds on the neediest students tends to doom federal student aid on the measure of efficiency. Programs have typically not been targeted to the neediest students because there is a desire to spread the benefits to a larger group of students in order to maintain political support for the programs. While this may be a politically correct judgment, the result is a relatively inefficient use of student aid program funds.

The overall evidence also suggests that student aid programs have not been highly effective. Participation rates in higher education have not improved despite massive investment in student aid, thereby suggesting a lack of effectiveness. Perhaps the best that can be said is that participation rates would have most likely dropped in the face of higher prices and the absence of increased aid. The lack of success suggests that student aid needs to be augmented by other strategies such as support services and simplification.

The degree of complexity in the student aid delivery system and the lack of early and accurate information on aid availability further detract from both the efficiency and effectiveness measures. The current system is too confusing to the consumer and too complicated to administer to be judged either efficient or effective.

Measuring effectiveness, however, is confused both by the diversity of goals and the lack of agreement over what is the objective for each program of student aid. In the case of Pell Grants, for example, they probably have been fairly effective in enhancing access to higher education, especially when their impact is combined with low tuition policies and grant programs in the states. On the other hand, the program has not been helpful in promoting choice among institutions, which is not surprising since choice was never intended as one of its primary objectives. The area in which Pell Grants may have been most successful is in promoting attendance in the proprietary sector, where over $1 billion in Pell Grants is now awarded annually, over one-quarter of all Pell Grant dollars. The other federal grant program, Supplemental Education Opportunity Grants (SEOG), was more intended to promote choice, and has probably been moderately successful in this regard, although limited funding increases have in turn limited the effectiveness of this program.

The GSL program has probably been the most important single effort for helping private institutions maintain their share of college enrollments over the past decade. Therefore, it could be said that it has been very effective in promoting the choice objective. The size of the current GSL subsidy, however, may lead to the program being less effective in the future in promoting choice in higher education for the following reason: these subsidies served as a constraint in raising loan limits in the reauthorization of the Higher Education Act and without an increase in loan limits, GSL over time will become less important in facilitating the maintenance or growth of private sector enrollments.

Federal Support of Campus-Based Research: Most observers would agree that federal research funds seem to be fairly effectively spent. The highly regarded research enterprise at the nation's universities has helped put America on the cutting edge in a multitude of scientific and technological areas. It seems fair to say that these efforts would not have occurred in the absence of the federal support.

Federal research support may be more questionable on the criterion of efficiency. The traditional peer review system is designed to help ensure that funds are spent on the most worthwhile projects. But criticisms of this system as too much of an old boy network and too concentrated in a few institutions (more than 60 percent of the funds go to fifty institutions) raise questions about the current system. The disturbing trend toward more pork barreling is also likely to reduce the efficiency in research funding as well as detract from the goal of effectiveness.

In addition, the system of indirect costs used in the funding of federal research is in some degree of disrepair. Indirect costs have risen over time as a percentage of total federal spending for research, suggesting that a smaller proportion of research funds are being provided directly for research activities, thus indicating a lower degree of effectiveness. Moreover, categorical federal funding for the construction and maintenance of research facilities has dramatically decreased over time, placing additional pressure on indirect costs to take into account facilities needs. This and other developments have led to increased padding of the indirect costs account, with the result of diminished accountability and effectiveness. A preferable approach might be to streamline the indirect cost account and to allocate funds for facilities as a direct cost of research, rather than depending on the current back door approach of using indirect cost allocations to pay for facilities construction and maintenance.

State Support of Public Higher Education: It seems fair to say that state support of public institutions has been a very effective public policy tool for enhancing access to higher education. It is difficult to imagine the expansion of American higher education since World War II in this country without low tuition policies. In combination with Pell Grants and other aid programs, relatively low tuitions in the public sector have certainly been instrumental in expanding access to higher education. But their strength as a vehicle for access has also meant that low tuition policies may have detracted from the goals of choice and diversity, at least to the extent that low tuitions make public colleges and universities a more attractive option compared to less subsidized private institutions.

The funds that are used to maintain low tuitions are also very inefficient in that large subsidies are provided to middle- and upper-income students who could afford to pay more. A preferable strategy from the viewpoint of efficiency would be to reduce the subsidies provided to all public sector students by raising tuition levels somewhat and to reallocate some of these resources in the form of more funding for grants to low-income students, which could reduce the out-of-pocket costs of these students below today's levels. This is by no means a new argument, but one that still needs to be made.

The way in which states provide funding for higher education typically has had a very large and inverse impact on the rate of increase in the tuitions that public institutions charge their students. This is because it has traditionally been the case that public sector tuitions serve as the "plug" that fills up the difference between state appropriations levels and the size of projected institutional budgets. Thus, when state funds increase rapidly, tuitions tend to increase less, since there is a smaller gap to fill between state funding and institutional spending levels. When the growth of state funds slows, then tuitions tend to increase faster to make up for the larger difference between institutional budgets and state funds.

To the extent that availability of state funds is tied to economic conditions in a direct way, then we find that a disturbing relationship exists between changes in economic conditions and tuition increases at public institutions. When times are tough, and a state cannot afford to add much to what its public institutions receive, that is when tuitions increase the fastest. As the economy improves, state funding increases and tuition increases abate. This seems to be contrary to an optimal policy in that students are asked to pay the highest tuition increases when times are tough and tuitions increase least when students can most easily afford to pay.

This is what has happened in the 1980s. Public tuitions shot up in the early 1980s when the economy was bad and state resources were strained. In the rest of the 1980s, the economy and state revenues recovered, and tuition and fee increases at public institutions moderated.

It is possible, however, that this traditional inverse relationship between increases in state funding and tuition levels may change as more and more states move to funding formulas that link tuitions with the amount of funds that a state provides or with the cost of educating a student. A dozen or more states have adopted such an approach in the 1980s. It seems reasonable to assume that in these states, tuitions will increase more directly with the economy and state funding levels: tuitions will increase faster when the economy is growing and more state funds are available than during economic recessions when funds are tight.

The outstanding question, however, is whether this kind of formula funding approach will hold up during an economic recession. If a state becomes strapped for cash and slows the growth of funds provided to public colleges and universities, will public institutions be willing to sacrifice by keeping tuition increases low, thus restricting their growth of spending. One way to address this issue is for states to establish mechanisms such as rainy day funds or borrowing authority that allows them to smooth out the patterns of revenue and expenditure fluctuations. But few if any states put in place such a safeguard mechanism when they shifted to a funding formula in the 1980s.

The recent experience in Virginia, one of the first states to move to a funding formula, does not augur well in this regard. Virginia experienced a revenue shortfall in 1989-90, which led to a slowdown in state funding for higher education. Many public institutions in the state, which had enjoyed the wave of expansion in the late 1980s, suddenly found themselves with less funding both from the state and from tuitions. A number of them reacted by wanting to raise their tuitions to make up for the shortfall, but Governor Wilder jawboned them into reducing their proposed tuition increases by threatening still larger cuts in state funding. Thus, it will be interesting to see what happens in Virginia and other funding formula states over the next several years.

State Student Grant Programs: State student grant programs appear to have been modestly effective in their role of supplementing other aid. To the extent these state programs are typically more tied to the financial need of the student than the federal Pell Grant program, they are particularly effective in introducing additional choice into the system in that state programs tend to be more favorable to private institutions than the federal grant programs. With regard to efficiency, state programs are probably slightly less efficient than the federal programs at this time because they are not as targeted on the lowest income students.

The federal SSIG program, however, is neither very effective nor efficient. It can more accurately be characterized as a special revenue sharing program for the states based on an enrollment driven formula. SSIG funds are not well targeted on the neediest students, and for most states, the funds appear to have no appreciable impact on the behavior of the states. The program should be phased out, and the funds could be better spent on other forms of student aid.

IMPROVING THE EFFICIENCY AND
EFFECTIVENESS OF GOVERNMENT SUPPORT

This final section discusses how federal and state government support of higher education might do better at meeting the goals of efficiency and effectiveness. I would place a further constraint on the discussion by asking how we can do better within the current level of government resources because this is a more realistic expectation for the future than to assume that funding will continue to increase as it has in the past. To address this issue, I would like to suggest a strategy—or actually a set of four strategies—to deal with the diversity of goals. These four strategies are: *targeting, diversification, experimentation,* and *evaluation.*

First, there should be more *targeting* of resources on the intended beneficiaries who would benefit the most from the use of these resources. Student aid dollars should go to the lowest income and neediest students. In the case of research, the bulk of the resources should be directed to the providers who are most capable of delivering the product. Targeting remains the best way to achieve both the objectives of effectiveness and efficiency.

Second, we should adopt more of a *diversification* approach in the way that public funds are distributed. To the extent that there are diverse goals, it makes little sense to put all of our policy eggs in one basket in the form of funding only one program. Funding of public programs should instead be diversified in order to meet diverse public policy goals. This is not unlike a private investment strategy in which one's portfolio is diversified between different instruments such as growth stocks, blue chips, and bonds in order to minimize risk while still earning a healthy return.

A third strategy would be to encourage more *experimentation* in public policies to see what works and what does not. There was a time not so long ago when experiments and demonstration projects, especially in a selected number of states, were viewed as a relatively inexpensive means to find out what policies might work. But the willingness to experiment has noticeably declined over the past decade. The one experiment in higher education during the Reagan administration was the Income Contingent Loan (ICL) pilot program, which was not much of an experiment since it provided very little leeway to the participating institutions. A renewed use of experiments and demonstrations might help greatly to improve the operation of public policies.

The fourth strategy is one of greater *evaluation*. Very little is written about the efficiency or the effectiveness of the current use of federal and state funds for higher education. This lack of knowledge is directly attributable to the reduced resources that are invested in evaluation efforts. Without more resources devoted to serious and objective evaluations, we should not expect to see better results from our public policies.

How do these strategies translate into future efforts in the field of government involvement and funding of higher education?

In student aid, it means that:

- Funds should be targeted on the neediest students as a means for enhancing both efficiency and effectiveness as well as improving equity.
- As important, student aid efforts should be diversified. If we seek to promote both access and choice, then the predominant share of all funds should not be directed at program(s) that are not designed to meet both goals simultaneously. Therefore, rather than place all our eggs in Pell Grants and GSLs, we should fund other efforts in graduate education and in student support services such as the TRIO programs, and also add a merit-based component to student aid and other areas, even at the expense of slightly less funding for Pell Grants and GSLs.
- More resources should be devoted to experiments and evaluation—a drop in the bucket compared to what we now spend on the programs themselves.

Research is not my area of expertise, and so I will not try to translate my four strategies into recommendations. But I would speculate that federal research efforts might benefit from the application of these strategies.

With regard to state policies:

- A targeting strategy would entail reducing the general subsidies provided to public institutions, establishing a funding formula that ties tuition levels to spending levels, and augmenting grants for low-income students, which would serve to reduce their out-of-pocket costs.
- State programs of challenge grants or other institutional incentives such as those in Virginia and New Jersey are good examples of what a diversification and experimentation strategy at the state level might reasonably entail.
- The growing call for more accountability is in many ways a call for better evaluation. But I would go further than providing greater accountability of institutions and students. States should also undertake to evaluate the use of their own funds by examining in a serious way the efficacy and the equity of low-tuition policies, funding formulas that are currently used to support public institutions, and student grant programs and new efforts such as Challenge Grants.

In conclusion, I believe adoption of the four strategies of better targeting, increased funding diversification, more willingness to experiment, and a greater commitment to evaluation are necessary if the efficiency and effectiveness of government support for higher education is to be improved. If these strategies are rejected and we instead stay on our current course of basic maintenance of the status quo with occasional tinkering, the results are predictable. The system will limp along with government funds operating at rates far from peak efficiency and with less than adequate results. This would seem to be an easy choice to make.

DATA SOURCES

Federal funding for student aid and total federal outlays: *Historical Tables, Budget of the United States Government, Fiscal Year 1989*, Office of Management and Budget, 1988.

Federal support of university R&D: *Federal Funds for Research and Development, Detailed Historical Tables, FY 1955-87*, National Science Foundation, 1988, and *Digest of Educational Statistics*, United States Department of Education, 1988.

State funding of institutions: *Higher Education General Information Survey*, United States Department of Education, various years.

State student aid programs: *Annual Survey*, National Association of State Scholarship and Grant Programs, various years.

Trends in the availability of student aid programs: *Trends in Student Aid: 1980 to 1989*, The College Board, August 1989.

11

FEDERAL SUPPORT FOR HIGHER EDUCATION IN THE '90S: BOOM, BUST, OR SOMETHING IN BETWEEN?

TERRY HARTLE

The 1980s turned out to be a pretty good decade for America's colleges and universities. Contrary to expectations, enrollments increased by more than one million students. The ledger sheets of most institutions remained balanced and, in many cases, improved dramatically thanks to aggressive fundraising. The Reagan administration was generally hostile toward education, but real federal support for need-based student aid increased, as did federal investment in research and development.

The coming decade looks promising. Enrollments are expected to remain steady, and, if they do, institutional budgets should remain on an even keel. Even more important is the high esteem accorded to higher education and its purveyors. Talk about "overeducated" Americans that was commonplace in the late 1970s has given way to a conviction that we are too poorly educated to compete in global markets. Seldom before have the contributions of higher education to the nation's economic growth and social progress been so widely recognized.

The future also looks good because a new administration, headed by a man who wants to be remembered as an "Education President," has taken office. His secretary of education is a former university president who knows firsthand the challenges facing America's colleges and the importance of higher education to the nation's well-being.

These are all good signs, and many observers believe that higher education will fare better in the coming decade than it did in the one

Reprinted from *Change*, January/February 1990, and based on 1988 conference paper presented at the College of William and Mary.

just passed. Perhaps. Lest we forget, higher education's overall health depends first and foremost on the condition of the nation's economy. Indeed, for colleges, the federal government's management of the economy may be the single most important variable in determining whether the 1990s are a boom, a bust, or something in between.

The most important short-term economic issue today is the enormous federal budget deficit. All economists believe that the deficit must be reduced, but there is no agreement about how to do it. Virtually all public policy debates revolve around this issue. Until the deficit is reduced, it will be difficult for the federal government to launch new initiatives (especially nondefense initiatives) or to increase funding for existing policies.

How will higher education fare in this environment? To make an informed judgment, it is first necessary to examine how the federal government's support for higher education has changed in the last decade. Then we can assess how the deficit will most likely frame the debate about federal social policy in the near future.

Student aid spending in the Reagan years: Proposed changes in student aid were a prominent and controversial part of the Reagan administration's efforts to reorder federal domestic priorities. The Reagan administration's ideas were generally variations on the same theme: cut, slash, and trim. However, with the exception of changes in the Guaranteed Student Loan program (now known as the Stafford Loan program) made as part of the 1981 budget cuts, Congress was unwilling to make wholesale changes in student aid. Moreover, despite the Reagan administration's best efforts, federal student aid spending, in real terms, increased by 33 percent in the last decade (see table 11.1).

Between fiscal years 1980 and 1990, appropriations for the Stafford Loan program increased by 48 percent in real dollars, and Pell Grant funding grew by 57 percent. Two of the campus-based programs, Supplemental Grants and College Work-Study, show increases in current dollars but, after adjusting for inflation, funding for the two dropped 18 and 28 percent, respectively. Federal capital contributions for the Perkins Loan program are 66 percent below the 1980 level.

College costs, by comparison, have increased 137 percent at public universities, 174 percent at private universities, 125 percent at public colleges, 163 percent at private colleges, and 114 percent at community colleges.

While the appropriations increases in the last decade failed to keep pace with the changes in tuition, it is essential to note that appropriations for the Stafford Loan program are used to cover interest subsidies, deferral and cancellation provisions, and defaults. This means that the appropriation figures do not show how much money was actually borrowed by students. The volume of loans in this program

TABLE 11.1. Federal Funding to Help Students Pay College Tuition Bills (In Thousands of Dollars)[a]

DEPARTMENT OF EDUCATION	FISCAL YEAR 1980	FISCAL YEAR 1990	PERCENT CHANGE FROM FY 1980	PERCENT CHANGE FROM FY 1980, ADJUSTED FOR INFLATION
Pell Grants	$2,441,328	$5,871,000	141.0	57.1
Supplemental Grants	370,000	465,000	25.7	–17.9
Perkins Loans	300,000	159,000	–47.1	–65.5
College Work-Study	550,000	610,097	10.9	–27.5
Stafford Loans	1,609,344	3,826,314	137.8	47.6
Total, Department of Education[b]	$5,270,672	$10,931,411	107.4	33.1
Social Security Benefits	$1,883,000	$ 0	–100.0	–100.0
Veterans G.I. Bill	$2,066,584	$ 235,657	–88.6	–92.2

Sources: Congressional Research Service; Department of Education; Social Security Administration; Department of Veterans Affairs

[a]Dollar figures for Department of Education programs are appropriations; Social Security dollar changes show outlays; and G.I. Bill figures show obligations.

[b]Appropriations for 1990 as specified in the Departments of Labor-HHS-Education Appropriations Bill for fiscal year 1990. These figures do not include the 1.4 percent reduction in domestic, discretionary programs enacted as part of the Omnibus Budget Reconciliation Act of 1989.

increased from $4.8 billion in 1980 to roughly $13 billion in 1990. This is an increase of 170 percent (49 percent in constant dollars).

At the start of the 1980s, two other federal programs provided substantial amounts of money to help students meet college costs. The G.I. Bill made more than $2 billion in tuition assistance available for veterans in 1980. Eligibility for this program and use of it have both declined, and in 1990 just $235 million was awarded. This represents an inflation-adjusted decline of 88 percent.

Another major student aid program at the start of the 1980s was the Social Security Student Benefit given to young dependents and survivors of social security recipients; in 1980, $1.9 billion was provided under this program. That program began to phase out in 1981, and no money is available through it for 1990.

Federal research and development spending: Federal support for research and development tells a different story. As table 11.2 shows, federal spending on R&D increased sharply in the last decade, with

TABLE 11.2. Federal Research and Development Spending (for Defense and non-Defense): 1965-1988, in Billions of Dollars

	DEFENSE R&D[a]	NON-DEFENSE R&D	TOTAL FEDERAL R&D	DEFENSE R&D AS A PERCENTAGE OF TOTAL
1965	$ 7.3	$ 7.3	$14.6	50.0
1970	8.0	7.3	15.3	52.3
1975	9.7	9.3	19.0	51.1
1980	15.1	14.7	29.8	50.7
1981	17.8	15.3	33.1	53.8
1982	22.1	14.3	36.4	60.7
1983	24.5	13.9	38.4	63.8
1984	28.3	14.9	43.2	65.5
1985	33.4	16.1	49.5	67.5
1986	36.5	16.2	52.6	69.4
1987	38.4	17.6	56.0	68.6
1988	39.5	19.3	58.0	67.2
1989 (est)	41.3	21.7	63.5	65.5
1990 (est)	44.0	23.3	67.3	65.4

Sources: Executive Office of the President, Office of Management and Budget; Special Analysis J; Budget of the United States Government; Fiscal Year 1990, p. j-16
[a]Includes defense-related research sponsored by the Department of Energy

federal support for it growing from $29.8 billion to $67.3 billion, an increase of more than 125 percent. Within this broad category, spending for basic research also grew, from $14.7 billion in fiscal 1980 to an estimated $11.3 billion in 1990, a growth of 140 percent.

Clearly these increases in spending are good news. But from higher education's perspective, there are two aspects to it that are problematic. First, most federal R&D support now goes to military or defense-related projects. As table 11.2 shows, between 1965 and 1980, federal funding of civilian and defense R&D was roughly in balance—about 50 percent went to each. Over the last ten years, however, a much larger share has gone to defense projects. In 1986-87, for example, almost 70 percent of the federal R&D spending went to military projects. Put another way, federal support for nondefense R&D increased 59 percent since 1980, while federal support for defense research increased 191 percent.

This shift in focus is important because defense-related R&D has an entirely different focus from civilian research and development. Most of the military's expenditures for basic research go to the development of weapons systems. The military's demand for relatively small quantities of highly sophisticated weapons encourages handicraft. By contrast, civilian R&D must pay greater attention to the costs of production and the implications of new discoveries for consumer markets.

TABLE 11.3. Government R&D Expenditures among Selected Objectives, by Country: 1987 (In Percentages)

Objective	United States	France	West Germany	Japan[a]	United Kingdom
Total	100.0	100.0	100.0	100.0	100.0
Agriculture, Forestry, Fishing	2.3	3.6	2.0	4.0	4.2
Industrial Development	0.2	10.6	15.3	4.8	8.7
Energy	3.6	8.7	8.7	23.2	3.5
Health	11.9	3.6	3.2	2.4	4.3
Advancement of Knowledge[b]	3.6	26.6	43.6	50.1	21.2
Civil Space	6.0	5.9	4.5	6.4	1.8
Defense	68.6	34.1	12.5	4.5	50.3
Other	3.8	8.9	9.6	4.2	6.1

Source: National Science Foundation, International Science and Technology Data Update, 1988 (Washington, D.C.: National Science Foundation, 1989), p. 6.
[a]Some data are National Science Foundation estimates.
[b]The "Advancement of Knowledge" category includes expenditures for general university funds for all countries except the United States. United States figures are for the federal government only; the federal government does not provide general university support.

The importance of the balance between civilian and military R&D is best appreciated by comparing the United States with its principal trading partners. Table 11.3 shows that in 1987 the United States spent almost 70 percent of its federal R&D funds on defense-related projects, while the United Kingdom spent 50 percent. West Germany and Japan spent 13 and 5 percent, respectively. The funds not spent on military projects by these countries were devoted to what the National Science Foundation calls "the advancement of knowledge" and "industrial development." Both West Germany (59 percent) and Japan (55 percent) devoted a much larger percentage of funds to these categories than the United States (4 percent) or the United Kingdom (30 percent).

The bottom line is that when expenditures for military projects are excluded, West Germany and Japan are spending a higher percentage of their GNP on research and development than France, the United Kingdom, and the United States (see table 11.4).

TABLE 11.4. Total and Non-Defense National R&D Expenditures as a Percentage of Gross National Product, by Country: 1985

	TOTAL R&D EXPENDITURES AS A PERCENTAGE OF GNP	NON-DEFENSE R&D EXPENDITURES AS A PERCENTAGE OF GNP
France	2.3	1.8
West Germany	2.7	2.5
Japan	2.8	2.8
United Kingdom	2.2	1.5
United States	2.7	1.9

Source: National Science Foundation, International Science and Technology Data Update, 1987 (Washington, D.C.: National Science Foundation, 1987), pp. 4-6. Some data are estimated by NSF.

Some analysts contend that military research generates many civilian spinoffs; they cite integrated circuits and aircraft technology. But other scientists maintain that such research does not create as many benefits because the knowledge generated by military research often doesn't transfer to the civilian sector or transfers much more slowly because of security considerations.

A second concern over recent federal R&D spending is that the proportion of funds directed to university-based research is falling. In 1980, the federal government spent $4.3 billion on university-based R&D, representing 14.3 percent of the total federal investment in research. The proportion of federal R&D funds going to universities dropped steadily in the 1980s, and in 1988 about 12.3 percent of federal support was devoted to university-based research. Thus, even though federal research spending rose substantially in recent years, higher education got a smaller share of it than before.

HIGHER EDUCATION IN THE POST-REAGAN ERA

Higher education will continue to be affected by a wide range of economic and social issues in the coming decade. The nation's rapidly changing demography will continue to exert a profound influence on enrollment patterns. Continued state support will be essential to the fiscal and academic health of colleges and universities. And, as always, the national and regional economies will continue to define the context for the fiscal health of higher education.

The deficit: The federal budget deficit will be the most important public policy consideration in shaping the future of our colleges. In fiscal year 1990, the federal government will have a $1.3 trillion budget. It will allocate roughly $300 billion for national defense, $205 billion for nondefense discretionary spending, $585 billion for entitlements and other mandatory spending, and $182 billion for interest on the debt. The deficit will be $110 billion.

Over the last decade, federal expenditures for national defense and interest on the national debt have grown from 7 percent of the nation's GNP (in 1980) to 8.9 percent in 1989. Entitlement spending is at 10.7 percent, roughly the same level as in 1980. Outlays for domestic discretionary programs have fallen sharply, from 5.9 percent of the GNP to 3.8 percent; the federal government is now spending a smaller share of the nation's wealth on discretionary social programs than it did before the Great Society.

Addressing the budget deficit is a monumental task. One major issue is timing. Trying to reduce the deficit too quickly could produce an economic slump if spending is cut back sharply or taxes increase rapidly. But not moving quickly enough may convince lenders that the deficit will never be reduced. This might well lead to much higher interest rates and an economic slump. If a slump occurs, the deficit will increase as the federal government spends more money to offset the social problems of the downturn.

The second thorny issue is how to reduce the deficit. There are two basic options: spending cuts and/or tax increases. Spending cuts are unpopular, and the easy ones were made years ago. Reducing defense spending may be possible, given recent developments in Eastern Europe, but it is unclear whether defense cuts alone will be sufficient to finance the backlog of high-priority spending demands in other areas of the federal budget. Cutting entitlements is difficult, especially for the biggest programs like Social Security and Medicare (Medicare expenditures are increasing at 12 percent a year, making this the fastest-growing program in the federal budget). Outlays for interest on the debt cannot be touched. Nondefense discretionary spending has borne the brunt of previous cuts but, as the "everything else" category of the budget, it may be a target for additional cuts. And, with the exception of Stafford Loans and R&D funded by the Department of Defense, most federal spending on higher education is in this category.

This is a very significant consideration. Expenditures for research and development are, according to the Congressional Research Service, about 15 percent of the controllable expenditures in the federal budget. This means that federal R&D spending—especially spending for "big science" projects like the Super Conduction Supercollider and Mapping the Human Genome—may be vulnerable.

Tax increases to help lower the budget deficit are, in theory anyway, another possible approach. But President Bush has made it clear that he is adamantly opposed to tax increases. As a result, it is unlikely that a Democratic-controlled Congress will raise taxes unless the president explicitly asks that it be done.

Federal Research and Development spending: The budget deficit is the single most important factor that will shape federal policy toward higher education. But even with the massive deficit, there are several important considerations that will influence federal policymaking.

In research and development, the most basic question is whether federal support will continue to increase and, if it does, whether the increases will be for civilian or military activities. A related consideration is whether the federal government will favor a "big-science" or "little-science" strategy—or whether it will try to accomplish both. So far, policymakers have not made a choice between large, expensive projects that focus on major areas of interest and the smaller projects involving a handful of scientists. Several major projects are underway or are on the drawing board. But if all the big-science initiatives are pursued, they will crowd out the little-science initiatives. Small research projects, the Congress knows, are vitally important—as the recent breakthroughs in superconductivity attest.

In the presidential campaign, President Bush committed himself to proceeding with both the supercollider and the manned space station. For fiscal year 1990, the Congress provided slightly less for Supercollider and space station than the president requested. But if these projects stay on their current schedule, huge funding increases will be necessary in the next few years.

The point here is that choices will have to be made soon about how many and what type of scientific projects to fund. The choices will be made by elected officials in a political context. The scientific community can play a major role in shaping these decisions, if scientists are willing to prioritize. In the past, this community has dodged budgetary struggles. Making hard choices is an unpleasant assignment, but one that is unavoidable. The federal government cannot afford all the promising scientific research that is possible.

A third issue is the quality of academic research facilities. In 1967, the federal government spent more than $700 million to help colleges and universities construct academic facilities. Today, we are spending a small fraction—roughly $70 million—of that amount.

Rebuilding academic research facilities is expected to cost at least $10 billion. In 1988, as part of the National Science Foundation Reauthorization Act, the Congress authorized an Academic Facilities Modernization program. This initiative, to be administered by NSF, is intended to help repair and renovate scientific and engineering facilities used primarily in research. A proposal to create a similar facilities program at the National Institutes of Health (NIH) for biomedical research facilities was not enacted.

The 1988 Republican platform said that "retooling" science and engineering labs at colleges and universities was "a key priority." However, when the Congress was debating the proposed facilities program, the Reagan administration indicated that it was "totally opposed" to such a program. Although the incoming Bush administration did not request funding for the new NSF program, Congress provided $20 million for it for fiscal year 1990. Whether appropriations increase in coming years will depend in large part on whether the Bush administration honors its campaign promise.

A fourth issue is the relationship between university-based R&D and industrial research. As noted earlier, the percentage of federal research funds spent at higher educational institutions has declined in the 1980s. At the same time, however, there is evidence that campus R&D funded by the private sector is increasing. But private-sector funding usually favors applied R&D because it offers more immediate economic returns.

Efforts to develop superconductors illustrate this point. At the present time, the United States and Japan are spending roughly equal amounts of money on this research. In the United States, however, three-quarters of this support comes from the Departments of Defense and Energy and is spent on military and high-energy physics projects. The Japanese, less concerned about military applications, have focused their efforts on consumer products; approximately 75 percent of Japanese funding comes from industry. In the United States, about 40 percent comes from industrial sources.

Finally, the United States is lagging behind other nations in producing graduate-level scientists and engineers. This is often explained as a "pipeline" problem. That is, too small a number of secondary-school students display an interest in and an aptitude for science and mathematics. Still a smaller number pursue that interest at the college level. Of those who do, many will be siphoned off for other careers or lucrative jobs that do not require an advanced degree; still others will decide against a scientific career because of the cost of getting an advanced degree.

Regardless of where the problem is most acute, there is little dispute that most secondary-school and college students do not acquire sufficient proficiency in science and mathematics. A recent analysis by the National Assessment of Educational Progress (NAEP) concluded that the scientific knowledge of our school children is "dismal." In the same vein, the National Science Board recently released a report concluding that undergraduate education in science and mathematics "contains 'serious deficiencies' that are harming this country's economy and security."

The Reagan administration initially reduced federal spending in this area and abolished the National Science Foundation's Science

Education directorate. Congress reestablished the directorate in 1983, which now spends about $210 million on science and engineering education, with approximately one-half of that devoted to precollegiate activities. There is widespread congressional interest in improving science and mathematics instruction and in attracting more students to careers that involve graduate-level science and mathematics. Still, it takes a long time to increase the stock of scientists and engineers; progress in this area will not come easily or quickly.

Federal student aid in the Bush administration: There are plenty of issues surrounding the federal student aid programs that will also be of concern in the years just ahead.

One issue is the enrollment of minorities in higher education and the role of student aid in increasing their participation. Between the mid-1970s and the mid-1980s, the percentage of minority high-school graduates enrolled in higher education fell and remains lower than it was a decade ago. Enrollment rates are just one aspect of this problem: minority students are less likely to complete their undergraduate degree than nonminorities and are much less likely to pursue graduate and professional education. In the last two years the participation of minorities has inched upwards. This is welcome news, but it is too early to tell whether these increases will be sustained.

Some observers believe that the way to increase minority participation is to expand outreach efforts to minority high-school students. Others contend that a high school focus is too late and argue for earlier intervention. Since we do not understand why minority participation fell, it is difficult to reach consensus about how to raise it. In any event, since federal student aid programs are designed primarily to increase the access of disadvantaged students to postsecondary education, federal policymakers will watch these trends closely.

Rapidly rising college costs will also be a matter of concern. As with minority enrollments, there are several explanations for the recent run-up in tuition prices. But unlike the recent trends in minority enrollments, there is very little good news on this front. One ominous development in this area are articles suggesting that colleges push tuition prices up to improve their image (see *Change*, March/April 1988). Such profit-maximizing behavior is, given the great demand for the limited seats available at selected colleges, not surprising. But it is hardly a flattering picture.

In recent years, Senator Paul Simon and Representative Pat Williams have both considered (from the same vantage point, chair of the House Subcommittee on Postsecondary Education) the possible use of "incentives" to help moderate college price increases. Both men are good friends of higher education. When they start thinking that college prices are rising too fast, the higher education community should pay close attention. Indeed, if the "rapidly rising tuition" issue is raised by a president who is not as openly hostile to higher education as President Reagan was, he may discover that efforts to restrain tuition increases have enormous popular appeal.

College tuition increases were in the news again in late 1989 when the Justice Department confirmed that it was investigating allegations that a small number of colleges had conspired to fix tuition levels and student aid awards. Fifty-five selective private colleges and universities have been asked to provide information about tuition, salaries, and financial aid policies since 1985. Antitrust experts predict that the inquiry will take at least a year. While the results of the investigation cannot be predicted, it is clear that tuition increases—which have always been a public relations nightmare—have become an even bigger problem.

The increasing reliance on loans as the foundation of student aid will also be a source of concern to policymakers. According to the College Board, in 1975-76 grants accounted for 80 percent of all student aid; this proportion declined to 56 percent in 1980-81 and 49 percent in 1988-89. There are growing fears that students are borrowing too much money and that this will distort academic, occupational, and personal decisions.

Perhaps surprisingly, while a small number of students borrow frightful sums to pay for higher education, there is no conclusive evidence to suggest that overborrowing has become a widespread problem. Moreover, because there is no nationally representative database that monitors student borrowing, we are not likely to have any such evidence in the next few years. Since Stafford Loans are a less costly form of student aid to the federal government than grants, loans will continue to be the predominant form of student aid in the near future. In other words, more and more students will leave higher education with ever-increasing debts.

Yet another concern is with the administration of current federal programs. One problem that seems to be getting worse is the complexity of the process. Student aid administrators can offer innumerable "horror stories." There are even suggestions that some students join the military and go to college later rather than try and wade through the sheaf of forms needed to receive need-based student aid. Few campus administrators outside the financial aid office appreciate the complexity of the entire system or understand how it works. Many financial aid officers freely admit the gaps in their own knowledge and the difficulty of staying current with ever-changing rules and regulations.

Some efforts to simplify the business of getting federal aid are underway. Under an experiment authorized by the Higher Education Amendments of 1986, the Department of Education is developing a simplified application form for students with family incomes below

$15,000. It will be several years, however, before the preliminary results of this project are available. In the meantime, student aid is unlikely to become any less complicated.

A final problem with the administration of the federal student aid programs is that the student loan default rate, and the cost of defaults to the federal government, are unacceptably high. In 1980, the cumulative default rate in the guaranteed loan program was 12.5 percent, and the federal government spent $263 million paying off defaults. A decade later the default rate was 14.4 percent, and the bill was about $1.8 billion. Some of the money paid out this year will eventually be collected from borrowers, but not all of it.

For the last three years, Congress and the executive branch have struggled to find a solution to this problem. In 1988, the Reagan administration proposed regulatory changes designed to tighten administration of the Stafford Loan program that would, among other things, have allowed the Department of Education to "limit, suspend, or terminate" the participation of schools with default rates over 20 percent. The proposed regulations were widely criticized. Both the House and Senate drafted legislation designed to reduce default costs while avoiding the harsh consequences of the Reagan proposals.

In June 1989, Secretary Cavazos withdrew the proposed regulations and issued a revised set of rules. The new regulations will be easier on colleges and trade schools than those proposed by Secretary Bennett. Nonetheless the new rules represent a major policy shift. Heretofore the federal government has not considered institutional default rates in determining a school's eligibility to participate in the student aid programs. But beginning in January 1991, the Department of Education will be able to remove schools with high default rates from the program.

Higher education groups have generally praised the revised regulations as more flexible and less draconian than the Bennett proposals. In addition, for the first few years, most of the ED default reduction efforts will probably be focused on private trade schools. It will be the mid-1990s before the new regulations are a major concern for most traditional colleges and universities.

The default problem is, in many respects, part of a broader matter that needs attention: what shall the term "postsecondary education" mean? Since 1972, federal student aid policy has tried to treat traditional colleges and universities and private vocational schools the same way. But in the last few years—as resources became scarcer and default costs soared—conflicts have emerged. Many in the traditional higher education community believe the default problem could be solved by eliminating proprietary schools from the Stafford Loan program. In addition, runs the thinking, some proprietary schools practice deceptive advertising and are more concerned with making money than they are with educating students.

The proprietary schools reject this view. They believe (often correctly) that they educate and train a higher percentage of low-income and minority individuals than do most traditional higher-education institutions. And many proprietary schools offer high-quality programs—as good or better than those available at selective colleges or at competing community colleges.

Ultimately, neither side can "prove" its point. The danger is that internecine warfare will detract attention from the important and complex questions about the most effective, efficient ways to provide post-high school education and training.

THE BUSH ADMINISTRATION MOVES IN: WHAT NEXT?

A year ago, most educators regarded the Bush administration with hope because of George Bush's pledge to be an "Education President." But one year after taking office, there are growing fears that the Bush commitment was little more than an election-year promise. The administration's legislative proposals for education were modest to begin with, and only one small part of the package dealt with higher education. Moreover, the administration has been slow to fill vacancies at the Department of Education.

Through the year, the news media progressively noted the President's lackluster commitment: "So Far, Educators Give Bush Just a Passing Grade," noted the *New York Times* in April. *Time*, which gave the administration a "B" for effort and a "C" for performance in March, awarded the president a "D" in May. *Newsweek* later called Education Secretary Cavazos a "do-nothing Education Secretary who is practically invisible . . . (a) wallflower" and predicted that he would soon be replaced.

The most visible education event in the administration's first year was the Education Summit held at the University of Virginia with the nation's governors. However, almost all the discussion at Charlottesville focused on elementary and secondary education. Other than hosting the event, higher education was absent from the proceedings.

Even in specific areas where Congress and the administration agree on the need to do more for higher education—such as increasing student aid, rebuilding research facilities, and training more scientists and engineers—efforts are fitful, and progress is slow. The basic problem is that the administration—like the Congress—is hemmed in by the budget deficit. In the absence of additional resources, new initiatives can be undertaken only at the expense of existing activities. But spending cuts are never easy: the first rule of politics is "do no direct harm."

Until the budget deficit is reduced, the administration will probably focus on low-cost high-visibility initiatives. For example, President Bush's much ballyhooed national service initiative—unveiled last summer at a White House ceremony attended by four thousand children—will involve very little federal money. Expect to see the president visiting lots of schools.

Educators should not underestimate the value of a president with a strong personal commitment to education—especially after eight years of a president without such an interest. Neither should they overestimate spending options in the current environment.

The federal deficit problems could hardly occur at a worse time. If nothing else, the economic uncertainty of the last decade has taught us that a society that invests heavily in the ability, talent, and knowledge of its work force will out-perform societies that do not. This lesson has become such an accepted part of public policy that it is no longer a debatable proposition. The challenge for the next few years will be to increase investment in human capital while continuing to reduce the federal deficit.

Colleges and universities have very little chance to help shape responses to the budget deficit. And this brings us full circle: in 1990, as in 1981, the biggest uncertainty facing higher education is an economic issue that will be addressed by policymakers a long way from the college campus. But whatever course is taken will have a major bearing on the future of higher education. Stay tuned.

12

IMPROVING HIGHER EDUCATION THROUGH INCREASED EFFICIENCY

WALTER W. McMAHON

Increased efficiency is one means of sustaining and improving quality and access. Increasing either quality or diversity at given levels of efficiency requires additional resources. So especially in the anticipated periods of budget stringency, there is need to focus on the third element in the uneasy triangle of quality, diversity, and efficiency. Should total resources for higher education grow significantly in real terms, it nevertheless continues to be in the best interest of universities and colleges to use resources efficiently and to the best possible advantage, thereby maintaining their competitiveness.

The persisting federal budget deficit, the $300 billion cost of the S&L bail out, and the ongoing struggle to meet the Gramm-Rudman federal budget deficit reduction targets continue to more than absorb the "Peace Dividend." This situation has been stressed by Terry Hartle, Arthur Hauptman, and others as well. It will result in continuing pressure to limit increases in federal support of higher education, R&D, and state-operated programs such as Medicaid, which in turn reduces the capacity of states to respond to the needs of higher education.

There is a broad concern with the slowdown in productivity growth in the United States, and some awareness of the relevance of investment in education at all levels as well as in R&D in order to reverse these trends. But even though there is far less conflict between the Bush administration and the Congress on education issues than there was during the preceding Reagan administration, the reluctance to introduce increases in taxes suggests that the budget facts are likely to remain grim.

But beyond this, Congress and state legislators want efficiency in the use of their tax dollars, just as parents want efficiency in the use of their tuition dollars. So seeking to improve quality as well as access by improving efficiency will continue to be a viable strategy. Delivering better quality and at the same time maintaining or improving access or diversity for whatever given amounts of resources that are available help colleges and universities to avoid waste and related sources of criticism. Through improved competitiveness it also positions them well to obtain additional support.

Efficiency is a difficult concept, however, for many in higher education. This is often because it is misinterpreted to be limited to only internal budget reallocation, which inevitably makes someone "worse off," leading to opposition and to disputes about what constitutes quality. The result is that efficiency decisions are either delegated to vice-chancellors of Academic Affairs to implement quietly and with a minimum of discussion or efficiency is merely ignored—and sometimes both situations occur.

Arthur Hauptman defines efficiency as the financial efficiency with which a particular federal student aid or research reimbursement program is administered within its own predetermined goals. Although this is one aspect of efficiency, the concept of efficiency in economics is considerably broader than that, in ways that will be addressed in this chapter. One can share his concern that the federal student Pell Grant programs are tending to be less targeted on the truly needy, although in the broader context of efficiency this would be thought of instead as a reduction in vertical equity. Hauptman's concern with excessive indirect cost charges by universities for research is an inefficiency in the system, especially if its source is a monopoly rent charged by some universities under the label of (padded) cost-based reimbursement for performance of the overhead functions.

Finally, the faster tuition increases by higher education institutions in those periods when state financial support is particularly tight are regarded by Hauptman as perverse and inefficient. The problem with this is that it ignores the devastating effects on the internal inefficiency of universities of off-again on-again financing. This efficiency loss must be weighed against the effects of irregular rates of increase over time in tuition rates used by colleges and universities as a means of stabilizing their revenues.

In what follows, this paper will consider efficiency in higher education more broadly, including:

- *The Concept of Efficiency*, or the internal and external efficiency of institutions as well as efficient investment strategies;
- *The Efficiency of United States Higher Education*, an evaluation of the trends in the social rates of return and some indicators of the relative efficiency of United States higher education compared to that of other countries; and
- *Remaining Potential Sources for Improvement in Efficiency*.

THE CONCEPT

Efficiency often is ignored because it either is not understood very well, or because it is defined too narrowly to mean only internal budget reallocations accompanied by cuts.

But efficiency to economists does not mean budget cuts. In fact, increased expenditure accompanied by increases in effectiveness that are as large or larger is one type of increase in efficiency. Specifically, Pareto efficiency in a college or university budgeting environment involves finding those changes that make some students or some programs "better off" *without making anyone "worse off."* Such moves therefore obviously require unanimous consent, a very tough standard. Although unanimous consent is sometimes possible in budget committees and program decisions, it is too demanding to be possible to achieve in all situations. The alternative is to arrange by various means to compensate those who are adversely affected. Since this compensation principle results in *no one being left "worse off,"* it reduces to the Pareto criterion. The Pareto criterion can be viewed as a kind of minimal ethical principle. But from an efficiency perspective it is also a means (hopefully at minimum cost) of reducing conflict and of facilitating change that otherwise could not occur.

Means of providing for compensation that are least costly and therefore frequently used in universities include allowing the budget cuts that may be necessary as part of reallocations to be handled through attrition. A second important means is by personnel reassignment, seen as a frequent (and often quite successful) practice when academic administrators or some tenured faculty change roles. A third means is the common use of a "grandfather clause," as when current students are not hit with new curriculum requirements but are instead expected only to meet the requirements printed in the catalogue as of the date they entered the program. Sometimes outright financial compensation is paid, as in the case of early retirements.

Finally, the most important and most common example of the search for efficiency in a dynamic context over time is an efficiency-increasing investment strategy that merely increases those budget lines more rapidly where the efficiency gain is the greatest, and increases all other budget lines more slowly. This also minimizes conflict. The economic criterion that is needed to implement this strategy involves making some estimate of the expected benefits in relation to the costs, or where possible, the social rate of return to the investment (which is a benefit/cost ratio). It is far less important (and sometimes quite impossible) to make a precise numerical estimate of the benefits and costs than it is to approach each budget decision with some qualitative judgment of the prospective benefits to quality or to access *in relation to the cost* of the investment if an efficient investment strategy is to be achieved.

Expenditures on higher education are in fact an investment in human capital formation. They yield returns later in the form of higher earnings throughout the life cycle and also higher productivity of the individuals involved to the extent that earnings reflect the individual's true productivity. The appropriate measure of the efficiency gain or benefit/cost criterion, under these conditions, is the social rate of return. It includes all of the cost to the society of the investment, including the tuition and foregone earnings (roughly room and board) costs to the family as well as the social costs to the taxpayers and donors who support the institution. The social rate of return is that pure internal rate of return that discounts the stream of earnings before taxes expected over the life cycle of each graduate back to its present value and sets it equal to the total private and social costs.

An efficient investment strategy therefore is not a one-time event decided upon by a special budget committee or a task force. It is a continuing process of annual and more frequent iterations, expanding by larger percentage amounts where the effectiveness and/or the quality is high in relation to the costs, and hence the social rate of return is highest, and increasing more slowly or not at all where the potential efficiency gain is negligible.

THE EFFICIENCY OF UNITED STATES HIGHER EDUCATION

Whether or not the United States is overinvesting or underinvesting in higher education as a whole depends primarily on the level and the trend of the social rate of return to higher education in relation to the investment alternatives. After considering this, an evaluation of the efficiency of some of the major features of United States higher education will be offered, while also comparing its efficiency to the structure of comparable institutions elsewhere in the world.

Is the United States Overinvesting in Higher Education?: The evidence is that the real social rate of return to investment in higher education in the United States has remained at a relatively high and steady approximately 11 percent rate of return since 1939. There was a dip in the 1973-79 period as the large wave of baby boomers were assimilated into the labor market, as has been developed by Welch (1979), McMahon and Geske (1982), and Murphy and Welch (1989). But this was temporary, and the relatively stable 11 percent real rates of return held up in spite of the huge influx of college-educated veterans entering the labor force between 1950 and 1955 as the result of the GI Bill, the dramatic expansion of community colleges in the 1960s, and the expansion of federal student grant and loan programs following the Education Amendments of 1972.

The reason that the social rates of return have not fallen, and that diminishing returns to higher education have not set in, is that the demand for college graduates simultaneously increased. It is also necessary that the internal efficiency of the higher education system cannot have declined substantially, or these rates of return over cost could hardly have remained stable. But the demand for graduates continues to grow in part because it is known that as technical change occurs, educated workers and managers hold a comparative advantage in the work place in implementing the new technology (Bartel and Lichtenberg 1987), giving an advantage in the job market to those aspects of American higher education that are technologically progressive.

Relative to the alternative uses of investment funds, this approximately 11 percent rate of return to investment in higher education is shown in figure 12.1 from McMahon (1989), where these estimates are discussed in detail in relation to recent careful calculations by Ed Mills (1989) of the real rate of return to investment in housing capital and to investment in non-housing fixed capital. The returns to higher education come out about in the middle. They are somewhat below the 15 percent or so real returns to non-housing capital, and significantly above the average 5 percent real rate of return to housing capital, both

TABLE 12.1. Ratio of Mean Income of College to High School Graduates

ALL MALES					YEAR				
Ages	1967	1968	1969	1970	1971	1972	1973	1974	1975
25-34	1.33	1.32	1.33	1.33	1.27	1.22	1.19	1.15	1.19
35-44	1.53	1.47	1.58	1.54	1.55	1.55	1.52	1.55	1.56

ALL MALES					YEAR				
Ages	1976	1977	1978	1979	1980	1981	1982	1983	1984
25-34	1.26	1.21	1.24	1.22	1.27	1.32	1.40	1.41	1.35
35-44	1.55	1.48	1.47	1.52	1.48	1.42	1.42	1.48	1.47

ALL MALES		YEAR	
Ages	1985	1986	1987	1988
25-34	1.46	1.51	1.45	1.45[2]
35-44	1.54	1.57	1.53	—

Source: Current Population Reports, Series P-60, Money Income of Families and Persons in the U.S., United States Bureau of the Census, June 1989 (for 1987 data) and earlier issues

[2]The 1988 figure is for median income, from *CPR,* Series P-60, No. 166, "Advance Data from the March 1989 Current Population Survey," for all male workers aged 25-44. For comparability of 1988 to earlier years, the median in 1987 (1.53) was the same as the mean (1.53) for the thirty-five to forty-four-year-old age group.

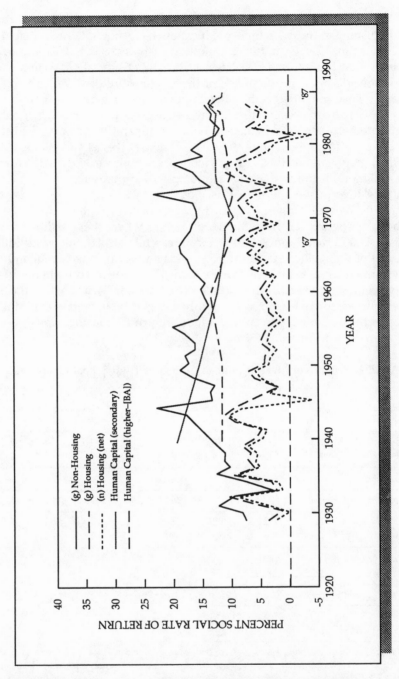

FIGURE 12.1. Real Returns to Human, Physical, and Housing Capital

Sources: Housing and non-housing capital: Mills (1989); human capital, 1939–69: Psacharopoulos (1981); human capital, 1967–87: McMahon (see text).

148

of which are calculated to include capital gains By this measure there is underinvestment in non-housing physical capital and significant overinvestment in housing in the United States. But the rate of investment in higher education (being in the middle) is about right.

We will return to this last point in a moment, but the temporary decline in the returns to higher education in the period between 1973 and 1982 deserves closer attention. Richard Freeman (1976) noted this decline in his book *The Overeducated American*, which got wide attention in the education community. But he did not develop its temporary nature. The United States fertility rates peaked in 1957 at 3.77 children per family, leading to a large cohort of college graduates entering the labor market and depressing the mean earnings of college graduates in the twenty-five- to thirty-four-year-old age group relative to the earnings of high school graduates from the 1.27-1.33 range between 1967 and 1972 to a trough of 1.15 in 1974 as seen in table 12.1. This same wave of baby boomers bid up housing prices and capital gains on housing as noted by Ed Mills (see figure 12.1). But then the relative earnings of college graduates recovered to their previous level of 1.32 by 1981 and have even risen above that since then to 1.45 by 1985-87. In terms of rates of return, Elchanan Cohn and Woodrow Hughes (1989), controlling for the extent to which college graduates differ in significant respects from noncollege graduates, find that the real rate of return declined to a low of 6 percent in 1978, but then started to recover by 1982 (e.g., Cohn and Hughes, 1989). For purposes of rate of return calculations, the earnings in the older thirty-five- to forty-four-year-old age range are also relevant. As can be seen in table 12.1 these also showed a dip, but only a temporary one between 1980 and 1982. This ratio of college to high-school earnings in the thirty-five- to forty-four-year-old age range recovered to its longtime average of 1.54 by 1985, and appears to be holding in the 1.53 to 1.57 range at least through 1987. The stability of this 50 percent premium in the earnings available to college graduates over high school graduates in the somewhat older age ranges stabilizes the rates of return somewhat since those workers aged thirty-five to forty-four whose earnings are included in the computation are less affected by transitory changes in the numbers of new entrants and the more transitory effects on their job opportunities.

Returning to the level of the real returns to various types of investment, the overinvestment in housing may be due to the large tax advantages to owner-occupied housing and the easier access to housing credit than to credit to finance investment in human capital (for which there is little collateral) or in non-housing fixed capital (which fluctuates more widely and is riskier). The real returns on those nonequity financial assets that carry somewhat less risk are also lower. The 1990 long-term Treasury bond rate is 8.47 percent, for example, and the prime rate is 10.04 percent. When corrected for the current inflation rate of 4.8 percent, these result in *real* rates of return of 3.7 percent and 5.6 percent, respectively (Data Resources Inc. 1990, p. 1), which are considerably below the returns to investment in human capital. Furthermore, these returns to investment in human capital are far more stable than the returns to investment in financial assets (McMahon and Geske, 1982, p. 161). The greater volatility of returns to housing capital has been noted by Ed Mills (1989) and can be seen in figure 12.1.

What evidence there is, therefore, with respect to the level, trend, and relative stability of the returns to higher education does not suggest that there is overinvestment. Instead there may be modest underinvestment in human capital (and in non-housing fixed capital) relative to the rate of investment in housing and in bonds.

Implications for the United States Saving Rate: The saving rate as conventionally measured is low in the United States by international standards, and there is great concern to learn how it can be increased. A new light is shed on this problem, however, when it is recognized that *total* saving, using the standard definition of saving as "refraining from consumption," includes the amounts provided by parents as they restrict their consumption to pay college tuition and room and board for their children. Total investment, similarly, includes these savings being invested in human capital formation.

The interesting point is that as public subsidies financed through taxation (which restrict consumption) encourage families to invest more in education than they might otherwise, the parents are encouraged to restrict their consumption even more to finance the total educational investment being made. *Total* savings and *total* investment are thereby increased. It is unlikely that as much would have been saved by the parents if the child had left home and gone to work after high school. The emotional attachment of the parent to the child, the concern for his or her future, and the public (tax and expenditure) encouragement to this instinct is a powerful force encouraging saving and investment toward the future.

The question is certain to be raised, since it has been of late, about whether especially federal, but also state, grant, loan, and subsidy programs are effective in inducing increased enrollments, and hence saving and investment in human capital by families. The question has usually been raised, however, by studies that do not control adequately for other effects on enrollment. When such controls are enforced, the effects of these programs are much more apparent.

For example, there was a 13 percent decline in the number of high-school graduates nationwide between 1979 and 1984. The anticipated decline in college and university enrollments, however, did not occur. According to C. Frances (1984, p. 3), "Enrollments grew between 1979 and 1984 by about 6 percent."

TABLE 12.2 Determinants of Investment in Education by Families (Three-stage least squares; t-statistics in parentheses)

A. MALES (WHITES ONLY)

Demand: $I_t = -62_r{}^* + .04A + 2.66S_M + .97S_F - 2.36\mu - 1.06N_1 - 2.55N_2$
(14.92) (.48)   (3.49)   (1.26) (1.36)   (1.31)   (2.21)
$+ .90N_3 - 3.45N_4 - 1.60N_5 - 4.13N_6 + 3.74N_7 + .30$
(.82)   (2.07)   (1.74)   (3.97)   (4.57)   (11.65)

Supply: $I_t = -4.44r + .43Y + .004S + .62L - .25B - .73W - .13O + .27$
(6.27) (21.82) (6.42) (23.18) (4.62) (45.41) (10.97) (22.33)

B. FEMALES (WHITES ONLY)

Demand: $I_t = -19_r{}^* + .19A + .47S_M + .29S_F - 1.19\mu - .18N_1 + 1.24N_2$
(6.71)   (4.42)   (1.21)   (.74)   (1.52)   (.42)   (2.07)
$- .57N_3 - .89N_4 + .51N_5 - 1.12N_6 + .97N_7 + .11$
(1.02)   (.83)   (.74)   (2.62)   (2.30)   (6.15)

Supply: $I_t = -2.01r + .25Y + .005S + .37L - .16B - .62W + 1.93O + 7.54$
(5.57) (21.79) (20.35) (20.08) (5.71) (31.47) (2.79) (10.79)

Investment demand, $I = I(r^*, A, S_M, S_F, \mu, N_1, ..., N_7)$,

I = planned investment in college. The number of years of education planned by the student and his family (e.g., two-year associate degree, bachelor's, master's, M.D., Ph.D., etc.) was multiplied by the expected costs per year. The latter were the sum of tuition and fees, reduced by the tax subsidies and endowment fund subsidies to tuition and room and board, plus foregone earning costs.

r^* = the expected rate of return. A pure internal rate of return to the planned degree program computed for each student by iterative methods. It equates the student's expected earnings over his or her life cycle (analyzed in McMahon and Wagner, 1981) to the family's total private investment costs as defined above by I. This is a *private* expected rate of return of the type relevant to private household investment decisions, which is developed further in McMahon and Wagner (1982).

A = ability, as measured by the ACT composite test score used for college admissions. Greater ability could be expected to increase the expected rate of return and hence shift the demand function upward as among different families.

S_M = schooling of the mother. The hypothesis is that home investments in children, when the mother has more education, raises the IQ or ability of the child (Liebowitz, 1974) and also, especially if the mother has been to college, shifts the utility function toward greater farsightedness. Both imply larger investment in education.

S_F = schooling of the father, analogous to S_M.

μ = degree of uncertainty. This was measured by asking the student to estimate his or her degree of uncertainty about future earnings on a scale from 0 to 1.

N_6 = expected nonmonetary returns from education—the contribution of education to greater efficiency in household production of satisfactions.

the supply-of-funds schedule $I = r(r, Y, S, L, B, W, O)$,

r = the rate of interest on student loans. In the rare instance that the family borrows in the nonsubsidized, nonguaranteed loan market to support human capital formation, r is the market rate of interest available to them.

Y = family disposable income, including earnings of the student, collected from parents and students separately in the survey.

S = tax subsidies and endowment fund subsidies to tuition, plus scholarship aid received from all sources.

L = student loans—the amount available to middle- or lower-income families, based on a means test, guaranteed by the federal government, and available at a subsidized rate.

B = the number of brothers ad sisters at home or in school. This is a limiting factor on the availability of family financial support.

W = work time spent in the market by the student, withdrawn from hours of study or leisure.

O = order of birth—a dummy variable, equal to 1 if the student is the firstborn. The hypothesis is that the firstborn male in some families (especially black families) is expected to help support the family, so that foregone earnings are less available for the support of further education.

Source: McMahon (1984).

This is not surprising when one examines the highly significant positive effects of public federal, state, and local subsidies on the amounts families decide to invest (after controlling for other effects). In the simultaneous equation results reported in Table 12.2, based on a sample of 5,200 individual students and their families in a nationwide survey sponsored by the National Institute of Education (NIE) and conducted by the author, these grant and subsidy programs are found to be highly significant. That is, table 12.2 controls for the reduction in the number of high-school graduates by reporting the results not in aggregate terms but on a per family, or per capita basis. The effect of ability (A) on the investment to be made *is* taken into account, although it does not turn out to be statistically significant. The effect of the mother's education (S_M) and father's education (S_F) is controlled for, as is sex and race by stratifying the sample. There are controls for other things, including the parents' income as reported directly by the parent with his or her signature that it could be checked by permitting access to IRS forms. The result was that Pell Grant and tuition subsidies (S) turn out to be very highly significant $(t = 6.42$ to $20.35)$, as are publicly supported student loans, $L(t = 20.08$ to $23.18)$. These key determinants of why families save and invest are the same for black females, but somewhat different for black males (McMahon 1976, p. 322). For black females, grants (S) give $t = 6.04$, similar to the $t = 5.69$ for black males. Similarly for loans, $t = 10.71$ for black females and $t = 10.65$ for black males, indicating that these policies have a very significant effect on the decision to save by foregoing earnings and investing in higher education. This suggests that in spite of the decline in the number of high school graduates from 1979 to 1984, and in spite of the 1980-82 recession and its effects on parental income, federal as well as state student financial aid was a stabilizing factor inducing investment by both blacks and whites.

A reasonable conclusion to reach, based on this evidence that controls for other effects, is that federal (and state) support is effective in inducing higher rates of planned saving and investment in higher education by families.

International Comparisons of Efficiency in Higher Education: This evidence of efficiency indicated by a satisfactory rate of return and by the effectiveness of public policy in encouraging total saving and total investment is put in broader perspective by considering the relative competitiveness of the United States higher education system in relation to higher education in other countries.

Research at Institutions of Higher Education: Some institutions have major research functions, whereas others have almost entirely undergraduate teaching functions. Most current research at all of these types of universities, however, is separately funded by the federal government or by donors on a project-by-project, user-driven, peer-group-review basis. There are exceptions, of course, and some relatively small state and private university sources of funds are provided to help younger faculty get started and to keep teaching faculty up to date in departments where there is little outside support (e.g., humanities). But apart from this, research time is financed by faculty who buy their time away from teaching, reimbursing their departments for time not spent teaching by separately funded outside user-driven research grants focused on finding useful solutions to problems.

The characteristics of this system in the United States, in contrast to the way it operates in many other countries, are that the research is largely *user-driven*, based on *peer-group review* in the attempt to insure its scientific merit, and *integrated with graduate instruction*. The procedures connected with each of these three basic characteristics are not perfect. But consider the alternatives.

Basic research in many other countries is concentrated in separate research institutes, rather than in the universities. These institutes are manned by salaried staff engaged in research that is not supported by the users of the output. The output often therefore sits on the shelf, and the research enterprise is less externally efficient.

Integration of the research with graduate instruction also is somewhat unique. By these means, the new technology gets transferred much more quickly as part-time graduate research assistants finish their programs and enter industry and other employments. In contrast, full-time, aging professional research assistants who are not graduate degree candidates are used in most British universities and some other countries. Although the quality of the research is often excellent from the point of view of its economic efficiency, it often does not get applied and used in industry or in public administrative practices.

The practice of not using graduate students as research and teaching assistants also makes graduate education more expensive, since the graduate students do not have the part-time support, and graduate education is therefore less accessible and less widespread. In Indonesia, most graduate students have to be sent abroad at high cost since the domestic faculties do not have the research support or the capabilities for advanced instruction. In some places this separation of research institutes into distinct cocoons is carried even further than in Indonesia and to logical extremes. In Pakistan, for example, the National Ministry of Research and Technology Labs are well financed for a poor country but are quite inaccessible to easy use by graduate students and faculty in what are often adjacent universities. The research output of these labs is not user-driven, often sits on the shelf, and has a short half-life. The semi-isolation of these institutes is also common in France, the USSR, and other places that are on the European pattern.

This lack of user-driven, peer-group-review research integrated with part-time graduate student support results in an externally inefficient system that is also internally so costly that it cannot be financed except at the cost of inefficient slower economic growth and much more limited access to graduate education.

Instruction of Undergraduates: Graduate student teaching assistants who assist with the instruction of freshmen and sophomores at most United States research universities are in a role that is very similar to that of apprentices or of interns who assist physicians. The practice is not going to change, because it is far less costly and a critical source of efficiency in instruction, at least at the major United States research universities (McMahon, de Groot, and Volkwein, forthcoming in 1991). It is sometimes abused, and has even been regarded by one critic as a "scam." But consider the alternatives.

The use of full-time faculty who are not engaged in research part-time frequently results in faculty that are out of date (as is common in Pakistan, some of Latin America, and Indonesia, for example). Graduate students in these places must go abroad. The system is so costly in part for this reason that access must be severely limited. Graduate student instructors in American universities are less experienced, as are interns, but they are in training, supervised by senior faculty, closer to the age of the undergraduates, and able to transmit the new technology being discussed in graduate seminars to undergraduates much more swiftly.

The practice as mentioned is sometimes abused. Some graduate teaching assistants, especially in the physical sciences, are unable to communicate well in English. But departments are developing more organized training sessions for first-time teachers. Even in the absence of training and supervision, the less effective teaching assistants are normally weeded out, but only after a semester or a year. The alternative of using full-time faculty at these beginning levels as is the practice throughout Africa, Asia, and some parts of Europe runs the cost of the instruction of undergraduates up so high that it results in a far smaller proportion of the population able to gain access to higher education than in the United States (McMahon 1988a).

External Efficiency: The activities of job placement offices located in virtually every college in the highly decentralized United States higher education system are in sharp contrast to the practice in developing countries and some European countries, where placement is not viewed as a responsibility of the universities and greater reliance is placed on a centralized manpower planning system. United States college placement offices channel students quite effectively to those fields and those industries where the need for their services is greatest. They also send a flow of information back to students in the pipeline who are well aware of where the opportunities lie and of expected salary levels (McMahon and Wagner 1981). Students tend to vote with their feet, gravitating to the fields and the education levels where the returns are highest, as Freeman (1971) found earlier. Admission standards rise in those curricula that are in highest demand, with the required grade point average acting as a nonprice rationing device. Then the budget money within universities gradually begins to be shifted, but with long lags. It is a highly decentralized system that does respond to local and occupational price signals, albeit sluggishly. It also appears to be reasonably externally efficient, with numerous college placement offices compared to most other countries.

There is a time dimension to the response that needs to be recognized however. For example, at the University of Illinois, 95 percent of the students in Engineering normally have jobs before they receive their diplomas. Only 54.25 percent of the Liberal Arts students do. But follow-up surveys find that when reinterviewed six months after graduation, 96.47 percent of these Liberal Arts graduates have jobs (McMahon 1987, p. 183). Furthermore, the age-earnings profiles of general education graduates tend to be steeper as learning on the job continues to occur (McMahon and Geske 1982, p. 173). Although this does not always apply to teachers and to those social and natural sciences that are dominated by public pay scales, the rates of return to many liberal arts and general education fields often are as high as that of engineering when this time delay in employment, followed by a more rapid growth of earnings later due to capacities to learn on the job, and lower educational costs are all taken into account (McMahon 1988b).

Financing: In relation to higher education financing patterns throughout Europe, Africa, Asia, and Latin America, parents and students in the United States pay a larger fraction of the total tuition and room and board costs. The federal student aid programs, although perhaps not adequately targeted on those most in need, are nevertheless much more equitably targeted than is the pattern throughout the developing countries and some parts of Europe.

Expansion of higher education in the United States to a larger percent of the population, therefore, is probably made possible not only by internal efficiencies that hold costs down (use of research assistants and teaching assistants, lower room and board costs for local community colleges), but also by financing arrangements that recover more resources from parents and students while limiting student aid funds to those situations where there is need and where enrollment is affected.

It is unfortunate that the lack of efficiency in the higher education systems in developing countries, such as those discussed, results in relatively high unit costs. The failure to use adequate methods of appraising financial need combined with low or free tuition also limits the resources available to finance access and quality. The weakness of the third pillar in the uneasy triangle, efficiency, pulls the props out from under the first two pillars, quality and access.

POTENTIALS FOR IMPROVEMENT

Although the United States higher education system appears to have many basic features that are conducive to its internal and external efficiency and that make it quite competitive and a major foreign exchange earner, there is always room for improvement. A few sources of internal inefficiency can be mentioned that merit further investigation.

1. *There is an increase in the amount of time it takes to complete a bachelor's degree.* In a recent study (1990) sponsored by the National Center for Educational Statistics (NCES) of 28,000 high-school graduates in 1980, it has been found that full-time students entering college directly after high school are taking 4.5 years on the average to complete a four-year bachelor's degree now. There are also many more part-time students, so if they are included, this trend is even more dramatic. The average number of courses taken per year by "full-time students" also appears to be falling. This slowdown is certainly even more true if part-time students are included in the average. Only 15 percent of the students now graduate in four years (Wilson 1990).

There are some hypotheses about the cause of this that merit further investigation, for it surely is a source of internal inefficiency. In some developing countries and in France where students are much more highly subsidized than in the United States there is less incentive to finish expeditiously. It is not much comfort to us that it takes six and one half years to finish a four-year bachelor's degree in Indonesia, six years in Nepal, about that long in Malawi, and seven years or over in Greece. Efforts to limit the large subsidies going to the sons and daughters of the highest income families and to reform the system in other ways led to major student protests in France and in Nepal, protests that also find support among influential parents.

In the United States parents and students pay a larger percent of the cost and the problem is not as severe. But since the late 1960s the rules permitting students to drop courses in the United States have become very lax at many universities, which encourages course shopping at the beginning of each semester. This operates to keep the average course load down, closer to the minimum of twelve semester hours each semester, and also to encourage dropping back to part-time enrollment to get tuition refunds. This has the effect of keeping opening fall enrollments up. But it would appear to be a source of growing internal inefficiency.

2. *A second problem is related sources of excess capacity on campuses that run up costs unnecessarily.* For example, the number of students in class before Thanksgiving or spring break, and the number of regularly scheduled classes that actually operate before vacations, have fallen dramatically in sharp contrast to when there used to be double cut rules. Very few faculty take attendance anymore (and those that do probably do so at their own peril on the student course evaluations that affect their salary). Although Saturday morning and evening classes were common until the late 1960s, now the average class attendance of undergraduates on Fridays is very low. There is therefore considerable excess capacity in the physical plant.

For example, the cost effectiveness of some degree programs is very low—often because of a very small output and lack of a critical mass. Others, including some that on the surface might be thought to be very costly, are very cost effective. In Britain the University Grants Commission has established uniform cost accounting categories among institutions that has made it possible to see this pattern across institutions much more clearly (Verry and Davis, 1976). Although comparisons across institutions are more difficult in the United States, there are some possibilities (e.g., the unique statewide Illinois Unit Cost Study). Within institutions, a Ph.D. dissertation by James Dyal (1975) found that among seventy-two academic departments, the benefit/cost ratios at the Ph.D. level were highest in the Chemistry and Chemical Sciences Departments. They were much lower in some fields in Agriculture, for example, where the output was only one or two Ph.D.s a year or in Veterinary Medicine where the output was small. A later study by McMahon (1979) included the research output of each department at the University of Illinois-Urbana, as well as a weighted measure of undergraduate and graduate instructional units, and a similar pattern emerged. Some of the departments or colleges that might appear on the surface to be the highest cost, such as the College of Law and the Chemistry Department, turned out, however, to be the most cost effective. Humanities, Psychology, Economics, History, Math, Library Sciences, and Business Administration were all cost effective units compared to the all-campus average. Engineering, Physical Sciences, and Life Sciences were at the all-campus average, and the smaller

and/or more costly programs in the Medical Sciences, Veterinary Medicine, Labor and Industrial Relations, and Dairy Science were far less
cost effective. The Aviation program was so cost ineffective that compared to the all-campus average it was off the map, but something has
since been done about that. The Chemistry Department, incidentally,
which is one of the most prestigious in the world, and has a large
output of Ph.D.s every year, makes very extensive use of teaching
assistants in the beginning courses and has one of the lowest instructional costs per instructional unit at all levels of any college level
department in the State of Illinois.

The basic point is that what is or what is not cost effective is not
always apparent on the surface. To improve cost effectiveness requires
a continuing search, and in large organizations, a commitment to do
the necessary analyses before making decisions.

3. *Allocative efficiency between public and private institutions.* The State
Student Incentive Grant program (SSIG) provides the federal government with a policy lever to correct the allocation between public and
private institutions whenever the need to do so exists. The fact that
federal grants to state scholarship funds have not been used extensively may only mean that the survival of large numbers of private
colleges has not been in serious jeopardy. It does not mean that this
tool is useless and should be abolished.

State scholarships in many states cover only tuition, and not room
and board as do the Pell Grants. This is not true in all states. Nevertheless, since the tuition at private institutions is considerably higher, and
since these state scholarship grants give more students the freedom to
choose private institutions, a larger percentage of these funds wind up
as aid to private colleges and universities. Perhaps the reason that
SSIGs have not been used more extensively to correct the allocation is
the rule of thumb "If it isn't broken, don't fix it."

The author does not believe in destroying centers of excellence. If
the survival of good quality private colleges should ever be in jeopardy, it would be desirable to keep SSIGs available for more extensive
use.

CONCLUSIONS

The evidence cited suggests that higher education in the United States
measures up pretty well on grounds of economic efficiency. One cannot say the same for United States secondary education, or for the
overexpanded and oversubsidized higher education systems in some
developing countries. The evidence is that the *real* social rate of return
to investment in higher education remains reasonably high at 11 percent, which is high in relation to the 5 percent real return on housing

or the 3.7 to 5.6 percent *real* rate of return on bonds. It is also reasonably stable and therefore less risky. Although there was a temporary dip from 1973 through 1982, the returns have recovered and there is therefore no evidence of a secular decline. Furthermore, the public encouragement to families to invest their foregone earnings in education induces private saving, and therefore probably increases the nation's *total* saving and total investment rates when these are defined to include human capital accumulation.

There are several major sources of internal efficiency that help to make the United States higher education system efficient and internationally quite competitive that are discussed above. They include emphasis on university-based *user*-driven research, the economically efficient use of part-time graduate student intern teachers, externally efficient decentralized placement offices, the sharing of financing with those parents that have the ability to pay, and faculty who are not full-time teachers but who are also involved with the development of the new technology. International students flock to United States higher education; it is a major foreign exchange earner, and the undergraduate enrollment ratios as a percent of each age group are the highest in the world.

Nevertheless, the time it takes to finish a four-year bachelor's degree is increasing, the average semester-hour load of students is falling, the internal excess capacity and the unit costs are rising, the high-cost low-output curricula that have not reached a critical mass are plentiful, and administrative leaders are not very well informed or concerned about the internal sources of cost-ineffectiveness.

All of us are concerned by the long-run secular slowdown in productivity and per capita economic growth in the United States. The higher educational system with its capacities for high-quality basic research, for the transmission of the results to industry and to the next generation, and for high-quality instruction, all within a relatively efficient and equitable structure, is a major asset. The more higher education chooses to get its house in order, and improve further its internal and external efficiency, the more it puts itself in a position to benefit, and the more it puts itself in a position to help the nation.

REFERENCES

BARTEL, ANN, and F. LICHTENBERG. "The Comparative Advantage of Educated Workers in Implementing the New Technology." *Review of Economics and Statistics* 69, No. 1 (February 1987): 1-11.

COHN, ELCHANAN, and WOODROW HUGHES. "Social Internal Rates of Return to College Education in the U.S., 1969, 1974, 1978, and 1982." Paper read at American Econ. Assn. Meetings, University of South Carolina, Columbia, December 1989. Forthcoming in the *Economics of Education Review*.

COHN, ELCHANAN. "College Education's Value." *Wall Street Journal*, 20 October 1988.

DATA RESOURCES INC. "Review of the U.S. Economy." Lexington, MA: Data Resources Inc., March 1990.

DENISON, EDWARD F. "Accounting for Slower Economic Growth: An Update." In *International Comparisons of Productivity and Causes of the Slowdown*, edited by J. Kendrick, pp. 1–46. Cambridge, MA: Ballinger, 1984.

DYAL, JAMES. *Investment in Graduate Education*. Ph.D. diss., University of Illinois, Urbana, 1975.

EISNER, ROBERT, and D. NEBHUT. "An Extended Measure of Government Product: Preliminary Results for the United States, 1946-1976." *Review of Income and Wealth* 27, No.1 (March 1981): 33–64.

FRANCES, C. "Major Trends Shaping the Outlook for Higher Education." *AAHE Bulletin 37* (December 1985): 5.

FREEMAN, RICHARD. *The Market for College-Trained Manpower*. Cambridge: Harvard University Press, 1971.

FREEMAN, RICHARD. *The Overeducated American*. New York: Academic Press, 1976.

FULLER, BRUCE. "What School Factors Raise Achievement in the Third World?" *Review of Educational Research*, Vol. 57, No. 3 (1987), 255-292.

LEIBOWITZ, ARLEEN. "Home Investments in Children." In *Economics of the Family: Marriage, Children, and Human Capital*, edited by T. W. Schultz, pp. 432–52. Chicago: University of Chicago Press, 1974.

MCMAHON, WALTER W. "Influences on Investment by Blacks in Higher Education." *American Economic Review*, 66, No. 2 (1976): 320-24.

———. "Why Families Invest in Higher Education." In *The Collection and Analysis of Economic and Consumer Behavior Data*, edited by Seymour Sudman and Mary Spaeth. Urbana: Bureau of Economic and Business Research, University of Illinois, 1984.

———. "The Relation of Education and R&D to Productivity Growth (in OECD Nations)." *Economics of Education Review* 3, No. 4 (1984): 299-314.

———. "Student Labor Market Expectations." In *Economics of Education: Research and Studies*, edited by George Psacharapoulos, pp. 182-87. Oxford: Pergamon Press, 1987.

———. "The Relation of Education and R&D to Productivity Growth in the Developing Countries of Africa." *Economics of Education Review*. 6, No. 2 (1987): 183-94.

———. "Potential Resource Recovery in Higher Education in the Developing Countries and the Parents' Expected Contribution." *Economics of Education Review* 7, No. 1 (1988): 135-52.

———. "The Economics of Vocational and Technical Education: Do the Benefits Outweigh the Costs?" *International Review of Education*, UNESCO, 34, No. 2 (1988): 173-94.

———. "Relative Returns to Human, Physical, and Housing Capital and Efficient Investment Strategies." Paper delivered at American Economic Association Meetings, December, 1989. Forthcoming in the *Economics of Education Review*.

———, et al. "Internal Budget Reallocations and Educational Policy." Report of the Senate Committee on the Budget, BG.80.2. Urbana: Senate Office, 10 December 1979.

————, and A. WAGNER. "Expected Returns to Investment in Higher Education." *Journal of Human Resources* XVI, No. 2 (1981): 274-85.

————, and T. Geske. *Financing Education: Overcoming Inefficiency and Inequity.* Urbana: University of Illinois, 1982.

————, and Alan P. Wagner. "The Monetary Returns to Education as Partial Social Efficiency Criteria." In *Financing Education: Overcoming Inefficiency and Inequity,* edited by Walter G. McMahon and Terry G. Geske, pp. 150–57. Urbana: University of Illinois Press, 1982.

————, H. DE GROOT, and J.F. VOLKWEIN. "The Cost Structure of American Research Universities." *Review of Economics and Statistics,* forthcoming (1991).

MILLS, EDWIN S. "Social Returns to Housing and Other Fixed Capital." *AREUEA Journal* 17, No. 2 (1989): 1-9.

MURPHY, KEVIN, and F. WELCH. "Wage Premiums for College Graduates: Recent Growth and Possible Explanations." *Educational Researcher* 13, No.4 (May 1989): 17-26.

PORTER, OSCAR. *Undergraduate Completion and Persistence at Four Year Colleges and Universities: Detailed Findings.* Washington, D.C.: National Institute of Independent Colleges and Universities, 1990.

PSACHAROPOULOS, GEORGE. "Return to Education: An Updated International Comparison." *Comparative Education* 17 (1981): 321–41.

————, and M. WOODHALL. *Education and Development,* Oxford: Oxford University Press, 1985.

VERRY, DONALD, and B. DAVIS. *University Costs and Outputs.* Amsterdam: Elsevier; New York: Oxford University Press, 1976.

WELCH, F. "Effects of Cohort Size on Earnings: The Baby Boom Babies: Financial Bust." *Journal of Political Economy.* 87, No. 5 (1979): 65-97.

WILSON ROBIN "Only 15% of Students Graduate in 4 Years, a New Study Finds." *The Chronicle of Higher Education* 36, No. 23 (21 February 1990): 75–91.

SECTION V

Conclusion: Coping with the Uneasy Triangle— the Tradeoff Continues

Coping with the uneasy triangle in higher education has not been easy and will continue to provide a challenge to public policymakers and to those involved in the production of and the lobbying for higher education. Tradeoffs always involve compromises, and choosing from among goods is difficult. As is apparent to most observers, the balance among the goals of quality, diversity, and budgetary efficiency varies with the economic and political environment. But these goals must continue to be on the forefront of discussion and policy concern.

There have been several recurring themes and "debates" in this book, including: (1) the balance between loans and grants in federal and state policy; (2) the difficulty of assessing quality of higher education versus the importance of accountability; (3) the role of the primary/ secondary education sector versus the higher education sector in dealing with minority access and participation in higher education; and (4) the role of policymakers as actively attempting to ameliorate the

163

problems in higher education versus a lesser role, one in which we expect policymakers to be either reactive or inactive or indirect (i.e., formulate policies that are designed to address other issues but that have the effect of aiding the higher education sector).

This closing section includes two chapters, one from someone involved with the major pipeline organization that deals with the high school/college transition as well as a variety of funding issues, and one from a college president (who happens to be from the private higher education sector).

In his chapter "The Education Pipeline and Public Policy," Lawrence Gladieux describes the role and functions of the College Board. He then examines "the education pipeline," suggesting that American education is all one system. Given the demographic changes, it will be increasingly the case that the higher education sector will be seeking to fill its classrooms with a more diverse student body (including an increasing number of ethnic minorities and other diverse groups from nontraditional age categories and those with educational handicaps). This will create new challenges for the public policy arena to sort out. Gladieux suggests that the pipeline view points to the importance of early intervention efforts so the high school dropout rate can be reduced and college participation rates can be increased. Innovative "I Have a Dream" programs (inspired by Eugene Lang's efforts in East Harlem to induce sixth graders to head toward college) provide a model, albeit an expensive one, for early intervention. Gladieux notes that efforts at the state level, as typified by the Liberty Scholarships and Partnerships Program in New York State, provide the assurance of financing, but also add important mentoring, counseling, and personal support. He cites the TRIO program as a likely early intervention vehicle to expand, but present budgetary problems raise questions as to the likelihood of such expansion.

Gladieux goes on to argue that financial aid to students "is not sufficient in itself to assure increased access to higher education by underserved groups." He suggests that other factors such as quality of prior schooling, family attitudes, motivation, and awareness of opportunities contribute to the explanation of college-going behavior. He thus questions others who suggest that student aid has failed because of the apparent lack of convergence in college participation rates. Gladieux argues for simplification of the student aid delivery system. He also suggests that "there is wide agreement in Washington that a better balance must be restored between loan and grant support for students." Gladieux raises important questions regarding targeting of student aid programs, and he questions the wisdom of combining, for student aid purposes, the proprietary sector with the college and university sector.

In his chapter "Needed: Creative Policy Ideas to Resolve the Competing Claims of Quality, Diversity, and Efficiency in Higher Education," Father William Byron agrees with others in referring to the uneasy triangle when he states that the "balance in that triangle will always be precarious." Byron suggests that educational quality "depends primarily on the presence of committed, competent classroom teachers." He then relates this to the importance of providing financial security for such professionals.

Byron views diversity as going beyond the student-body mix, faculty, staff, and administration. He also argues for the importance of pluralism among institutions, including a strong independent higher education sector.

Byron suggests that to help maintain a balance in the uneasy triangle, we must seek a "value reversal in America...against a very basic problem in contemporary society, the problem of materialism." As an example, we must find ways to raise the ranks of primary- and secondary-level teachers if we are ever to prepare students, especially minority students, for participation and success in higher education.

Byron offers two policy proposals that have to do with root problems in the primary/secondary education sectors: (1) the use of innovative break-away strategies to offer high motivation "camp" environments to break the cycle of inner city schools that produce high dropout rates and (2) the provision of teacher tax credits designed to attract and retain good teachers at all levels and sectors of education. The annual tax credit would go to teachers who demonstrate competence by completing five years of supervised and certified teaching service. This view suggests that the private return to educational investments by teachers significantly understates the return teachers bestow upon society by educating others. Byron argues that the tax credit would help to provide the proper rewards to insure an adequate supply of qualified, professional educators.

The 1988 conference at the College of William and Mary that led to this book benefited from the remarks of two well-known speakers from the political and policy arena who have contributed much to higher education and public policy, but who have rather different points of view on the issues—the Honorable Thomas Kean (R-NJ) (former governor of New Jersey and recently appointed to the presidency of Drew University) and the Honorable Paul Simon, United States Senator from Illinois (D-IL).

In his remarks, Governor Kean commented on budgetary efficiency being addressed by saying, "I don't believe that higher education needs to be a victim of those winds of austerity." He went on to say that "never has it been more apparent . . . that our economic health and the security of this country . . . depend on having simply the best system of higher education in this world. But it's also true that the American public is not going to stand anymore . . . for the waste of a single dollar, on things that don't work." Governor Kean also emphasized that "access and equity . . . cannot be sacrificed on the altar of budgetary efficiency."

Senator Simon was critical of public policy toward higher education and asserted that the budgetary commitment indicates that education is not much of a priority in America. Senator Simon particularly questioned "the shift away from grants to loans." Among Senator Simon's recommendations were that: (1) "the growth in expenditure ought to be on grants, rather than loans . . . making the Pell Grant program an entitlement" and (2) "we need more assistance for graduate education . . . we ought to be providing assistance for specific national needs."

The public policy debate in higher education continues. The issues surrounding quality, diversity, and budgetary efficiency are complex and very often conflicting. Nevertheless, these represent the critical goals that policymakers will continue to try to keep in balance.

13

THE EDUCATION PIPELINE AND PUBLIC POLICY

LAWRENCE E. GLADIEUX

THE CEEB CONTEXT

This paper is billed as a response by a representative of the "higher education sector." In fact, I represent an organization that is something of a bridge between *two* sectors—secondary and higher education. Let me first say a word about the College Board (CEEB) and thus the vantage point for my remarks.

The College Board (or, officially, the College Entrance Examination Board) was founded in 1900 to create a better match between what the high schools were teaching and what colleges and universities expected of their entering students. It started as an elite association of mostly eastern colleges and feeder preparatory schools; ninety years later College Board membership is nationwide and includes about twenty-six hundred postsecondary institutions of all types (public and private, two-year and four-year) as well as secondary schools and school systems. Its growth and history mirror the growth and democratization of American education in this century, and the interplay of meritocratic and egalitarian values along the way.

The College Board's mission and services continue to focus on the transition of students from high school to college—and the preparation, counseling, testing, sorting, selection, placement, and financing of students in that process. It is most known, of course, for the Scholastic Aptitude Test, or SAT. The Board also sponsors the Advanced Placement and other credit-by-examination programs, and we operate the College Scholarship Service (CSS), which annually processes several million forms filled out by students and parents applying for financial aid from federal, state, and institutional sources.

When I talk to international groups, educators from other countries find it a curiosity that these functions are handled not by a ministry of education but a private, voluntary organization in our system. I try to explain this in the context of American pluralism and our untidy, decentralized arrangements for governing education as well as most other things in this country, though I add that government does increasingly influence College Board programs and procedures. A growing body of state legislation, for example, is designed to regulate the educational testing process (including the SAT), while the federal government increasingly shapes the student aid delivery system (including CSS operations).

ALL ONE SYSTEM: THE EDUCATION PIPELINE

But that is another story and enough background on the College Board, an organization that spans secondary and postsecondary education. And that provides a segue into my first observation in response to the foregoing papers: The governance of American education is decentralized but in a larger sense it is "all one system." Higher education cannot afford to ignore problems earlier in the education pipeline; its strength depends heavily on an annual supply of academically prepared high-school graduates ready to enter college. By all demographic indications, problems in the academic pipeline will intensify in the 1990s and beyond. One-third of the nation's young people by the year 2000 will come from minority backgrounds, many from poverty and unstable home environments, many from an economic underclass that appears to be expanding, many with severe learning and linguistic deficiencies (Hodgkinson 1985).

I need not belabor this message; we hear repeatedly these days about the burgeoning numbers of "at-risk" children straining the capacity of school systems across the country. Every sector of American education has a stake and responsibility in preparing for and absorbing the demographic shifts that are underway. American higher education has graduated the postwar baby boom. The middle-class majority students who have flocked to college campuses for the past twenty-five years will be in much shorter supply in the next twenty-five. To fill college classrooms, somehow the flow of college-ready young people coming through the pipeline will have to be increased, and many are going to have to come from that emerging "one-third of a nation"— nonwhite, nonmajority, increasingly diverse and educationally handicapped.

For higher education, addressing this challenge will be a matter of enlightened self-interest. For public policy, it will be a matter of both social justice and assuring that the country has an adequately educated and skilled work force to meet the needs of a competitive, changing global economy.

EARLY INTERVENTION EFFORTS

What does addressing the "pipeline" issue mean for colleges and universities? It means developing partnerships with school systems to strengthen the quality of secondary education. It means a broader, longer-range approach to student recruitment, including intervention programs at the middle school and even earlier grades to insure that more at-risk young people stay in school and get the academic guidance, counseling, and support to make higher education a realistic possibility for them later on. It means expanding the potential college-bound pool through outreach and enrichment programs that bring young people to campus during summer and vacation periods. In short, it means many things, all of which require considerable effort and resources and not all of which come naturally to traditional institutions of higher education. But there are not many institutions that will be able to continue business as usual in the face of the demographic trendlines of the 1990s.

Early intervention programs to reduce the school dropout rate and boost the educational skills and aspirations of disadvantaged young people have drawn growing support from the business world in recent years. Eugene Lang started something of a movement in 1981 when he promised a class of sixty East Harlem sixth-graders in New York City that he would pay their college tuition bills if they graduated from high school. He soon expanded on this commitment by becoming a mentor and advocate for the students, seeing them through the high-school years, making sure they had the necessary counseling, tutoring, and social services for their families. Lang's formula, combining the financial incentive of an *early* guarantee of college financing with sustained guidance and support to keep the students from falling between the cracks along the way, apparently has worked. Over half of the students started higher education two years ago. Lang-inspired "I Have a Dream" programs are now being sponsored in a number of cities, reaching an estimated five thousand plus students nationwide.

Lang and other philanthropists are investing considerable private wealth and personal commitment in such programs. The effort is admirable, yet it is at best a wheel of fortune for the millions of youngsters across the country whose life chances are dim and could be lifted by an "I Have a Dream" program. A youngster must be lucky enough to be in the right city, the right school, the right classroom.

EARLY INTERVENTION: STATE AND FEDERAL PROGRAMS

What about public policy to address problems in the educational pipeline? A "thousand points of light," to borrow a 1988 campaign slogan,
are well and good. The Eugene Lang model of direct-intervention
philanthropy, along with the development of enlightened recruitment
policies by higher educational institutions, will help. But clearly the
reach of government, both state and federal, is necessary to get at
these problems in any reasonable proportion to their depth and
magnitude.

At the state level, an emerging model may be the Liberty Scholarships and Partnerships Program enacted by New York State. Inspired
by Lang's example, the program aims to couple early (beginning in
junior high) assurance of college financing with the critical element of
mentoring, counseling, and personal support. State officials originally
projected that by 1994 over ninety thousand students would be receiving assistance from Liberty Scholarships, closing the gap between student needs and what is provided from existing federal and state aid
resources. State budget austerity has since clouded the outlook for
implementation of the scholarships. How the companion Partnerships
Program will be fostered, and whether the state will be able to replicate
the continuity of support services that seems to be a key to the success
of the "I Have a Dream" movement, also remains to be seen.

At the federal level, a deficit-ridden national budget continues to
leave little room for expansion of existing programs or new initiatives
that cost money. So far the "education presidency" has consisted
primarily of good intentions. But if additional federal resources do
become available for education, a high priority in my estimation would
be to expand support for the programs known as TRIO, or Special
Programs for Students from Disadvantaged Backgrounds. The TRIO
programs, authorized as a companion to the student aid programs
under Title IV of the Higher Education Act of 1965, are designed to
identify, counsel, motivate, and help to achieve postsecondary access
and retention for disadvantaged students who would be the first generation in their families to attend college. The appropriation for these
programs is over $240 million in fiscal year 1990, a level of support
sufficient to reach barely 20 percent of the eligible and needy population.

Whether or not new funds become available for TRIO, greater
emphasis should be given under these programs to early intervention
strategies. Most of the current TRIO effort focuses on helping students
at the transition point from high-school to college, either eleventh and
twelfth graders who need encouragement and support in the college
application process or those who have already enrolled in higher education and need tutoring and other support services on campus. The
federal TRIO programs ought to be intervening earlier in the education

pipeline as well, to widen students' horizons and increase their options as they enter high school.

THE ROLE OF STUDENT FINANCIAL AID

Much has been said in this volume about student financial aid, the principal mechanism (along with sponsored research) of federal support for higher education. State governments are the largest source of *indirect* aid to students in the form of subsidized, low tuition at public institutions. But for at least the past twenty years the federal government has contributed by far the most *direct* aid to help students meet their costs of attendance, including tuition, living costs, transportation, books, and supplies. The great bulk of such aid is awarded progressively according to some measure of family and student financial need.

Terry Hartle's paper for this volume sketches what has happened to budgetary support for the federal student aid programs during the 1980s. Suffice it to say here that the Reagan administration, beginning in 1981, succeeded in drastically slowing the real growth of federal assistance and even cutting or eliminating some major programs. As the new decade starts, however, the federal government continues to invest more than $10 billion annually in programs that generate almost $20 billion in aid to students in postsecondary education. State governments also put money into direct student aid, almost $2 billion for scholarships and grants in 1989-90, but Washington remains the principal source of such funding (Washington Office of the College Board 1989).

I will devote the balance of this paper to problems and prospects for federal student aid policy in the post-Reagan era.

First, it is clear that student financial aid is not sufficient in itself to assure increased access to higher education by underserved groups. Too many variables other than finance—quality of prior schooling, family attitudes, motivation, awareness of opportunities—help to determine college participation rates. And that is precisely why we need the early intervention efforts that I have described earlier in this paper.

For the same reasons I quite disagree with two fellow authors, Bob Zemsky and Art Hauptman, who have asserted, in effect, that student aid has failed because college-going rates have apparently not been significantly equalized in the past fifteen years. A similar interpretation gained currency early in the Reagan administration based on a study by W. Lee Hansen, who concluded that federal financial aid had operated largely as a transfer program, relieving some of the burden of college costs for parents and students but failing to induce or influence the mix of enrollments in higher education (Hansen 1983). Then and now this kind of analysis is one-dimensional, based on Census data for a young age cohort of recent high school graduates that tell nothing about the growing proportion (well over one-third) of older undergraduates who are deemed self-supporting. Differing conclusions might be drawn from analysis based on different data, age groups, and historical periods.

A penetrating discussion of the conceptual and data-related difficulties in such investigations is contained in a recent College Board monograph prepared by Michael McPherson titled *How Can We Tell If Federal Student Aid Is Working?* (1988). McPherson reviews the studies that have been done, looking at college participation data in the 1970s and 1980s, and says there are just too many other factors at work to draw any inferences from such data about the efficacy of student aid.

By thus responding to some critics, I hardly want to imply that the design of student aid is satisfactory. Quite the contrary. In fact, there was a standoff during the 1980s between the Reagan administration, alternately bent on slashing and reforming the programs, and bipartisan student aid supporters in Congress, who battened down the hatches to weather the Reagan years. The result was to freeze existing policies and to neglect underlying policy problems. I will be brief in suggesting a few that should and hopefully will be addressed as Congress debates the reauthorization of the Higher Education Act, scheduled for 1991-92.

SIMPLIFICATION OF THE STUDENT AID DELIVERY SYSTEM

Nearly everyone associated with student aid administration—campus aid officers, state and federal program managers, congressmen who authorize the programs—are aghast at the complexity of the forms and procedures students and families face in applying for assistance. The system itself seems to have become a barrier to educational opportunity for the very students, low-income and disadvantaged, that Pell Grants were originally intended to reach. Yet federal requirements, combined with what states and institutions feel they need to determine eligibility for their programs, continue to balloon the application forms students and parents must fill out.

Some of the complexity can be traced to the Middle Income Student Assistance Act of 1978, which extended eligibility for the federal programs to a population with more involved financial circumstances, calling for more detailed questions to be asked to determine need for aid. Congress has also in recent years encumbered the student aid process with extraneous requirements unrelated to determining financial eligibility. Selective Service registration compliance is an example. Recent anti-drug legislation is another; a provision barring federal student aid to convicted drug offenders could force a whole new set of questions onto application forms.

Congress and other parties to the student aid process need to take a hard look at these and other data requirements, with a particular eye to streamlining procedures for low-income applicants. The College Board has proposed in testimony to Congress, for example, establishing virtually automatic eligibility status for certain classes of students—for example, recipients of AFDC benefits, who have already proven their need, or applicants with family income below a certain level who file a simple tax form. Such applicants would bypass complicated and unnecessary income questions on the standard form.

THE LOAN/GRANT IMBALANCE AND THE NEED TO RESTRUCTURE STUDENT LOAN FINANCING

As on the need to simplify the delivery system, there is wide agreement in Washington that a better balance must be restored between loan and grant support for students, but there is more lip service than practical consensus on how to bring this about.

Twenty-five years ago the federal government undertook a policy of trying to remove financial barriers to higher education for the disadvantaged through grant programs, while helping the middle class with access to credit (loans) to meet cash-flow problems. In the 1980s this policy was turned on its head. The Stafford Student Loan program is by far the largest source of student assistance, even for low-income students, providing more than twice as much aid as Pell Grants, which were originally designed as the foundation of support for needy students. Meanwhile, the loan program is no longer a reliable source of credit for great numbers of middle-income students and their families. To cut costs, Congress has excluded from eligibility many of those for whom the loan program was originally intended.

Congress has made stabs at reversing this policy drift, to no avail. Any proposal to boost the buying power of Pell Grants to significantly higher levels (the current maximum award for the neediest students is $2300, 20 percent less in real terms than was being paid ten years ago) runs into a stonewall of budgetary constraints. Proposals to turn Pell Grants into a true entitlement program have met the same fate. By contrast, the Stafford Student Loan program does operate as an entitlement; in fact, it is the only item under the Higher Education Act, or administered by the Department of Education, for which annual appropriations are nondiscretionary.

Over the long haul my own view is that federal policymakers need to rethink the structure and uncontrollable expense built into the student loan system. The government's cost exposure in Stafford Loans makes this program a shaky foundation for student assistance—and erodes support for grant programs. Rising default claims projected for the years ahead, combined with higher payments to lenders if interest rates rise, could generate another crisis-driven search for cost savings and destabilize program operations, as students and institutions experienced in the early 1980s. Whether through restructuring or tightening of the current system, federal policymakers should be looking at ways of reducing loan subsidies that are not targeted on needy students and stabilizing the multiyear obligations that the government incurs when it guarantees loans to students and parents. A recent publication by the College Board, *Radical Reform or Incremental Change?*, explores a number of options for federal student loan policy in the 1990s (Gladieux 1989).

QUALITY CONTROL: RETHINKING THE DISPARATE MIX OF PURPOSES AND TYPES OF EDUCATION SUPPORTED BY FEDERAL STUDENT ASSISTANCE

Two statements by speakers at the 1988 conference at which this paper originated help to crystallize a final concern I want to put on the table about the design and drift of federal student aid policy. The late Frank Keppel recalled a Carnegie Commission book of fifteen years ago, a British-authored evaluation of American higher education titled *Any Person, Any Study*, and said this seemed to him an apt description of underlying United States government policy toward higher education today (Ashby 1971). I agree—cryptic but on the mark. Then Gordon Davies cited an apocryphal definition of public policy as "whatever we can get away with."

My concern has to do with quality control in the education and training supported by government subsidies—and what types of education and training should be fostered through the mechanism of student aid. Beginning in the early 1970s, "postsécondary education" rather than higher education became the watchword in federal student aid legislation. Eligibility was broadened to include short-term career training offered by for-profit institutions as well as collegiate education offered by public and independent nonprofit colleges and universities. Both are, of course, appropriate objects of government support, but I know of no other country where the two policy streams—job training and higher education—are run together in this way. And I wonder if it has been a wise decision. Simultaneously regulating the use of student subsidies by several thousand proprietary schools and twenty-five hundred collegiate institutions has been awkward at best.

The student aid amendments of 1972 were inspired by a marketplace philosophy. Congressional sponsors envisioned Pell Grants operating like vouchers: Students would "vote with their feet," taking their federal aid to institutions meeting their needs. Schools that met the market test of attracting students would flourish, others would wither.

Eligible programs included proprietary institutions providing training of at least six months duration for students with a high school diploma or "ability to benefit" from the offered training.

But, no one foresaw that this policy—and the substantial incentives built into the aid programs as they grew in the late 1970s and 1980s—would stimulate such a burgeoning of the vocational training industry. Hundreds of new profit-making programs have been created during this period. It is said that the federal government has never directly sponsored or established institutions of higher education, other than the military academies and a few specialized schools like Gallaudet University for the hearing impaired. But the growth of proprietary trade schools during the past decade, much of it sparked and fueled by the availability of Pell Grants and Stafford Loans for students, is surely another exception.

About one quarter of Pell Grant funds are now going to the proprietary sector; the proportion of Stafford Student Loan funds is probably higher, but no national data are available to confirm this. Some proprietary schools are financed almost entirely by federal tax dollars through these programs. Alongside traditional, established training programs in secretarial and business fields, refrigeration, welding, or auto mechanics, new programs have sprouted offering such things as truck driver, security guard, retail clerk, and nanny training. Cosmetology programs have mushroomed.

I am no expert on vocational education, but it strikes me that the marketplace, students-voting-with-their-feet rationale begs important questions about the expenditure of government funds, the locus of accountability for such training programs, and the social and individual returns on the federal taxpayers' investment.

Very few states have followed the federal government's lead by extending eligibility for state scholarship programs to proprietary schools, and many state policymakers have become resolute in *not* yielding to political pressure to do so as they have watched problems develop at the federal level. In fact, state officials responsible for licensing postsecondary programs complain that they are often saddled with regulatory problems that the federal government will not address but has itself helped to create by subsidizing the proprietary sector so heavily.

The concern I am raising is *not* a matter of the worthiness of collegiate versus vocational training. Both are important in the nation's human capital agenda; both warrant government support. Likewise, I am not saying that all the problems in student aid program administration, such as high default rates on student loans, are confined to the profit-making schools. My point is that the same rules, delivery systems, and regulatory mechanisms are not necessarily appropriate for both sectors. Accountability for job training efforts should probably be consolidated in the United States Department of Labor and counterpart state and local agencies.

One would have to strain to find a more tangled issue politically and bureaucratically than this last that I have put on the table. Sorting out the mix of purposes served by federal student aid policy will hardly be easy. Vested interests powerfully reinforce current program arrangements, and in practice the distinction between vocational and collegiate in American postsecondary education is far from cut-and-dried. I am simply suggesting it is past time to debate the issue squarely.

There will be no better opportunity to do so—and no better opportunity to address the challenge of strengthening the "education pipeline" through public policy—than the upcoming reauthorization of the Higher Education Act.

REFERENCES

ASHBY, ERIC. *Any Person, Any Study: An Essay on Higher Education in the United States.* New York: McGraw-Hill Book Co., 1971.

GLADIEUX, LAWRENCE E., ed. *Radical Reform or Incremental Change? Student Loan Policy Alternatives for the Federal Government.* New York: College Entrance Examination Board, 1989.

HANSEN, W. LEE. "Impact of Student Financial Aid on Access." In *The Crisis in Higher Education,* edited by Joseph Froomkin, pp. 84-96. New York: Academy of Political Science, 1983.

HODGKINSON, HAROLD. *All One System: Demographics of Education, Kindergarten through Graduate School.* Washington, D.C.: Institute for Educational Leadership, 1985.

MCPHERSON, MICHAEL S. *How Can We Tell if Federal Student Aid Is Working?* New York: College Entrance Examination Board, 1988.

WASHINGTON OFFICE OF THE COLLEGE BOARD. *Trends in Student Aid: 1980 to 1989.* New York: College Entrance Examination Board, 1989.

14

NEEDED: CREATIVE POLICY IDEAS TO RESOLVE THE COMPETING CLAIMS OF QUALITY, DIVERSITY, AND EFFICIENCY IN HIGHER EDUCATION

WILLIAM J. BYRON, S. J.

THE UNEASY TRIANGLE AND THE NEED FOR VALUE REVERSAL IN AMERICA

There are, quite obviously, three sides to the "uneasy triangle" that is closing in on higher education today. They are: quality, diversity, and budgetary efficiency. From a public policy standpoint, the focus naturally falls on the role of government in balancing these three objectives. Balance is the key. Achieving balance between and among desirable policy objectives is an unending challenge for policymakers.

In the 1960s, the uneasy triangle confronting macroeconomic policymakers was defined by three objectives: price stability, full employment, and economic growth. As a nation, we were unwilling to concede then that one of these objectives had to be sacrificed in order to achieve one or both of the others. A balanced solution, however uneasy that balance might be, was then and is now our overall policy objective.

My concern at the moment centers on *coping* with the competing claims of quality in higher education, on campuses characterized by racial and ethnic diversity, in a fiscal environment (institutional and federal) marked by budgetary efficiency. Balance in that triangle will always be precarious.

Quality in education at any level depends primarily on the pres-

Some of the ideas presented here are drawn from William J. Byron, S.J., *Quadrangle Considerations*, Loyola University of Chicago Press, 1989.

ence of committed, competent classroom teachers. It also depends on strong family motivation and encouragement, but there will be no quality if there are not dedicated, skilled professionals in the classroom. Financial security for these professionals and their programs is another prerequisite for quality. Also important for the maintenance of quality is the availability of adequate facilities and support services. But the point cannot be overemphasized that quality people—committed, competent professionals at work in the classroom—are the sine qua non of quality education.

Policymakers must think first, therefore, about how they can most effectively attract and retain quality professional for teaching at all levels. Next they should consider how best to prepare those persons for their classroom responsibilities.

Diversity from a public policy perspective cannot be limited to student-body mix. It surely must extend to faculty, staff, and administration—rich diversity throughout the institution. And in the world of higher education, the notion of diversity should consciously include pluralism among institutions. Policymakers cannot stand by and permit the range of institutional diversity to shrink. Those committed to independent higher education cannot be left simply to their own resources to preserve the independent sector. Sound public policy requires the maintenance of a strong independent sector along with publicly supported community colleges and state colleges and universities. Otherwise cultural pluralism will diminish in our nation and the principle upon which our nation was founded—independence—will be correspondingly diminished.

Coping with budgetary efficiency is a local challenge on every campus; it is also and quite obviously a challenge in the realm of public finance. Not to be overlooked is the individual student in the coping environment; students in the independent sector are coping with their inability to obtain state and federal grant money by working for pay on or off campus, and often in two jobs. Sadly, we are finding that many of them cannot cope medically or academically with this added burden.

The coping mechanisms on individual campuses focus naturally enough on the battleground of the budget. I have often remarked that a university budget is really a theological document—long on mystery and short on revelation. Faculty are understandably concerned with budgetary assumptions and allocations. Far more than narrow self-interest is involved when the faculty voice is raised; in addition to their own compensation, faculty members have to argue for budgetary attention to library, stipends for graduate students, and an array of necessary support services. Although it has no voice of its own, the physical plant speaks out in the sign language of deferred maintenance. Caught in the middle, the administration tries to cope.

The coping challenge for the federal budget planners is quantified annually in deficit figures. At the end of the first month of a new federal fiscal year, newspapers give a firm count on the year-end deficit as of 30 September. The federal government ended the 1988 spending year, for example, $155.1 billion in the red. The deficit has worsened since then. How should the federal government cope? Most economists would say there must be a tax increase and spending cuts. They would also add that attention must be paid to the trade deficit and the key in that regard would be increased productivity in the United States economy.

Higher education, which enjoys a much more favorable trade balance than any other major industry in America, can help the nation with its productivity problems; it must, however, attend to productivity gains within its own individual "firms." Not much is being said about that on the campuses these days.

It would be good for higher education and for the nation, I believe, if, whenever the federal lawmakers and budget planners confronted this uneasy triangle, they were surrounded by an atmosphere of political will that held strongly to the following convictions: (1) that education is an investment, not a consumption expenditure; (2) that an educated population is our first and most important line of defense; and (3) that tax policy should be used to reward classroom professionals, renew and equip educational plants, and reinforce parental and individual determination to pursue higher learning by qualified students who deserve both access and choice in postsecondary education.

Assuming that we have quality diversity, and budgetary efficiency in balance, how now, from a public policy perspective, do we continue to cope with the challenge of keeping them in balance?

At bottom, the question calls for a value reversal in America. We must value quality in all things educational. This pits us against a very basic problem in contemporary society, the problem of materialism. Let me explain.

Education deals with immaterial reality. Knowledge is immaterial. Two persons can set out on a competitive expedition to learn all the biology there is to be known. It is not necessary for one to have less in order that the other have more. Immaterial reality like knowledge can be widely and fully shared. Not so with a stack of fifty-dollar bills, or a pizza pie, or a plot of land. Start dividing up material reality and it becomes evident that one must have less if another is to have more.

As a nation we value the material. Without realizing it, we are drowning in a sea of materialism. There is a difference, of course, between material possessions and materialism. We all need material possessions. The question arises, however, whether or not we are possessed by our possessions. If we are, we have become materialists. A person can certainly use alcohol without becoming alcoholic. Similarly, a person can use material things without becoming materialistic.

Materialism means an overemphasis on the material side of existence to the exclusion of the immaterial. It is a lopsided attachment to material possessions. It is an addiction that impedes the life of the mind, that vital area of immaterial reality. I warn students that I am posing an unfair question when I ask, "Which do you value more, your library card or your credit card?" They always laugh when the question is asked: I pose it simply to make the point that material concerns and immaterial values must be kept in balance for a meaningful human existence.

In America, sad to say, we value persons more for what they have than what they know. Indeed, if knowledge is not directly related to income, we question the value of knowledge. The American value system is distorted by what can only be called heresies like: you are what you have, and if you have nothing you are nothing; or, you are what you do, and if you do nothing you are nothing. We tend not to value people for what they are in themselves, or what they know as the result of application of intellect in the wonderful world of immaterial reality—memory, understanding, knowledge. This is not to say there is no material basis for memory, understanding, or knowledge; it is simply to suggest that it is helpful from time to time in policy discussions to separate, for purposes of analysis, the life of the mind from the trappings of a materialistic society.

We will have to achieve a value reversal that bestows occupational prestige on those who commit themselves to elementary and secondary education as classroom professionals. Otherwise, we will never have the quality there to prepare youngsters well, particularly minority children, for higher education. Indeed, we have to reinforce the prestige of the professorate—value it, reward it—if we are to continue to attract and retain quality professionals in our college and university classrooms. We must, moreover, look to the immaterial side of human existence—to the world of ideas—if we are to find solutions to the most pressing social, political, medical, and economic problems in contemporary society. We must become more ready to spend for basic research than we are for conspicuous consumption. In a word, we have to value education and all surrounding life-of-the-mind activities more than we value our material abundance that now distracts us from the life of the mind. Unless and until we do, we cannot seriously speak about quality in education.

We also have to, seriously and honestly, value pluralism in both institutional diversity and the mix of personnel in individual institutions. This will require value reversal on another level. The majority population will have to come to value heterogeneity in a single educational community. We do not now value fully integrated schools that foster pride in difference and respect for various cultures. When we value difference, instead of protecting homogeneity, we will translate our respect for other cultures, races, and nations into new interest in the study of foreign languages and exposure to foreign cultures.

Underlying our efforts to cope with budgetary efficiency, we simply have to be willing to pay for progress on the two other sides of the triangle—quality and diversity. Unlike immaterial reality, budget dollars can only be distributed by a calculus that respects limits. And the only way to expand budgetary limits is through the building of consensus and the expression of political will. A more generous distribution of the achievement of both quality and diversity cannot happen without sacrifice.

We must, of course, think creatively in dealing with these issues. Creative ideas may well be the best we educators have to offer to the ongoing policy debate. In the spirit of that suggestion I offer two concrete policy proposals to fuel the policy debate. The first is aimed at the apparently intractable problem of America's inner-city public schools. I think of that problem as a quicksand pulling youngsters out of the reach of the admissions offices of our colleges and universities. The second policy idea is aimed at making classroom life more economically rewarding for the committed, competent professional. Without better compensation for teachers at all levels of education, the profession will not attract and retain the best people. Without good teaching at the lower levels, higher education will not get well-prepared students ready to meet college-level academic challenges. Higher education has its proper place on a ladder of achievement. The policy suggestions offered below look, in the first instance, to a broken rung lower on that ladder, which. accounts for some who could bring racial diversity to college campuses, never gaining the competence needed to reach the higher rungs. The second policy option outlined below gets to the heart of the quality issue, namely, the attraction and retention of quality faculty at every rung on the education ladder.

IN SEARCH OF CREATIVE POLICY IDEAS

Of Camps and Classrooms: "Rochester Asks Teachers for 'Extra Mile,' " according to an 18 February 1988 *New York Times* headline. The story reports the failure of the upstate New York community of 240,000 to educate poor inner-city children, and its plan to provide financial incentives that will "push the student-teacher relationship beyond the classroom, into the community." Essentially, the plan invites teachers "to accept increased accountability and responsibility." They will have a "personal responsibility" for a group of approximately twenty students for several years—this, of course, in addition to normal teaching duties. The newspaper account provides a statistical picture of the problem: "In a system with 33,000 students, 68 percent from minority groups, one in three does not finish high school. Twenty percent are absent at least one day a week. Among girls fifteen to nineteen years old, one in eight becomes pregnant each year, or almost 1,400 a year."

On 25 January 1988 the *Washington Post* headlines an experiment "Where the 3 Rs Stand for Rowdy, Rebellious—and Redeemable." The acronym is PAUSE (Providing an Alternative Unique School Environment). The school, created by the school board of the District of Columbia in the wake of a widely publicized series of high school drug raids in 1986, has had a difficult beginning and has met with less than modest success. It is, according to the *Post*, "filled entirely by students who have been nabbed carrying weapons, attacking other children, selling drugs, assaulting teachers or simply disobeying virtually every rule of decent comportment."

Experiments like these are not to be dismissed lightly. But, in my view, they miss the point. They do not go far enough. They should eliminate the pretense that the classroom is the place for disconnected, disruptive youngsters whose development needs could be better served by a temporary relocation to a camp-like environment. The D.C. school building dedicated to the PAUSE program could be redesignated as a "camp." Sedentary moments would be rare in the camp environment. Supervised activity in creative urban experiences would be the daily routine. Individual achievement in camp-style, not classroom activities would be the goal. The hope, of course, would be to generate achievements, one on top of the other, that would literally raise the sights of the achiever to a clearer view of the need for *academic* achievement in literacy and numeracy. Once this perception is clear—namely, that literacy and numeracy are the twin roots of achievement in a better and exciting world that need not remain closed to the camp-based achiever— then the youngster will be motivated to return to the classroom.

Curiously, the efforts of educators to prevent dropouts from school might become more effective if they encouraged, even mandated, dropping into a camp-like setting *for awhile*. This would eventually and effectively lower the dropout rate by substituting a "stopout" experience designed to build motivation to return to school. The hoped-for return mechanism would be a positive peer pressure among the out-of-school "campers" to get back in the classroom in order to acquire the skills necessary for higher and more satisfying achievements. If academic achievers and nonachievers are forced to coexist in chaotic classrooms, the peer pressure, sad to say, works in a negative direction. The achievers tend to pull back; overall classroom performance declines. Teachers quite literally run for cover.

The United States Department of Education's Office of Educational Research and Improvement published in 1987 *Dealing with Dropouts: The Urban Superintendents' Call to Action*. It represents the collective experience and reflection of the superintendents of thirty-two major urban public school districts with a combined enrollment of 4.6 million students. Six drop-out prevention strategies are offered: (1) Intervene early; (2) Create a positive school climate; (3) Set high expectations; (4) Select and develop strong teachers; (5) Provide a broad range of instructional programs; and (6) Initiate collaborative efforts. There is virtually no room in these recommendations for a break-away strategy that would take the students out of the school setting altogether in the hope of building nonacademic achievement while heightening motivation to return to school.

There is an obvious need for sensitivity to the needs of different age groups as break-away strategies are planned. Intensive "resuscitation" efforts in an in-school environment would clearly be preferred for younger children. But, whatever the strategy, both the effort and the environment should respect the feelings expressed by one dropout quoted in the Department of Education pamphlet: "I didn't like (the school). I hated it there. It felt like a dummy zoo."

The urban school superintendents agree that parental involvement is crucial to keeping students in school. "Parents who encourage their children to succeed in school beginning in the early years exert a powerful influence over who stays and who leaves. Unfortunately, the bond between school and home is characteristically weak for potential dropouts." Camp has been used to reinforce the home for generations of children in America. It might be helpful in filling an obvious gap where the dropout problem is most pronounced.

Each year I am invited to a dinner in Washington honoring the forty finalists in the Westinghouse Science Talent Search, an evening of recognition and reward for the nation's most gifted high-school science students. Each year I note the preponderance of Asian-American youngsters in the top ten. There are normally forty tables in the hotel ballroom where this recognition-of-talent dinner takes place. At each table one of the forty winners sits surrounded by adults from universities, foundations, the federal science agencies, and similar organizations. Several years ago it was interesting to me to hear the reply of a bright and vivacious Floridian, not in the top ten, to a table-talk inquiry about what, if anything, she might have learned from the group of Asian-American youngsters (all ten gathered in front of the head table receiving handsome college scholarship awards) with whom she had spent those several days in Washington. "Wow," she said. "You wouldn't believe how hard their parents make them work!"

What if there are no parents to "make" their children work in school? What if there is no parental support for in-school disciplinary requirements? What if there is no parental reinforcement against peer pressure to disrupt, to drop out? The United States Department of Education recommends heroic efforts on the part of teachers, counselors, and principals to contain the problem in school. I applaud those efforts, but I also have a feeling that this kind of containment policy will not work. All of us who are fortunate enough to have had a camp experience in our younger days would do well to reflect on the applicability of that experience—summer, autumn, winter, or spring—to the challenge of conditioning our young people to want to remain in or return to school.

Mention "camp" to kids in school, and watch the surge of enthusiastic expectation. Mention "school" to kids at camp, and brace yourself for a deluge of disappointment.

Both reactions are quite likely to be stored in the memory of childhood experience of those who now set the policy for our nation's schools. Reflection on that experience suggests a policy alternative to our present system of schooling the young for personal fulfillment and productive citizenship.

Camp is a confidence-building experience. Most kids come to love it because they find there some competitive exercise in which they can excel, a craft or skill through which they can produce a measurable, portable, displayable result, and some victory over fear (going off the high-diving board, walking alone through the woods at night). Every camper returns home knowing more and feeling better—in ways that have nothing to do with fresh air, exercise, milk, or cookies. School, on the other hand, is viewed by children as more cage than camp. School need not be, but often is, a lead-pencil laboratory for the discovery of failure. Everyone is "marked," but not all are encouraged and, failure of failures, not everyone learns.

Children of white parents with higher incomes tend to score better on the Scholastic Aptitude Test (SAT), the exam that each year establishes a college-entrance credential for about a million high school seniors (the achievement-oriented, mostly from the eastern United States). Those are the same youngsters most likely to have enjoyed repeated summer camp experience in their earlier years. The low-income, minority students who may have had a poverty program, week-in-the-woods escape from the ghetto as a summer alternative to fire-hydrant surfing on city streets, are, with few exceptions, at the bottom of the SAT scorecard. To what extent does the lower half of the SAT profile make the top half possible? That is a serious question of social justice requiring attention of both scholars and policymakers. To what extent are low-income, minority students, who could run a good academic race, being held back by the presence in school of other kids who ought to be in camp? There's another one for the policymakers, who really do not need the scholars to tell them that students will learn more under the direction of teachers not doubling as prison guards, and in the company of other students who are eager to learn.

Could it be that state laws mandating school attendance to a specified age are hurting the schools and the youngsters who want to learn? I think they are. Am I suggesting that the schools should clear the classrooms of unwilling and uncooperative learners and dump their problems on the streets? Clear the classrooms, yes; turn them loose on the streets, no. Simply send them to camp.

This could be the salvation of the public schools, particularly those large urban public high schools that, in many cases, have become warehouses of defeat and social malaise.

Residential camp? Day camp? Rural environionment? Urban setting? Let the policymakers work it out. Public education available to all who seek it, and accredited education for all up to a certain age, would remain a matter of public policy. The style of education would change for some, but only for a while, in most cases. The camp experience should develop in the young a sense of worth, together with an internalization of a sense of entitlement to academic development. Thus motivated, they can return to school. The classroom door will be open always, and only, to those who want to learn.

In many school districts close to urban centers where the quality of public education is eroding fastest, teachers are facing layoffs and school buildings are being retired from service because of demographic declines. Why not reemploy both these resources, the human and the plant, in this alternate delivery of care and cultivation of young persons (the sort of thing the camps have been doing for generations)? Some teachers will need retraining, a nice alternative to unemployment. Other professionals—counselors, social workers, coaches—will find expanded employment opportunities in the camps. So will persons skilled in arts and crafts and those prepared to manage not-for-profit organizations.

Will the camps reinforce racial segregation? No more than the schools do now. Will they have the effect of foreclosing academic advancement for minority youngsters? Transfer from school to camp could mean the end of academic training for some; but for those same youngsters it could mean the beginning of real, but nonacademic, education. Others, most I would hope, would return to the schools after a confidence-building and maturing camp expericnce, even if that experience in alternate education took several years. That would mean graduating from an academic program a few years later than the expected age today. But a high-school diploma that means something at age nineteen or twenty-two is better than functional illiteracy through a long, unhappy, and unproductive life.

Can the nation afford both camps and schools? Of course it can. All we need is the political will.

Somewhere, and I would hope, sometime soon, a courageous school board will bite the pencil. It will decide that its classrooms are open only to those who want to learn. The need for camps will then become apparent. The school board dedicated to the educational needs of all its young will find a way of providing alternate education, to those who need it, outside the classroom walls.

Teacher Tax Credits for Better Schools: Teacher tax credits represent a new idea for financially troubled United States education at all levels in both the independent and public sectors. Not tuition tax credits (an old idea without widespread political appeal), but teacher tax credits, designed to attract and retain good teachers in elementary, secondary, and higher education, public and private.

Education enlarges a nation's economic productivity even more effectively than investment in new plant and equipment. If the federal government has noticed the possibility of encouraging enlargement of productive capacity by granting an income-tax credit to those who invest in plant and equipment, why should it not acknowledge the link between education and economic productivity by granting an income-tax credit to those whose classroom services transform students into more capable producers of goods and services?

Who would qualify for the credit? Any teacher, at any level, in any subject area, who had demonstrated his or her competence by completing five years of supervised and certified teaching service. The credit would be taken every year thereafter.

Although the idea looks directly to the federal income tax obligation, it could also apply in those state and local jurisdictions that impose a tax on personal income.

The cost to government would depend, of course, on the value of the credit and the number of teachers at work in the nation's classrooms. By any count, the cost would be much less than that associated with tax credits to parents of children in school. The return to government would be measured by the conventional calculations of tax income generated by increased economic productivity.

Teachers who opposed tuition tax credits for parents of children in private schools are not likely to oppose tax credits for teachers. Public-sector teachers stand to gain, so do private-school teachers. And so do the schools themselves—private and public. They all need relief from the understandable pressure placed on their already strained funding sources by demands for higher teacher pay.

As the policy debate continues over merit pay, mediocrity, and educational outcomes, the world's best-educated nation should consider giving credits where credit is long overdue.

The teacher tax-credit idea has the potential to become a political issue capable of gaining support from all educational interests in the United States. As a new initiative, it could spark fresh cooperation between and among all the schools—lower, middle, high, and higher.

It is time to look for issues that will unite, not divide, the private and public sectors at all levels of education. Caught as it is on a rising tide of criticism, education in America is waiting for all the educators to come to some consensus on the purposes and goals of education itself. But instead of talking about education, they argue endlessly over money.

Alternatives to internecine feuds over funding in the academy must be found. Tax credits for teachers are not proposed as alternatives to existing forms of aid. They offer a remedy to an unappreciated and undercompensated profession as new and increased aid to that profession's clients, the students, is also on the public policy agenda. Also in the policy conversation will be the question of finding funds for educational facilities. But the faculty function is central to the success of the whole educational enterprise. So policy options designed to strengthen the economic security of the teachers deserve careful and sympathetic consideration.

Education is an investment, not a consumption expenditure. Those who provide education are not vendors (whose high-volume sales net of expenses would be taxable income); nor are they fee-for-service professionals (whose high-incomes net of expenses are protected by all available shelters yield high tax payments to Treasury). Those who provide education—the teachers—are low-salaried professionals who create the environment for investment in education to take place. They nurture its growth and guide it to maturity. Except for psychic income— the satisfaction derived from seeing youthful talent develop under one's tutelage—the teacher receives no return on the investment. The dollars invested (the costs of education) are not his or her personal outlays; hence the teacher has no claim on the appreciated value. The higher lifetime income earned by the educated person (the "finished product" or "mature asset" to emerge from the educational process) does not return to the teacher. All he or she has claim to is the agreed-upon payment for classroom work. That work can be described as fostering the growth of an income-producing asset—an asset to the national economy, an addition to the national stock of brainpower, an enhancement of the national supply of skill, and an enlargement of the national potential for productivity. The teacher does much more, but no more need be said to make the point that an enormous national investment takes place and appreciates because of what a teacher does, and yet no financial return on that investment accrues to the teacher who makes the investment possible.

The educated person receives a return in the form of higher lifetime earnings. The government shares in the return through higher tax revenues derived from higher earnings that are a function of more and better education.

The teacher tax-credit idea provides a simple device to put a return to the teacher at the front end of the process. Without the teacher the process will not happen. The process is, in fact, now in trouble. It is experiencing difficulty in attracting and retaining superior teachers. Other nations with other systems pay their teachers better than we do in the United States. We need not change our system—economic or educational—to strengthen our teaching ranks. We need only use our familiar, workable, and much-maligned tax-and-transfer system to reward teachers, at the front end of the educational investment process, for the indispensable work they do.

Index

INDEX

191